THE NOVEL IN INDIA

This is one of the volumes sponsored by
the Asian Literature Program of the
Asia Society, New York

THE NOVEL IN INDIA

ITS BIRTH AND DEVELOPMENT

edited and with an Introduction by

T. W. CLARK

UNIVERSITY OF CALIFORNIA PRESS

Berkeley and Los Angeles · 1970

UNIVERSITY OF CALIFORNIA PRESS
Berkeley and Los Angeles, California

ISBN 0-520-01725-0
Library of Congress Catalog Card Number: 70-119719

PRINTED IN GREAT BRITAIN

Dedicated by his fellow contributors
to the memory of

T. W. CLARK

who died while this book was
in the press

CONTENTS

INTRODUCTION

by T. W. CLARK

The essays in this book are designed as a contribution to the history of the literature of six of the major languages of what then was India, now India and Pakistan: Bengali, Hindi, Malayalam, Marathi, Tamil and Urdu. They do not include the greatest names in Indian letters, but confine themselves to an examination of the beginnings of prose fiction and the stages by which it reached that point in time, which is different in the different languages, at which the great writers of novels and short stories emerged. Even these great men are little if at all known beyond the confines of the language area or community in which they were born. Only Rabindranath Tagore, who was awarded the Nobel Prize for Literature in 1912, is of repute outside India, and he is better known as a poet than as a writer of prose fiction. There are however, others: in Marathi, H. N. Apte; in Hindi, Premcand; in Urdu, Rusva; in Tamil, Kalki; in Malayalam, C. V. R. Pillai, T. S. Pillai, V. M. Basheer; in Bengali, in addition to Tagore, Saratcandra Chatterji and Bibhutibhushan Banerji, to mention only the most famous. Their works will, when adequately translated, bear comparison with those of many of the novelists of other nations. At present unfortunately they lie unheralded behind a language barrier which few western readers are ever likely to surmount.

Yet in some of our languages prose literature including fiction is less than 100 years old, and in none does it antedate the early decades of the nineteenth century. The first experiments were made in Bengal, the chief city of which, Calcutta, was the political capital of British India and the matrix of commercial and industrial enterprise and cultural development. The pioneer was William Carey, a Christian missionary, who in 1801 was appointed Professor of Bengali in Fort William College, which had been established the year previously to instruct British personnel in the languages and cultures of India. At the outset Carey was faced with the problem of providing text book material for use in his classes. To meet this need he assembled a small group of pandits who under his guidance set about the task of writing essays, stories and dialogues in Bengali prose. They worked mostly by translation and adaptation from Sanskrit and other languages, but their collection included an important original composition, *Pratāpādityacaritra* (1801), which has some claim to be considered the first historical novel in Bengal. Carey himself contributed a small book of conversation pieces. At about the same time another missionary, John Gilchrist, who was Professor of Hindustani at Fort William College, undertook the provision of material in Urdu and Hindi. We are told 'he travelled in the regions where the choicest Urdu was spoken, and from Delhi, Lucknow, Cawnpore and Agra, he collected a band of men who were masters of the Urdu idiom'. They produced translations from Sanskrit, Persian and English, as well as some original compositions. A little later Carey turned his attention to Marathi, in which language he wrote a grammar (1805) and initiated some prose translations from Sanskrit (1814–15). These new prose works were printed in their various scripts in the printing press Carey had set up at Serampore, a suburb of Calcutta, whence they were distributed to other educational institutions in Bengal and other parts of North India. The task of distribution was later eased and extended by the inauguration of two School Book Societies, one in Calcutta in 1817, the other in Bombay in 1820.

Thus did prose composition get under way in four north Indian languages, Bengali, Hindi, Urdu and Marathi; but there was no comparable initiative in south India. A Tamil translation of the Bible was completed in 1793, shortly to be followed by a Tamil version of *Pilgrim's Progress*; but it was not until the end of the nineteenth century that the first original and worthwhile compositions in the area of prose fiction are recorded. Madras and Kerala had no William Carey to give the lead.

The initial impulse to prose composition thus generated by missionary school teachers was continued and strengthened by journalists. And again the centre of innovation was Calcutta. The first newspaper in the Bengali language was edited and published by John Marshman, a colleague of Carey's, in 1818. It was followed within four years by two others, the *Sambād Kaumudī* of Ram Mohan Ray and the *Samācār Candrikā* of Bhavanicaran Banerji, both of which were due entirely to

Bengali enterprise. Within the next decade there were journalistic ventures in other languages, Hindi, Urdu and Persian. Many of these ventures were short-lived, but by 1832 the Bengali newspaper was firmly established in Calcutta and its immediate hinterland. The newspaper provided Bengalis with a wider scope for literary activity, and soon prose narrative contributions, some of which may be described as social tales or serialized social novels, began to be published. Progress in other languages and in other parts of north India was slower, and in general it was not until well into the second half of the century that the opportunities afforded by newspaper publication began to be realized.

Meanwhile, proficiency in the English language was extending and deepening, especially among the emergent middle classes in the cities of Calcutta, Bombay and Madras; and with command of the language came a voracious interest in English literature. Shakespeare, Defoe, Johnson, Lamb, Scott and Lytton became very popular, as did Burton's version of *The Arabian Nights*, and, curiously, the works of G. W. M. Reynolds, a writer of melodramatic novels, who though famous for a time in some parts of India, is virtually unknown in England. Moral tales, so popular in Victorian England, acquired a certain vogue among fourth and fifth decade authors in Bengal and Maharashtra, but little else did. There was during this period a slowing-down in the production of original material in Bengali, and it was not until after 1850 that there was in either language any significant output of narrative prose for which literary merit can be claimed. The initial impulse was thus weakened in north India, but in the south Tamil and Malayalam had not yet made a start. In Bengal and Maharashtra one delaying factor was unquestionably the low prestige of the indigenous language *vis-à-vis* English among the reading public. Western influence in both areas was strong, and many Bengalis and Marathas were by now so proficient in English that they preferred to read books in that language, as they considered them to be far superior to anything which was available in their own languages. Furthermore, as economic benefits increasingly accompanied proficiency in English, it is not surprising that educated people, to whom social status was important, should seek their entertainment in the works of fashionable English authors and withhold their support from the immature and, to them, unentertaining literary products of their fellow-countrymen. To this cult of English must be added another factor which told against the prestige of some of the local languages among the people who spoke them, namely the fact that many leaders of orthodox thought were strongly of the opinion that Sanskrit, and not the vernaculars, was the only Indian language which was suitable for literary writing. In Bengali, it was not until the late 1850s and the early 1860s that writers were able to contrive a style which was distinctively literary and yet intelligible and attractive to the ordinary reader, and not until 1865 that Bankimcandra Chatterji's novels won the day for it, though the pandits were still far from placated.

Further inland, in the central areas of Hindi and Urdu, widespread proficiency in English came a good deal later than it did in Bengal and Maharashtra, but for Urdu the prestige of Persian, the classical language of much of Muslim culture, played a role similar to that of Sanskrit for Bengali. When Urdu prose did begin to develop, the process was delayed by a conflict between two literary styles, that which evolved in Calcutta under the guidance of Gilchrist and the other which derived from ornate Persian models. The former style was easy and flowing, and its vocabulary and grammar approximated fairly closely to Urdu as it was spoken; whereas the latter used a more artificial vocabulary and was characterized by regular recurrences of rhythmical phrases and rhymes. The Fort William style proved so unattractive to many readers in the Urdu-speaking centres that it was some thirty years before it was used on any significant scale in publications there. 'Every gentleman of taste', its opponents affirmed, 'knew that this was not the way to write literary prose.' And to demonstrate what literary prose should be like these 'gentlemen' published a work in ornate prose which had attracted little attention when it was first written some years earlier, and commended it to their readers. Russell tells us how Rajab 'Alī Beg Sarūr, the author of this work, says that he wrote in Urdu only because he found he could not excel in Arabic or Persian, and that he consoled himself for this failure by making his Urdu as close as he possibly could to the ornate Persian style then in fashion.

What he achieved resembles an amalgam of the eccentricities of Lyly's *Euphues* and the rhythmical, rhyming prose of Burton's *The Arabian Nights*. This conflict of prose styles continued well into the period 1870–90, as the first two works cited in the section on the transition to the Urdu novel exemplify. Naẕīr Aḥmad's *The Bride's Mirror* (1869) was written in near colloquial prose on the Fort William model, whereas Sarshār's *Tale of Āzād* (1878–79) has rhyming passages and other conventional features. Yet both works present contemporary situations. The resolution of the debate about language and style may well have been delayed in the case of Urdu because prose had, and still has, a lower prestige than verse as a medium of literary expression.

The evolution of a literary prose style in Hindi was also marked by conflict, but the conflict was of a different order. It was conducted at two levels. It took several decades before Hindi was able to establish for itself a separate identity in contradistinction to Urdu. Furthermore its development was to some extent restricted by a dialect difficulty. The traditional literary dialects of the Hindus of northern India were Sanskritized Braj Bhāṣā and Avadhī, but by 1800 the Khaṛī Bolī dialect which formed the basis of Hindustani and Urdu was more widely known colloquially. It was inevitable that a style of language intended to supplement Persianized Hindustani and Urdu as a general means of communication with the mass of the Hindu population in northern India should now be based on Khaṛī Bolī. The first powerful impetus towards its development came from Fort William College. Here it was decided that alongside Hindustani a form of language should be studied which did not rely on the Perso-Arabic vocabulary of the lingua franca, but came nearer in its vocabulary to the various dialects of the Hindi language area. Such a form of language would draw where necessary on Sanskrit, rather than on Persian or Arabic loanwords, and would naturally be written in the Devanāgarī script. For a time the name Khaṛī Bolī, anglicized then as *Khuree Bolee*, was retained; but later the name Hindi was adopted. Sanskrit texts were translated into this modified language and distributed by the Calcutta Book Society. They were later distributed from Agra when a School Book Society was opened there in 1837. Nevertheless the prestige of Hindi in comparison with Urdu remained low, and when in 1837 Urdu replaced Persian as the official language of the departments of law and revenue in the Agra presidency, it declined even more. A significant extension of its use *vis-à-vis* Urdu only began thirty years later. As McGregor comments: 'The increased importance of Urdu meant a corresponding diminution in the attention paid to Hindi as a formal style of expression; and the use of English from 1835 onwards for higher government business and in the higher law courts was an even more important factor discouraging the cultivation of Hindi.' The predominance of Urdu also inhibited the circulation of Hindi language newspapers until the influence of the Ārya Samāj, founded in 1875, began to be felt in the area. 'There is, however,' McGregor continues, 'evidence from the late 1860s onwards of an increasing desire on the part of Hindus for a greater measure of recognition and public use of Hindi and the Devanāgarī script, and it is to this feeling that the ensuing gradual expansion of the sphere of use of Hindi can be traced.'

In Tamilnad the writing of original prose fiction began later than was the case with most of the north Indian languages we have considered. The opportunities were there. A printing press had been established in Tranquebar as early as 1710, though it was not used outside the mission field until some fifty years later. There was a missionary presence, and the need to supply schools with text books, similar to that in the north, also existed from the beginning of the nineteenth century. A number of books were translated from Sanskrit to meet this need. But writers remained unaware that this type of prose composition had any literary potentiality. On the contrary there was a strong feeling that literature and verse were synonymous terms. Indeed, so Asher tells us, as late as 1875 a long narrative poem was described as 'an original Tamil novel'. It was not until 1879, when the novel was already an established art form in north India, that the first work of prose fiction was produced in the area.

Narrative prose writing in Kerala, where missionaries began printing in the sixteenth century, started late, but when it did it seems not to have been beset by the conflicts which obstructed and delayed its development in the north and in Tamilnad. There were no problems of language style or literary medium to be solved. The novel came, as it were, in one stride, inspired directly by one man's interest in English literature. Chandu Menon wrote the first Malayalam novel in 1889 after reading Disraeli's *Henrietta Temple*. He wrote it in a language and style akin to the colloquial speech of his readers. He was not at all concerned to prove the superiority of one language, dialect or style to another, but only to entertain his public and to awaken their interest in prose fiction generally and in the novel as an art form in particular. If he had any further motives they were to instruct his readers and by displaying the attractions of English literature to demonstrate the benefits of a good education in English, especially for women.

It is clear therefore from what has been said so far that the adoption of prose as a literary vehicle was for all our languages a nineteenth-century innovation. The forms used for narrative fiction, the novel, the novelette and the short story, were new also. New subjects too were sought out by the majority of authors. In spite of the persistence for a while in some languages of traditional themes, the prince–princess romance and semi-magical hero of superhuman strength and mobility, the innovating writers tended to find their topics in situations drawn from contemporary life. The development in Bengal illustrates the process which, in one way or another, was paralleled in most of the other languages too. Contact with western culture and literature had made the literate population more aware of the present and its problems, and less interested in the past. The age-old monopoly of verse as the sole literary medium was broken. Great poets there were, and continued to be, but they no longer had the field to themselves. Furthermore the coming of the printing press had changed the method of transmission of literary creations. In the cities first and later in country towns and villages, recitation at religious festivals, *kīrtan* singing and *yātrā* plays, lost popularity to the printed book; and the patron to whom the medieval poets had turned for support was in time displaced by the reading public who paid for what they wanted to read. Letters to newspapers reveal that the public was interested in current affairs and world news, and authors responded to the demand. The divine or semi-divine heroes and heroines of the medieval epics and ballads, Rām, Sītā, Lakṣmaṇ, the Kauravas and the

Pāṇḍavas, Behulā and Kālketu, Hasān and Husain, Yūsuf and Zulaikhā, Hanifā and Amīr Hamzā, gave place to local heroes and heroines taken from town and village society, and later to warrior heroes who came to fame during the period of India's more recent history, the Rajput and Moghul princes, Śivājī, and local leaders of more modern times. The new writers were concerned with social problems and with the awakening of patriotic sentiment. Some took religious belief and practice under critical review.

Moral tales for the edification of the young were at an early stage represented in all six literatures, though particularly so in Bengali and Marathi. Two reasons for this vogue spring easily to mind: many authors were concerned with the production of text books for schools, and moral teaching, including as it did simple hygiene and some general knowledge, was considered excellent pabulum for the young; and secondly, certain writers in Victorian England who were very popular in nineteenth-century India were likewise concerned with moral teaching. Samuel Smiles, for example, was widely read and indigenous authors were quick to imitate him. It was natural that virtue should always be applauded and vice condemned. The characters created to exemplify different virtues and vices were uniformly white or black, and right always triumphed in the end. It was tedious stuff very often, but it won popular approbation.

The prose narratives which are based on social situations share a common didactic purpose with the moral tales; and often the method of presentation is similar too. Characterization for example is generally typified by the same black-and-white method of delineation. The themes selected varied from language to language and from generation to generation, but some evoked universal interest, particularly those dealing with the family, marriage and education. In Hindi, Malayalam and Tamil there are stories which describe the joint family system and the marriage procedures which were practised within it. In Urdu, we have a novel in which a girl was instructed in the role she would be called on to play when the time came for her to marry. In Bengali the existing social system was described by many authors, the method often being that of satire. On the one hand we are shown the evils which could result from flying against time-honoured customs, particularly with regard to marriage and the upbringing of the children; on the other hand there are authors who inveighed against rigid adherence to custom, and who described with considerable emotion the suffering involved in child-marriage, the sale of brides to elderly husbands, the ban on widow remarriage, the practice of polygamy by certain kulin brahmins, and the debarring of girls from obtaining a good education. Filial piety and the dangers of the spoiling of sons—not be it noted of daughters—by indulgent parents are frequent themes in Bengali fiction as early as the 1820s. Also prominent are the dangers to religion and family life of a western education, the aping by young men of western modes of behaviour, chiefly the vices of drink and immorality. The theme of the 'new babu', a term coined in Calcutta about 1825, is found also in Marathi, Hindi and Urdu literature, though in Urdu it is expressed mainly in satirical verse, and does not bulk large in prose literature. These westernized youngsters are depicted as wearing clothes alien to their own culture, eating forbidden foods, drinking alcoholic beverages, frequenting brothels, and as either atheists or near-atheists who pay only lip service to the rules of their own religion as a form of social insurance. The different portrayals of the conflict between tradition and innovation within contemporary society in the nineteenth century are often crude and over-simplified, but they are powerful and supported by a wealth of detail. Their importance to the social historian can hardly be over-stated.

The social novels and stories of this period were not however restricted to the consideration of the domestic scene. From time to time reference is made, if only tentatively, to certain political and social consequences of the British presence and to relations between Hindus and Muslims. On the political side, though some British officials are presented in an unfavourable light, there is little before the last decade of the century to suggest that thoughts of *svarāj* were being entertained. Indeed in *Ānandamaṭh* Bankimcandra Chatterji considered the case for independent government and rejected it as not being feasible yet. Education was seen as an outcome of British influence, and to some it was beneficial, to others it was harmful. In Bengal, several authors, some Hindu, some Muslim, commented on the oppressions of the indigo planters and the support they received from the British magistrates. The regard of the Hindu for the Muslim is variously voiced in the historical novels which first appeared in the 1860s.

A striking feature of narrative prose writing on historical subjects was hero-worship, the admiration of great warriors from India's past. The first historical novel in Marathi (1871) naturally enough had as its hero the national figure of Śivājī, who had some years previously been so sympathetically portrayed by Bhudeb Mukherji in *Angurīyavinimay*, which being written in 1862 is probably the first creation in this genre. The wars between the Rajput kings and the imperial Muslim power, which later found expression in Hindi works, were first treated in the novels of Bankimcandra Chatterji, whose *Durgeśnandinī* was published in 1865. The works of these two Bengali authors owe much in respect of form and method of treatment to the British novelists Lytton and Scott respectively. The early Indian historical novels have little political motive or bias; and, except in the case of the Marathi novels, in which the heroes were Marathas and the villains Muslim, there is no indication of hostility against Muslims, though the authors were Hindu. It is true that in the Hindi novel *Jayā* and in Chatterji's early novels victory for the Hindu heroes is desired, but the Muslim soldiers are presented as brave and honourable men. Nothing could be more impartial from the point of view of both communities than the treatment of Śivājī and Rośinārā, the Hindu hero and the Muslim heroine, in *Angurīyavinimay*. In Bengal this impartiality did not last; nor was it general in Hindi historical novels. In his later novels Chatterji lost no opportunity to vilify his Muslim characters. He unfailingly presented their soldiers as poltroons. The British characters, though few in number, were also treated unfavourably. They are depicted as arrogant, unfeeling bullies, though unlike the Muslims they always fight bravely. Christianity too was weighed in the balance and found wanting in comparison with a new, idiosyncratic version of Hinduism. The admiration of Hindu heroes and the association of them with their Hindu faith had now reached a point at which it is possible to discern the seed, as yet unfertilized, of nationalistic sentiment. In Malayalam literature, fifty years later, the seed had come to bloom, and the politics of independence and revolution were freely discussed. In Urdu literature however, with its overwhelmingly Muslim background, the historical novel has rather a different theme. The portrayal of the Muslims' glorious past for the most part removes them altogether from the Indian scene. There is thus little antipathy to Hindus, and it is medieval Christendom, rather than the British in India, which is the most common target of attack, though this clearly had implications for the current scene.

It is not our purpose in this book to show Indian prose fiction at its full maturity, but only to demonstrate the stages by which, and the manner in which, that maturity was attained. We have indicated that in all our languages there was a break with the past, in some abrupt, in others more gradual. Much has been said of the struggle to develop a prose style of literary merit, and of the slow acquiring, chiefly by reading the works of western authors, of the techniques of the novel as an art form. Naturally there is much in these early writings that is crude, laboured and unconvincing. Characterization is over-simplified and lacking in an ability to portray those individual attributes which are the essence of the man and which distinguish him from other men. Descriptions too tend to be stereotyped. Landscapes are often the same, with the same trees and flowers, the same bird-song, the same clouds and rivers. Dialogue is too often artificial; and the novels themselves are weak in structure. All this was to be expected, and has not been glossed over. It must be borne in mind however that the earliest English novels, which unlike those in India had generations of literary prose writing behind them, were not free from like blemishes. They too reveal weakness of structure. Some are long tales, told either by direct narration, as in the case of Smollett and Fielding, or by correspondence between the characters, as in the case of Richardson. It was not until a later school of British novelists was born that the novel was seen as a coherent, integrated structure, in which all the parts, large and small, subserve a total plan. The working builder, it seems, precedes the architect. The building of Indian novels on a sequence of episodes was to a large extent rendered inevitable by the necessity of conforming to the requirements of the newspapers, which were for many the only avenue to publication. Yet they should not be criticized too strongly on these grounds, for serial production was then, and if the present practice of television producers is a valid comparison, can still be conducive of much excitement by anticipation. Tagore bears eloquent testimony to this fact.

'Now he who will may swallow at a mouthful the whole of *Chandrashekhar* or *Bishabriksha*, but the process of longing and anticipating, month after month, of spreading over long intervals the concentrated joy of each short reading, revolving every instalment over and over in the mind while watching and waiting for the next: the combination of satisfaction with unsatisfied craving, of burning curiosity with its appeasement; these long-drawn-out delights of going through the original serial none will ever taste again.'[1]

Nevertheless the practice of serialization did delay the realization of the structural potentiality of the new literary form.

All this however is natural and predictable in a period of young growth. What is astonishing in the works we have under review is not that there should be evidence of immaturity, and indeed much bad writing, but that there should be so many flashes of good writing, however short, of tender and moving characterization, of lively description, and so many interesting stories.

Note: Five of the essays included in this book were first presented as papers to a seminar on Asian Literature held in the School of Oriental and African Studies, in the University of London. The only exception, R. E. Asher's essay 'Three Novelists of Kerala', was presented as a paper to the Michigan State University, U.S.A.

[1] The two works mentioned are novels by Bankimcandra Chatterji. The passage occurs in *Reminiscences*, the English translation of Tagore's autobiographical work *Jibansmriti*.

BENGALI PROSE FICTION UP TO BANKIMCANDRA

by T. W. CLARK

Bengali literature had had a long and distinguished history before the period we are going to examine, but it had consisted solely of verse compositions. The muse of poetry had blessed the land abundantly, but the other harmony, that of prose, was entirely unheard. During the eighteenth century however, after four centuries of prolific creative activity, the springs of poetic inspiration began to flow with less and less power and freshness. The waters of Baru Caṇḍīdās, Kṛttibās, Mukundarām, Ketakādās, Kaśirāmdās, Govindadās, Alāol and many others, were tending to run dry, until the changes of time brought forth new tributaries which were fed from different sources. The medieval past seemed suddenly to have ended; and there was, as far as literature is concerned, a dead period of several decades before the modern future began.

This intermission can in large measure be ascribed to far-reaching political and social changes which took place in the eighteenth century. The old ways of life in Bengal were disrupted by these changes, and it took some time before a new and settled pattern can be seen to have emerged. The following three factors combined to put an end to the old and to inaugurate the new. Political power passed from the Navāb and other princes, some of whom had been patrons of art, to the East India Company. Secondly, the uncertainty and insecurity which the transfer of power engendered were further enhanced by a severe natural disaster, the catastrophic famine of 1768, and by the wide-spread dacoity which accompanied it. Both are referred to in some of Bankimcandra's novels.[1] And thirdly, that new economic Mecca, the growing metropolis of Calcutta, had already like a magnet begun to draw to itself a vast new population, composed of Hindus and Muslims, men of all castes, and from all levels of society, migrants looking for a new home and a new life. From them was born the modern Bengali, a man cut off from the life and culture of the past, which he was rapidly forgetting. He began to shape his life in a new political,

[1] Particularly in *Debīcaudhurānī* and *Ānandamaṭh*.

social and economic mould, out of which grew in time a new culture, a new literature, part of which was a creation hitherto unknown in Bengal, that of prose.

The gestation of prose as a literary mode was not easy. It had no ancestral models on which to shape itself, and consequently had to struggle into being by a process of trial and error. It is true that a few prose documents have survived the earlier period, but they are mostly legal notes, set out in long unanalysable paragraphs and using a vocabulary which few, even among contemporaries, could have understood outside the professional scribes who drafted them. They certainly were no guide to the pioneers of the early nineteenth century, even if they knew of them, and they probably did not. The problems which faced these pioneers were numerous, complex and fundamental. They included such primal elements as vocabulary, word form and spelling, the structures of phrase, clause, sentence and paragraph, not to mention aesthetic considerations associated with style. The only established literary vocabulary in existence at the time was that of verse, and this was seldom able to supply the prose writer with the word material he required. Moreover, the condition of this verse vocabulary at the time was far from ideal. By the beginning of the eighteenth century poetic diction had lost its early freshness and capacity for growth and adaptation. It had to a large extent degenerated into a stereotyped jargon, relieved now and then by ingenuity, as in the case of Bharatcandra Ray, but seldom brightened and energized by original creativeness. The only important exception was Rām Prasād Sen. He was a lyrical genius and quite unique in the eighteenth century, but his musical ecstasies were conveyed in words which no prose writer could hope to adapt to the different purposes and styles of his medium. The vocabulary of prose therefore had to be built up without help from that of the verse literature which preceded it. The case with regard to sentence structures was similar. The sentences of verse composition did not run beyond the end of the couplets in which much of medieval verse was composed and it is not uncommon to find as many as four sentences in one couplet, one to each half line. Indeed few sentences run continuously as far as the end of the couplet. The *tripadi* metre, a variant of the rhyming couplet, and the various lyric metres in frequent use allowed the sentence no greater length or freedom. Subordinate clauses, so necessary in prose writing, were rare. In consequence the prose pioneer had to build up his own phrase, clause and sentence structures, as well as develop his own vocabulary. It is hardly to be wondered at that the process was slow, and that the first efforts were at times crude, unrhythmical and lacking in the cultured graces of later writers.

Another factor which complicated the birth of Bengali prose and delayed writing of a literary quality in it was the humble status the Bengali language held at the time in polyglot Calcutta.[1] Bengali was, at the end of the eighteenth century, one of seven languages which in varying degrees were in use in the city. The other six were Arabic, English, Hindustani, Portuguese, Persian and Sanskrit. Portuguese had virtually disappeared by the turn of the century. Arabic, English, Persian and Sanskrit were highly esteemed in different circles; and all four were literary languages. Hindustani and Bengali had a very low prestige even among the people who spoke them, and no literary status at all. Though Bengali was the mother tongue of the majority of the inhabitants of Calcutta and its hinterland, it had little or no currency beyond the domestic context. Persian and English were the languages of government, commerce and the law. Sanskrit and Arabic were the languages of Holy Writ. No way to advancement or distinction was open to those who knew only Bengali, and it is not surprising therefore that it soon came to be despised by many whose mother tongue it was. It trailed no clouds of glory from its distinguished past, and even the sunset glow seemed to have faded away.

The first attempts to extend the use, and enhance the status, of Bengali came from a few British civil servants. One, Charles Wilkins, with his own hands cut a fount of Bengali type for printing official papers. This was the first successful Indian language press in east India,[2] and its construction made a major contribution to the development of Bengali culture in

[1] For a fuller treatment of this subject see *The Languages of Calcutta, 1760–1840*, by T. W. Clark, BSOAS, 1956, XVIII/3, pp. 453–9.

[2] Preface to *A Grammar of the Bengali Language*, N. B. Halhed, pub. Hugli, 1778; and *History of Bengali Literature*, Sukumar Sen, Sahitya Akademi, New Delhi, 1960, p. 178.

the nineteenth century. Wilkins's fount was first employed in 1778 to print part of a Bengali grammar which had just been completed by another civil servant, Nathaniel Brassey Halhed.[1] In the introduction to this important work Halhed praised the elegance and beauty of the Bengali language. He asserted that it was potentially a superior language to Persian and urged upon his fellow countrymen the wisdom, indeed the practical necessity, of learning it. A little later the edicts of Sir Elijah Impey and the Cornwallis Code were translated into Bengali, and an English-Bengali word list was composed and printed.[2] The orthodox leaders of Bengali society had no hand in these developments. They viewed with disfavour any attempt to elevate Bengali to literary dignity. In their eyes Sanskrit was the only language suitable for the purposes of literature, and Bengali was a mere vernacular, a 'barbaric' vernacular. They were powerless to hinder the work that was being carried out by the civil servants, but they did nothing to encourage it.

The second phase in the rehabilitation of Bengali belongs to that great missionary, William Carey.[3] It was his scholarly genius and enthusiasm which created the circumstances in which Bengalis were able to experiment with prose writing in their own language. As soon as circumstances permitted, Carey took up the study of Bengali and Sanskrit, and made such phenomenal progress in both that within two years or so he was able to commence a translation of the Bible. In 1800 he moved to Serampore; and here by happy chance he was joined by the blacksmith, Pañcānan Karmakār, whom Wilkins had trained in type-cutting and printing. Together they set up a printing press, later to become the Baptist Mission Press, and took in hand the publication of a Bengali version of the New Testament which was now completed. The same year Wellesley, then Governor-General, opened the Fort William College in Calcutta with the declared aim of providing young civil servants with a probationary training in the languages and culture of the country, and in 1801 he appointed Carey professor of Bengali and Sanskrit. This appointment gave Carey his opportunity. The immediate need as he saw it was to write

[1] Halhed, *loc. cit.* [2] Sukumar Sen, *loc. cit.*

[3] *The Life and Times of Carey, Marshman and Ward* (abbreviated CMW), Longman, London, 1859, 2 vols.

text books for his classes, and with a small group of Bengali scholars he faced the task with remarkable assiduity. Within twelve months, one of his colleagues, Rām Rām Basu, had written *Pratāpādityacaritra*, a fairly lengthy prose work which is part history and part fiction.[1] About the same time Carey himself completed his *Dialogues*, a book of class lessons set in the form of imaginary conversations.[2] In 1802, Mṛtyuñjay Bidyālankār completed *Batris Siṃhāsan*, a narrative work translated from Sanskrit. Other works followed: some, like Mṛtyuñjay's *Hitopadeṣa*, were translations; others, like Carey's *Itihāsmālā*, Basu's *Lipimālā* and Mṛtyuñjay's *Rājāvalī*, were original or partly original works. Carey also contributed a grammar and an English-Bengali dictionary.

The age of prose writing had commenced. As one Bengali critic has put it, 'The foundation of prose and of literature generally was being laid'.[3] The works themselves show clearly the difficulties of the labour with which the birth was brought to fruition. Carey and his colleagues resolutely set about the problems of amassing a vocabulary and a variety of sentence structures suited to the requirements of the new literary medium. It is not to be wondered at that they had failures. What does arouse astonishment is the measure to which efforts were successful. They built up their store of words from spoken Bengali, including some dialect forms, from Persian, Arabic, Sanskrit and Hindustani, and in some cases by neologisms wrought in Sanskrit by translation from English. The introduction of a later edition of *Dialogues*, which was published in 1818, throws light on the vocabulary problem and how they attempted to overcome it.

'A Khansaman, or a Sirkar, talking to an European, generally intermixes his language with words derived from the Arabic or Persian, and some few corrupted English and Portuguese words: examples of this, in several varieties occupy the first thirteen pages of the following work. From the thirteenth to the nineteenth page are instances of the grave stile. At the twentieth

[1] *Bengali Literature*, J. C. Ghosh, OUP, 1948, pp. 101–2.

[2] This work of Carey's was published without a title, but it is described as 'Dialogues intended to facilitate the acquiring of the Bengali language'; see Ghosh, *op. cit.*, p. 100.

[3] Ghosh, *op. cit.*, p. 104.

page is an instance of the common talk of labouring people. Women speak a language considerably differing from that of the men, especially in their quarrels: instances of this, both in the friendly and contentious stile, will be found. . . . The dialogue, page 56, . . . is the language of fishermen, and is peculiar to that class of people.'

Similarly, the authors attempted to meet the problems of sentence structure by marrying patterns of phrase and clause culled from English, Sanskrit, Persian and spoken Bengali.

Assessment of the achievements of the Fort William group is not easy. It will depend ultimately on the level at which critical judgement is made. Their purpose was to provide text books for their classes, and this they fulfilled. They did more than this, however. What they wrote was prose, the first prose with literary promise ever written in Bengali; and as such what they did is historically important, as all first things are important. Some modern Bengali critics are of the opinion that what they wrote can hardly be treated as literature. We are told that their style is unformed and crude, unrhythmical and lacking in aesthetic appeal.[1] This judgement is in the main true; though the writers did improve with practice. Even in as early a work as *Pratāpādityacaritra* there are passages of clear and simple narrative.[2] Mṛtyuñjay's writing shows variety, ranging from what Carey called the 'grave stile' to passages of a live and racy quality approaching very nearly to the flavour of speech.[3] Bengali literature had known narrative in verse for centuries, but here for the first time was narrative in prose, and Carey added conversation, which also was a beginning however pedestrian its content. So whatever may be said adversely, Carey, Rām Rām Basu and Mṛtyuñjay contributed to Bengali literature prose narrative and conversation, the embryo of the novel and short story which were to come: and they did it with the minimum of raw material to hand.

In 1815, an important personage entered the arena of Bengali prose writing, Rām Mohan Rāy. From this time until his death

[1] Ghosh, *op. cit.*, pp. 102–3.

[2] The literary quality of this work has been carefully assessed in a thesis, as yet unpublished, by R. R. Van Meter, South Asia Dept., University of Minnesota.

[3] Sukumar Sen, *op. cit.*, p. 181.

in 1833 he was probably the most influential scholar and thinker in India, and his example in adopting Bengali as the language for much of his work went some way to countering the disfavour with which some contemporary scholars regarded it. His early works belong to the sphere of theological exposition and religious polemics. Later he entered also the field of public education, but he was first and foremost a religious reformer. Rām Mohan Rāy however did not make any contribution to the history of prose narrative, but he must be mentioned because his name and work lent some prestige to Bengali prose writing in general.

It is not a digression to mention the Hindu College at this point. It was founded in Calcutta in 1816 by a group of men, some Bengali, some English; one of them was Rām Mohan Rāy. The purpose of the institution was 'the education of native youths in European literature and science' through the medium of English.[1] It was financed privately, most of the subscribers being Indians. The Hindu College, which was an immediate success, became the *alma mater* of the new urban middle class, which later was so prominent in the social, political, economic and cultural life of the city. The curriculum comprised the same subjects as were taught in English schools of similar standing. The alumni of the college began to read English and European literature, and soon many of them spoke and read English in preference to, and more proficiently than, Bengali. Bengali literature to them was non-existent. The only literary forms they knew were those they were becoming familiar with through their reading of English; and one of these forms was the novel, which had been established in Britain for over half a century. Scott was already writing and his works soon became popular in Calcutta. It is understandable that minds thus nurtured found little to their satisfaction in Bengali prose literature until Bankimcandra Chatterji burst into their world in 1865 with his first novel, *Durgeśnandinī*.

Nevertheless prose writing still went on and gathered momentum. The year 1818 marks the beginning of journalism in Calcutta. The first regular newspaper in Bengali, the *Samācar Darpan*, was published in that year from Serampore. Its editor

[1] *Saṃbād Sekāler Kathā* (abbreviated SKK), ed. Brajendranath Bandyopadhyay, Bangiya Sahitya Parisad, Calcutta, vol. I, p. 710.

was John Marshman, a missionary colleague of Carey's.[1] Three years later Rām Mohan Rāy initiated another important paper, the *Sambād Kaumudī*, which he used as a platform from which to launch attacks on orthodox Hinduism and the Trinitarian doctrine of Christianity. In 1822, Bhabānīcaran Bandyopādhyāy left the staff of the *Sambād Kaumudī* because of its anti-Hindu bias and published his own paper, the *Samācar Candrikā*, which supported the orthodox Hindu point of view. Others followed, and so the age of the newspaper was inaugurated. There were over forty new ventures in less than twenty years.

The newspaper was important in the evolution of prose writing and prose style for a number of reasons. Firstly, it brought written Bengali into even closer contact with English usage than it had had even under the tutelage of Carey. Much of the copy was translated from English, and translated at speed, with the result that Bengali words tended to be fitted into a syntactic mould the basic shape of which owed much to English. As this tendency has persisted and is still operative today, it is not surprising that the style of some of the early newspapers has a more modern flavour than that of Rām Rām Basu, Mṛtyuñjay and Rām Mohan Rāy. Secondly, as the success of any publication depended on popular support, writers had to ensure not only that their matter was of topical interest but that it was written in a style simple enough to be understood easily by the ordinary reader. The need to satisfy popular taste compelled the adoption of a simple vocabulary by the avoidance of learned Sanskritisms. Sentence structure also was simplified; phrases and clauses were linked together more smoothly.[2] Thirdly, the newspaper opened the way for the professional writer. Journalism provided a large number of authors with an opportunity to write and have their articles tested against the opinion of an impersonal judge, the general public; and in time it killed the custom of private patronage so long prevalent in the history of Bengali literature. By 1840, many writers had begun to test their ability in the columns of

[1] CMW, vol. II, p. 162.

[2] This statement is true of only some of the papers published at the time. A more detailed examination may disclose some correlation between numbers of publication failures and editors' inability to appreciate public preference in respect of language and style.

the papers, among them men whose names were shortly to be known in their own right.

There is little however which was produced during these first twenty years of journalism that can be said to have marked literary merit; and though there was scope for narrative writing, original stories or anything that falls within the general definition of prose fiction were rare. Bhabānīcaraṇ Bandyopādhyāy, the editor of the *Samācar Candrikā*, is credited with two social satires, *Nababābubilās* and *Nababibībilās*,[1] which are historically significant and which by reason of their content deserve mention. They hold up to ridicule the *nouveau-riche*, westernized Bengali, the Babu, who was becoming more and more prominent in Calcutta society, and whose excesses provided ample material for the satirist. It has been said of Bhabānīcaraṇ, and not without justification, that 'he was the first writer who made an effort to use prose for creative work and for giving literary pleasure'.[2] Though he may not have been the first to write in a satirical vein and on a social subject, he was clearly aware at an early date of the literary possibilities of satire, and it is probably true to say the influence of his example can be seen in the more famous satirical works of Pyāri Cā̃d Mitra and Kālīprasanna Siṃha, who wrote some thirty years later. The credit for the first known prose satire goes to an unknown author who contributed two chapters of what he calls an *upākhyān* to the *Samācar Darpan* in February and June respectively, 1821.[3] Dictionaries define the term *upākhyān* as *imaginary incident, story, anecdote.* The writer ridicules the way rich fathers spoil their sons and the absurd extent to which young men go in their efforts to imitate western ways of life. The following excerpts are typical both of the content of this *upākhyān* and of its style. The translation is as literal as is feasible and the punctuation of the original has been preserved.

'In this way the boy began to grow up he was a great talker spoke rudely to everybody and beat them instead of checking him they were all delighted with him if Tilakcandra (the boy)

[1] Ghosh, *op. cit.*, p. 121; and *The Bengali Novel*, Humayun Kabir, Calcutta' 1968, p. 6.

[2] Ghosh, *ibid.*

[3] It has been suggested that this unknown writer was Bhabānīcaraṇ Bandyopādhyāy, but the suggestion has not finally been authenticated. See S. K. De's *Bengali Literature in the 19th Century*, 2nd edn., 1962, p. 564.

did anything wrong instead of punishing him Cakrabarti Devan (his father) told him to say I did not do it.[1]

'Babu knew nothing about reading and writing yet he was everywhere respected and pandits said you can interpret all the Scriptures and understand the finer points as a result of all this Babu became very conceited he thought he knew all the Bengali customs practices sciences ordinances and all that had to be done in respect of them had been done. I shall now become like the sahebs and show forth their customs practices purposes religion culture judgements. Consequently all Babu did was to dance like a cock sparrow. For example.

'The sahebs had a custom in the morning and evening they used to ride about in a carriage or on a horse.

'Babu gave instructions to his servant wake me up before the gun in the early morning I shall go out mounted on a horse. Babu spent practically the whole night in a brothel he got home in the early hours and went to bed later the servant woke him consequently he had to get up with his eyes full of sleep he was mounting the horse when he saw the sun was up now he felt ashamed to go along the road the sahebs ride. Therefore he went another way horses know their riders well taking note of Babu's seat it threw him off its back on to the ground Babu fell on the cinder track getting his hands and face scratched with cinders he came home leaning on the groom's shoulder the horse was running away a saheb saw it he gave orders to his own groom having caught it he took it to the pound.

'The sahebs if they quarrel with anyone usually go to war they fight with fists or pistols etc.

'If Babu was angry with a dependent uncle or other aged relative or manservant or maidservant he hit them in the English way with his fists and said (in Hindustani) bring my pistol he made this kind of terrifying noise whereupon the miserable wretches ran away. Babu at the time thought to himself that this was the peak of human achievement.'[2]

This is not great writing; but it is a beginning, and for all its clumsiness it shows that the author had a sense of the ridiculous and the ability to hold it up to scorn.

[1] SKK, vol. I, p. 109.

[2] *Ibid.*, pp. 112–13.

The most important newspaper of the 1830s was the *Saṃbād Prabhākar*. The editor was Iśvarcandra Gupta. He is best known as a poet, but he did write a few biographies which have a historical importance. His prose style is heavy and lacks distinction, but what he was unable to do himself he tried to encourage others to do. Some of the outstanding writers of the next generation served their literary apprenticeship on the staff of his paper.

In 1843, Debendranāth Tagore, father of Rabindranāth, and successor to Rām Mohan Rāy as the head of the Brāhmo Samāj movement, founded an influential newspaper, the *Tattvabodhinī Patrikā*. Its purpose was to serve as a means of propagating the teachings of the Samāj.

As the first editor of the *Tattvabodhinī Patrikā* Debendranāth appointed Akṣaykumār Datta, a young man who was introduced to him by Iśvarcandra Gupta. Among the number who wrote for the new journal was Iśvarcandra Śarma, better known as Vidyāsāgar. The fifth decade of the century belongs almost exclusively to these three. Debendranāth himself was a writer of ability. He has to his credit an autobiography, which has been translated into English,[1] a number of sermons and some letters. His prose writings merit further study, though as most of what he wrote is didactic and expository little need be said of him here. Even his Autobiography is almost wholly concerned with his religious beliefs and practices but there is a certain amount of narrative writing. One example may be given.

'Thus the days and nights wore on in my forest exile. Two Bengalis, a Ghose and a Bose, were employed in the post-office here, after their return from the Kabul War. They came to see me. Bose said, "I narrowly escaped with my life, on my way back from the Kabul War. In the course of my flight I saw an empty house on the road to Kabul, entering which I hid myself on the top of a sort of loft. The Kabulis found me out there, and very nearly killed me. I managed to come away alive with the greatest difficulty. And now there comes this fresh trouble!" As long as I stayed there, Ghose used to come

[1] *Autobiography of Maharshi Devendranath Tagore*, trans. by Satyendranath Tagore and Indira Devi, Macmillan, London, 1914.

and make enquiries every day. One day I asked, "Well, Ghose, what news today?" "Not very good news", he replied. "They have set fire to the mails." Next day I asked, "What news today, Ghose?" He said, "Today the news is not very good. The rebels must be coming today from Jullundur." One never got good news from Ghose. Every day he would come with a long face. I spent eleven days in this way, in great anxiety. Then news came that Simla was safe, and there was no longer any fear.'[1]

The translation reads awkwardly, but the narrative is clear and reveals an ability to handle conversation. It represents a considerable advancement in technical skill from the clumsy *upākhyān* in the *Samācar Darpan*.

Akṣaykumār Datta was a considerable contributor to the *Tattvabodhinī Patrikā*. His work in the main consisted of essays on moral and scientific subjects, which, it seems, were well received at the time. Didacticism was popular in Bengal as it was in contemporary England, whence it came. 'The English books that were most widely read, and had the most influence, were of the type represented by Isaac Watts's *Improvement of the Mind*, Maria Edgeworth's *Moral Tales*, Chambers's *Moral Class Book*, and Samuel Smiles's *Character* and *Self-Help*',[2] the first three of which were translated into Bengali. Most of what Datta wrote seems dull today, but it clearly did not appear so to his contemporaries, who were only too ready to be moralized at and to be impressed by scientific information provided it was purveyed in readable form; and Datta was and is easy to read. 'His style had no pretension to literary polish, but it brought . . . coherence in diction and precision.'[3] Debendranāth thought very highly of him: 'In those days few men possessed his beauty of style.'[4] A number of his essays were incorporated into school readers, where some of them are still to be found. He had that quality of simplicity which is invaluable in the classroom; and moralizing and elementary science were considered excellent pabulum for the young. It has been said that with him 'a new age . . . had

[1] *Autobiography of Maharshi Devendranath Tagore*, pp. 232–3.
[2] Ghosh, *op. cit.*, p. 123 and fns.
[3] Sukumar Sen, *op. cit.*, p. 187.
[4] *Autobiography*, p. 72.

already begun, and a new prose, one that was a fit instrument of literary artistry, had already been created'.[1] Nevertheless he made no direct contribution to the development of prose fiction in Bengali; that was reserved for his greater contemporary, Vidyāsāgar.

Vidyāsāgar's career as a writer extended from roughly 1840 until well into the 1870s. His literary work comprises narrative prose on subjects many of which were drawn from Sanskrit sources and religious treatises, though he is also credited with two satirical sketches 'impugning the private morals of some of the leading pundits who supported the continuance of polygamy'. His polemical writings, which have both eloquence and power, show him wearing the mantle of Rām Mohan Rāy in his opposition to polygamy and the ban on widow marriage. The passing of the Widow Remarriage Act in 1856 was due in no small measure to his advocacy. Vidyāsāgar was an alumnus of the Sanskrit College. He was a pandit by training and inclination, but a journalist and text book writer by profession. His first important work, *Vetālpañcavimśati*, was published in 1847. It is a set of twenty-five tales based partly on Sanskrit originals. His greatest works are *Śakuntalā*, 1854, *Sītār Banabās* (Sita's Exile), 1860, and *Bhrāntibilās*, an adaptation of the theme of *A Comedy of Errors*, 1869.

The greatness of Vidyāsāgar's prose lies in his ability to combine the sonorous phraseology of the Sanskrit element in the Bengali vocabulary with that fluency and ease of comprehension which two generations of journalism had succeeded in inculcating. He was an assiduous critic of his own writing. He devoted much care to revision, changing words, remodelling phrases and adjusting the order of both, with the result that in his best compositions he achieved a rhythm and a propriety of diction hitherto little known in Bengali prose.

'Sītā was pondering these things in deep distress of mind, when Kusa and Laba suddenly came into her room, and said, "Mother, the Rishi has told us that he will take us to see King Rāmcandra's Horse-Sacrifice tomorrow. We were curious so we went to those people who had received invitations and asked them many things about King Rāmcandra. We discovered that

[1] Ghosh, *op. cit.*, p. 123.

everything about King Rāmcandra was out of the ordinary. But, Mother, about one thing we were puzzled and astonished. The deep devotion we felt towards him on reading the Rāmāyan has now increased a thousandfold. People have told us that in accordance with the wishes of his people the King has put aside his beloved consort. Consequently, we asked, "Will the King then take to himself a second wife, as otherwise there will be no consort at the celebration of the sacrifice". One of them said that Basiṣṭadeb bearing the celebration of the sacrifice in mind had strongly urged the King to marry again, but that the King was by no means disposed to agree. He had caused them to make a golden image of Sītā and was going to marry that image as his consort.'[1]

A more truly representative passage could have been chosen, but the above has been extracted from *Sītār Banabās* because of its conversational content. Much has been lost in translation of the rhythm and diction of the original, but sufficient remains to reveal that here exists an easier control of sentence structure and a greater degree of comprehensibility than was accomplished by Rām Mohan Rāy and the earlier scholarly writers of Bengali. The courtly conversation with its great frequency of Sanskrit words is still far removed from the conversation of colloquial speech, but some advance has been made in that direction. There is here greater simplicity than any other pandit had hitherto achieved; indeed it is relevant to note in this connection that one contemporary critic condemned Vidyāsāgar for the surprising reason that he was 'quite easy to follow'.[2] Compound words on the Sanskrit model are less frequent and not so long. The archaic verbal nouns, a marked feature of the syntax of the writers of the Carey school have largely disappeared—there is not a single example in the passage quoted—and been replaced by participles. The use of participles and the increase in the number of nominal inflections give Vidyāsāgar's writing a more modern flavour, for both are common features of present-day spoken and written Bengali. Noteworthy also is the introduction of English marks of punctuation. The original of the extract contains eleven commas, three marks of exclama-

[1] *Vidyāsāgar-racanāsambhār*, ed. P. N. Biśī, Calcutta, 1957, see Sītārbanabās, p. 45.

[2] Sukumar Sen, *op. cit.*, p. 189.

tion and one question mark. To Vidyāsāgar and Akṣaykumār Datta must go the credit for establishing marks of punctuation in Bengali. The newspaper of the twenties and thirties had failed to do that. The adoption of punctuation marks accompanies, as it was occasioned by, an increase in the use of subordinate clauses, as a result of which the sentence acquired a greater variety and flexibility. Vidyāsāgar's achievement however is not limited to technical innovations: he was a writer of genius, a master of style and diction, and to his prose creations we can assign the term literature. 'The true Bengali prose has at last arrived.'[1]

Nevertheless in one important respect Vidyāsāgar was backward-looking. The subject matter of his literary, as opposed to his polemical writings, was drawn from the past. The stories he told and the characters he portrayed were already well-known to the Bengali public, and there is evidence to suggest that the educated middle-class was getting tired of the same old thing so oft repeated. One thinks, not without sympathy, of the tired sigh of Hippolyta, 'I am weary of this moon. Would he would change!' The newspaper had brought the reading public up to date, and it clearly required of its authors something more than a re-telling of the old puranic stories. His ability to provide something new was one of the reasons for the electrifying effect Bankimcandra had on Calcutta a few years later.

So in the history of Bengali literature Vidyāsāgar marks the end of a phase, not the beginning of a new one. The judgement of history is clearly expressed by Bankimcandra in an essay he wrote on another author in 1892.[2]

'Before or after Vidyāsāgar no one wrote Bengali prose of such sweetness, but in spite of that his language was far removed from what was easily intelligible to ordinary people. . . . It was much Sanskritized and difficult to understand, and later writers being bound to old custom and being fascinated by the charm of Vidyāsāgar's language had neither the desire

[1] Ghosh, *op. cit.*, p. 125.

[2] *Bāṅgālā Sāhitye Pyārīcād Mitrer Sthān*, in *Bibidha*, by Bankimcandra Chatterji, ed. Brajendranāth Bandyopādhyāy, Baṅgīya Sāhitya Pariṣad, Calcutta, 1941, pp. 144–5.

nor the courage to use any other kind of language. In consequence Bengali literature moved along the narrow path of the past. And even more serious, if the language of literature was so confined, its subjects were even more confined. There was no Bengali literature except such as was borrowed or translated from Sanskrit or English books. There is no doubt that Vidyāsāgar was a writer of genius, but his *Śakuntalā* and *Sītār Banabās* were taken from Sanskrit, and his *Bhrāntibilās* from English. His followers consistently plundered the treasury of English and Sanskrit. From the point of view of literature there was no greater disaster than this.'

A change however was coming, and it began in the 1850s while Vidyāsāgar was at the height of his powers. Bankimcandra's essay above quoted continues as follows:

'It was Pyāricā̃d Mitra who rescued Bengali literature from these two great handicaps. He was the first to write a book in language which was not only understood by all Bengalis but which was also the language they themselves used. Moreover he was the first who did not go hunting in the treasury of English and Sanskrit as his predecessors had done, but found his material in the store of his own experience and feelings. Both these purposes were achieved in a book named *Ālāler Gharer Dulāl* (The Spoilt Child of a Rich Family).'[1]

In 1854, Pyāricā̃d Mitra published a penny paper, which was called *Māsik Patra*. It was intended for the edification and amusement of women, who were not likely to have known any Sanskrit. To it he contributed a series of chapters from the narrative which was published as a book in 1858. It was very well received in Calcutta. E. B. Cowell, who was consulted about its publication, wrote that it had 'great charm'.[2] Beames, the grammarian, has this to say:[3] 'Babu Piari Chand Mitra, who writes under the *nom de plume* of Tekchand Thakur, has produced the best novel in the language. He stands high as a

[1] *Bāngālā Sāhitye Pyāricā̃d Mitrer Sthān*, pp. 144–5.

[2] *Ālāler Gharer Dulāl* by Pyāricā̃d Mitra, ed. Brajendranāth Bandyopādhyāy and Sajanīkācitā Dās, pub. Baṅgīya Sāhitya Pariṣad, 1940–47; Intro., VIII.

[3] *A Comparative Grammar of the Modern Aryan Languages of India*, 1872. Pt. I, Intro., p. 86.

novelist; his story might fairly claim to be ranked with some of the best comic novels in our own language for wit, spirit and clever touches of nature. Mitra puts into the mouth of each of his characters the appropriate method of talking, and thus exhibits to the full the extensive range of vulgar idioms which his language possesses.' Bankimcandra writes of it at length.

'Ālāler Gharer Dulāl has a lasting and memorable place in the Bengali language. Better books may be written now or in the future, but I am confident that no book has conferred or in the future will confer such benefit on Bengali literature. It is beautifully written, and was the first to demonstrate that a book could be written in the Bengali which is spoken by ordinary people. Its language has a natural quality which can hardly be obtained by the Sanskritized language which all seem to like. . . . Pyāricā̃d Mitra was not a prose writer of the first order, but he was first and foremost responsible for directing Bengali prose into the path of progress. That is his undying claim to fame. His second glory is that he showed for the first time that the natural material of literature is to be found at home, not by going begging to English and Sanskrit for it.'[1]

Ālāler Gharer Dulāl may not be 'beautifully written', as Bankim averred. It is not a great novel either, but it is important because it is the first work in Bengali which can be described as a novel. Moreover it has much intrinsic interest and merit. It narrates the story of the son of a very rich father, who spoiled him outrageously from birth. The boy very soon fell into bad company who flattered him and egged him on through a series of discreditable and sometimes unsavoury escapades, while at the same time helping him to squander his large patrimony, until it was entirely dissipated. Thereupon of course his companions forsook him. Reduced to penury, he lived for a time in want and distress until he was rescued and miraculously converted by his virtuous younger brother whom earlier on he had banished from the family home.

The structure of the novel bears the marks of its serialized origin. It is a series of episodes which follow one another in

[1] *Bibidha, loc. cit.*, p. 145.

chronological sequence. It is true that the retention of the same set of principal characters throughout gives the book coherence, but the episodes are discrete, and as a whole it lacks structural unity. This however is a minor criticism in so early a work.

Bankimcandra's comment on the language of *Ālāler Gharer Dulāl* has been quoted above: it is, he wrote, a language 'which was not only understood by all Bengalis but which was also the language they used themselves'. This statement is important both as a judgement on Pyāricā̃d's language and by implication as a definition of what in Bankim's view constituted the colloquial style in written Bengali. Pyāricā̃d's vocabulary stands in marked contrast to that of Vidyāsāgar and others of the 'pandit' school of writing. It contains few words which a Bengali would regard as 'Sanskrit'. Apart from occasional archaisms and dialect words there is little that the modern reader would have difficulty in understanding. Nevertheless the colloquial forms of verbs and pronouns, which are formally different from those known as the literary forms, are used only in conversational passages. Yet in this respect *Ālāler Gharer Dulāl* represents a marked advance towards a more colloquial diction and style, for Vidyāsāgar and other contemporary writers did not use the colloquial forms of verbs and pronouns at all. The colloquial flavour of Pyāricā̃d's writing is further increased by his employment in some contexts of a mixed dialect, known as *do-bhāṣī*, which reflects the speech forms of Bengali Muslims.[1] Ṭhak Cācā, the arch-villain of the story, regularly speaks in this dialect.

It is in the portrayal of character that the novel is weakest. All the persons are either black or white. The majority, including the hero, are bad, without redeeming features. They never, even by accident, deviate into a kindly thought or a charitable action. The remaining few, including the younger brother, are unbelievably virtuous. All that can be said is that the bad characters are not all bad in the same way; but nevertheless they are inadequately distinguished as individuals. The boon companions of the young hero are an undifferentiated band of profligates. We do not know how many they were or who

[1] *The Emergence and Development of Dobhāṣī Literature in Bengal to 1855 A.D.*, Q. A. M. Mannan, University of Dacca, 1966.

they were. The others too lack individuality as persons, and what they say is often so much of a piece that the reader has to turn back to remind himself who the speaker is. The only exception is Ṭhak Cācā. This is due to the fact that as a major character he is given greater prominence than some of the others, and that being a lawyer he is on that account occupationally distinguishable; and secondly, he speaks a peculiar dialect. Though I hesitate to disagree with so distinguished a critic of his own literature, I cannot feel with Sukumar Sen that Ṭhak Cācā is 'an immortal rogue'.[1] He has not the stature which makes for immortality, even in roguery; and what stature he has is diminished and loses clarity by being depicted against a background which is peopled by so many other rogues.

The *dénouement* of the plot also is unconvincing, because it is so entirely improbable. It may be granted that a happy ending was necessary. Right conduct had to be justified, but not so abruptly and without reasonable time for preparation. Until the last chapter the hero had been utterly bad. Nothing touched or interested him except the gratification of his own selfish desires. He had, for instance, been quite unmoved by his father's death, and his behaviour to his mother in her sorrow was inhuman and callous in the extreme. Then suddenly, at a turn of the page, without even a decent period of time for the 'sweet uses' of adversity to teach him their salutary lessons, he ceases to be a rogue and becomes completely virtuous. It makes a poor ending even to a study in caricature.

There is nevertheless something to be said on the other side. The extremes to which Pyāricā̃d has pushed his caricaturization accord with his major purpose, which was didactic. He wrote to compel the reader's derision. *Ālāler Gharer Dulāl* may be regarded as a farce, but it is a farce with a moral. It is not the characters we are asked to judge, but the characteristics they typify. Discipline for the young is good, so we are invited to deride the situations which in the author's view are bound to occur when it is denied. Affection for parents is good, so we are invited to condemn those children in whom it is lacking and applaud those in whom it is found. And so the lesson goes on through a long list of virtues and vices. The author's purpose

[1] Sukumar Sen, *op. cit.*, p. 230.

is a moral one, and exaggeration of character and situation to the point of absurdity is his method. Bankim's praise of the book can only be taken as proof that it was acceptable to part at any rate of the contemporary reading public. The Calcutta Bengali of that age, as has been said earlier, was ready to be moralized at, and Pyāricā̃d gave him moralizing through the medium of ridicule which was probably a welcome change from the more pedantic moralizing of Akṣaykumār Datta.

The setting of *Ālāler Gharer Dulāl* is not contemporary. The society depicted is that of the early nineteenth century. It belongs roughly to the same period as that described in *Nababābubilās*. Babuism was beginning to emerge. Westernized education had not yet begun. It was before the Hindu College. There are however passages in the book in which Pyāricā̃d inveighs against social ills in his own day, sometimes with light satire, but sometimes with bitterness. One such was the mercenary practice of polygamy by kulin brahmins. It is only a short extract but it speaks volumes. The speaker is a young wife.

'Listen to me for a moment. I had a bad go of fever a year or so ago, and was confined to bed day and night. I was too weak to stand. While I was still in bed my husband turned up. I did not know what a husband was like beyond knowing as everybody knows that a husband is a wife's sole wealth. I thought that all my pains would leave me if only he would sit by me and talk for a few minutes. If I tell you what he did, you will never believe me. He stood by my bed and this is what he said. "It is 16 years since I married you, and therefore because you are therefore my wife I have come to you for money. I cannot stay long. I spoke to your father about it, but he made some excuse. So give me the jewels you are wearing." I said, "Let me ask mother. If she says so I will give them to you." He barely let me finish speaking before he grabbed at my bangles and began to pull them off my arms. I pulled my arms away from him, so he kicked me and made off. I fainted, and mother had to fan me for some time before I came round.'[1]

The subject was very much of a public scandal at the time

[1] *Ālāler Gharer Dulāl*, pp. 24–5.

Vidyāsāgar was writing about it, and in 1854 a reward was offered for a play on the evils of kulin polygamy. One cannot doubt that the publication of the above extract in the popular *Māsik Patra* must have been a powerful contribution to the movement for reform.

Regret for lack of proper parental discipline is the note of the next extract. The author is comparing the different upbringing children receive in English and Bengali homes.

'English children are taught all sorts of games by their parents, games which strengthen their minds and bodies and yet are harmless—some paint pictures, some look after flowers in their gardens, some go out hunting or play manly games. All these are harmless, and the child is free to choose which he will. The Bengali child does whatever he likes the look of. They love to deck themselves out in fine clothes and jewels, to play in the garden with bad companions and harlots, to ape the Babu and show off . . . this sort of behaviour can only lead to utter ruination.'[1]

A third extract deals with a topic which was much in the public mind at the time, the behaviour of some of the indigo planters. Sukumar Sen summarizes the situation. 'Indigo cultivation was then the most important industry in Bengal and was entirely controlled by British interests. The masters of the plantations and attached factories were Britishers with little education and less sympathy. With the passive indulgence of some of the administrative officers of the government or encouraged by their indifference, the indigo planters did what they liked to the peasantry.'[2] Pyāricād made several references to the subject, and it is important to note that he did so some four or five years before Dinabandhu Mitra wrote his play *Nīldarpaṇ* which caused such a stir in Calcutta.[3]

'The magistrate takes the attitude that the indigo planter can do no harm because he is English and a Christian, and that it must be the black man who is the guilty party'.[4]

[1] *Ālāler Gharer Dulāl*, p. 41.

[2] Sukumar Sen, *op. cit.*, p. 200.

[3] *Ibid.*

[4] *Ālāler Gharer Dulāl*, pp. 106–7.

In another passage on the same subject he attacks both Muslim and Christian teachers.

'There are only two ways of thwarting the landlord and the indigo planters: first, to seek the protection of a moulvi; and second, to become a Christian. Many peasants I know, once they have the protection of a padre, feel that they are free to go where they want and do what they want like any sacred bull, because the padre always looks after the brethren. Sometimes he gives them money, sometimes he gives them a letter of recommendation, sometimes he helps them in other ways. It is not that the peasants all become Christian because they believe in it, but because all sorts of advantages come their way if they attend the padre's church.'[1]

The attitude revealed by Pyāricā̃d in this passage is symptomatic of the strengthening resistance to Christian proselytization which was the first overt sign of the revival of orthodox Hinduism. In his protagonism of a purified but still orthodox Hinduism, then in competition with Christianity, Islam and the Brāhmo Samāj, Pyāricā̃d was the forerunner of Bankimcandra.

The writing of prose satire was to continue. The next important work, *Hutom Pyā̃cār Nakśā* (Sketches by Hutom the Owl),[2] consists of a number of sketches which were first published separately. The first of them appeared in 1862. The anonymous author was later discovered to be a well known Calcutta figure, Kālīprasanna Siṃha. The discovery must have come as a shock to many people, for Siṃha was prominent in the city as a scholar, a patron of the arts and a generous dispenser of charity. He had already won literary fame for his prose translation of the Mahabharat, and it was Siṃha who paid the fine imposed on the Revd James Long, who had been prosecuted and imprisoned for translating Dinabandhu Mitra's play, *Nīldarpaṇ* (1860). Such was Siṃha's standing in Calcutta society at the time, and it was some time before it leaked out

[1] *Ālāler Gharer Dulāl*, p. 113.

[2] *Hutom Pyā̃cār Nakśā*, by Kālīprassana Siṃha, ed. Brajendranath Bandyopadhyay and Sajanikanta Das, pub. Baṅgīya Sāhitya Pariṣad, Calcutta, 1948.

that he was also Hutom the Owl. Indeed so carefully was his identity concealed that in 1863 a caustic reply to his sketches, *Āpnār Mukh Āpni Dekhun* (Look at your own Face), was published by one Bholānāth Mukherji, who was a tenant of Siṃha's and a man who was under considerable financial obligation to him.

Why Siṃha was attracted to the writing of satire is not known, but some hints are given in his brief introduction to the first issue.

'The Bengali language nowadays has become material for the use of poets who like us are as lifeless as statues. It is like the kneaded flour left over from the making of pancakes or the wet clay which idle boys take over for fun and fashion into dolls of various kinds. Like these things the Bengali language is a left-over. . . . If there were a true heir to take it over, it would not be mauled about by schoolboys and asses like us. . . . We have therefore taken up the writing of sketches.'[1]

He continues with a short illustrative anecdote which suggests that sketches of the type he had in mind were a new creation. 'I offer them to readers', he says, 'as something new.' From this it can be inferred that he did not see himself as the inheritor of an established tradition. The most significant paragraph in the introduction gives his own assessment of his sketches and the purpose he had in writing them.

'The sympathetic reader need turn over only a couple of pages to be able to appreciate the purpose of this publication, because there is nothing in these sketches which is untrue or not founded on fact. It is true that many people may think that they can see themselves in what I have written, but I ought not to have to explain to the reader that this is not so. My target is not any particular individual but everybody in general; and I have not even left myself out.'[2]

It is doubtful however whether all of his readers were convinced. Some of his characterizations must have been very life-like for in the introduction to the second edition he speaks of readers

[1] *Hutom Pyā̃cār Nakśā*, Intro., p. v. [2] *Ibid.*

looking at the sketches surreptitiously to see if he had put them in.[1]

Hutom's canvases depict life in Calcutta as he saw it, with its vulgar, *nouveau-riche* population. The central figure in one sketch is the Babu, ostentatious in his dress and ridiculous in his aping of Western ways, living a superficially respectable life by day but devoting his nights to all forms of riotous living. The Babu is anxious at all times to appear to be an orthodox Hindu. He pretends to pay meticulous attention to the demands of his creed and in particular to take his full share in all religious festivals; yet in his private life he is utterly profligate, hard drinking and lecherous. And the background is Calcutta, with its crowded, noisy and ill-scavenged streets. The picture is realistic and very convincing, for the author had his subject ever before him, and he had a fine eye for the telling detail. Pyāricā̃d's Calcutta could have been any large town, and his village any village; but Hutom's Calcutta was the Calcutta that he and his contemporaries lived in and knew, and it was peopled by men and women they met every day, or every night. It is not surprising that some of them felt that the cap had been made to fit themselves.

'There were hawkers on the pavement, their baskets full of rotten lichis and mangoes, and jack-fruit which were cracked and oozing and black with flies. There were mango stones everywhere, and some small boys were picking them up, rubbing holes in them to make them into whistles, and blowing them too. Suddenly it began to rain, a heavy shower, and Chitpur Road soon shone like the polished leaves Brahmins have just eaten from. A few office workers were carrying their shoes in their hands; some took shelter on the verandahs of the brothels, others in the doorways of shops. It was a good day for coachmen.

'The drivers shouted out coaxingly. "Four annas, four annas! Dalhousie Square! Terajuri! The petty court, Babu?" One or two office workers had already got in, and were sitting waiting as self-consciously as a bride in her carriage, but no fellow turned up to share the fare. Some government clerks were haggling with the drivers about the price. But most

[1] *Hutom Pyā̃cār Nakśā*, p. xxi.

went by on foot, and the drivers jeered after them, calling out with mock politeness, "You can't afford a coach? Then why not go home in the cook's basket?" '[1]

No other book of this period has described life in Calcutta as vividly and with such a wealth of detail as this. It is all there, the sights, sounds and in places even the smells. What a background for the central character, Hutom's Babu! The following extract of a Babu and his Śiva festival is typical, though only of one aspect of the hero's life.

'The Babu's festival was being held in the garden, and it was crowded with people. Drums were beating, and near the Śiva emblem many heads were swaying to and fro. The holy men were sitting straight up, moving their heads round and round. Some ordinary people were kneeling devoutly, their bodies bent low to the ground. The brahmins were sprinkling water. For nearly half an hour this head swinging went on, but still the flower on the emblem did not fall. There was nothing they could do. The news reached the house, where the women's faces showed how distressing the situation was. "Somebody has committed a sin", they said; and they covered their faces with their hands. There were some guests there too. They said, "The head holy man must have taken something to eat. When this sort of thing happens that's always the cause." Then followed a long argument. Finally the teacher of the house, the priests and the women decided that the tidings had to be imparted to the master of the house. A brahmin, who usually went with the Babu on his escapades, and four or five of the holy men ran into the house. "Sir," they said, "you must get up and come to the Śiva shrine. The flower won't fall." It was dark and the Babu was just going out. His carriage was waiting. He was all dressed up and his handkerchief was scented. He was taken aback when he heard what they said, but he had to do something. There mustn't be anything irregular in these rites in honour of his ancestors. So much against his will he went, just as he was, pineapple-coloured coat and all. The head door-keeper ran ahead and cleared a way for him. His boon companions were obviously most distressed that the

[1] *Hutom Pyãcār Nakśā, Kalikātār bāroiyāri pūjā*, pp. 14–15.

Babu should be put to all this trouble, and they followed on behind.

'The drums near the shrine beat even more loudly. Everybody shouted at the top of his voice. "Śiva, Mahādeb, Bhadreśvar!" The Babu bowed low before the shrine. Large hand fans wafted him on both sides, and if you had not known what was going on many of you would have thought it was a human sacrifice. Finally the Babu raised his hands in salutation and a garland of flowers was placed around his neck. Then with tears in his eyes and a silk scarf round his throat, he moved to one side. The priest at the shrine began to call out, "Father, give us the flower, give us the flower!" And with the gracious permission of the Babu a pitcher of Ganges water was poured over the head of the god. The holy men swung their heads violently. They kept it up for about half an hour when there slipped from the head of Śiva a twig with a couple of leaves on it. Their joy knew no bounds, and they shouted, "Bhadreśvar, Śiva!" Everyone agreed that it could not fail to happen this way, for it was such a distinguished family.'[1]

The sketches which make up *Hutom Pyācār Nakśā* vary considerably in length. The longest, *Bāroiyārī Pūjā* (Community Festival), contains 34 pages. Some which are included in a section known as *Hujuk* (gossip)[2] are only a few lines long. These latter treat of local items of gossip and describe rumours which were currently in circulation in Calcutta. The rumours are varied, and some of them fantastic though not, it would appear, incredible. One such concerns the Kabuliwalas, traders from Afghanistan who are so well known in Calcutta. They, it is said, kidnap children, fatten them up and then eat them. Another was to the effect that Dilip Singh, son of Ranjit Singh, has become a Christian, and that the entire Sikh community had followed him; and nearer home, that the Brahmins of Bhātpāṛā had been converted to Christianity, and many people in the district likewise. Another curious rumour had it that Vidyāsāgar's campaign against the ban on widow-marriage was the cause of the Mutiny. Naïve they may be, and Hutom saw to it that they lost none of their naïveté

[1] *Hutom Pyācār Nakśā, Kalikātār caṛakpārbbaṇ*, pp. 2–3.
[2] *Ibid., Hujuk*, pp. 48–79.

in the telling. In these, as in his other sketches, one gets the feeling that Hutom was enjoying himself.

Hutom Pyãcār Nakśā is not a single work. It is a collection of separate sketches, each of which is complete in itself. When they were published together in one volume, no attempt was made to unify them. They have nothing in common beyond the author's satirical purpose, which informs them all, the city of Calcutta in which they are set, and the rich, naughty and foolish people the author delights to pillory. *Ālāler Gharer Dulāl* can be called a novel, however rudimentary in form. *Hutom Pyãcār Nakśā* is in no sense a novel, but its contribution to the history of prose fiction in Bengal is no less important on that account, even though, as has been stated previously, some contemporary readers were not convinced that it was a work of pure fiction.

Three features of the content and form of Hutom's work are worth stating. The first is the organic unity he achieved between narrative and descriptive writing. By welding the two so closely the author is able to demonstrate the important place description, whether detailed and realistic, or general and impressionistic, can play in heightening the effect of a story. In this regard he was far in advance of his time. The paucity of apt and properly integrated descriptive passages is one of the faults of *Ālāler Gharer Dulāl*. Secondly, at a time in the history of Bengali prose when writers were uncertain which subjects were suitable for prose composition, Hutom established once and for all the fact that contemporary life, whether of individuals or of society at large, can supply endless material for the writer of fiction, be he novelist or short story writer, satirist or moralist. The vogue of satirical or farcical writing based on contemporary society which followed is clear proof that the lesson had been learned. No fewer than seven other works of this type were published in less than ten years after Hutom. It is true that the appeal of satire then began to weaken, but the writing of real-life novels and short stories went on in a tradition which embraces some of Bengal's greatest names, Bankimcandra, Rabindranāth, Śaratcandra and Bibhūtibhūsan.

The third feature of importance in *Hutom Pyãcār Nakśā* is linguistic. Siṃha was the first Bengali to make exclusive use of the language and word forms of the colloquial style for literary purposes. The shorter forms of verbs and pronouns are employed consistently throughout, not in conversation only as in *Ālāler Gharer Dulāl*. The vocabulary is that of spoken Bengali, and I noticed no Sanskrit words other than those which had become fully naturalized in Bengali. Siṃha pursued his desire to impart a colloquial flavour to his sketches to the extent of employing coarse and sometimes obscene words. Bankim describes his language as 'racy and vigorous, not seldom disfigured by obscenity'.[1] Sukumar Sen says that it is often vulgar.[2] Terms such as 'vulgar' and 'obscene' are notoriously difficult to define, but however they are defined it is certain that some of the words used by Hutom would not have been used in polite speech. Whatever may be said on this aspect of his writing, there can be no doubt that Siṃha's language was nearer to that of speech than had been achieved by any previous or contemporary writer. He went so far as to use 'phonetic' spellings, a device previously unknown, though it has been adopted by a number of later authors. These phonetic spellings demonstrate in certain cases that he had a remarkably acute ear, e.g. *kacci* for *karchi*, *śād* for *śādh*, *haẏece* for *haẏeche*, *lāldiki* for *lāldighi*. He also regularly wrote *gyālen* [gælen] for *gelen*.

Siṃha was not a great writer. The intrinsic merit of *Hutom Pyā̃cār Nakśā* judged objectively as a literary work is not high. He is little read today, and the tricks of language which made what he wrote so colloquial in 1862 are now outdated and difficult to understand. Nevertheless he was an early traveller along the road many later and greater writers of prose fiction were to tread: and therein lies his importance.

The prose fiction of Bhūdeb Mukherji, who was a contemporary of Siṃha's, was different from Siṃha's in style, language and subject matter. Siṃha, as has been seen, wrote in a racy style, used colloquial language, and found his subjects in the life of contemporary society; whereas Mukherji wrote more formally, perhaps stiffly, used a more Sanskritic type of Bengali, and drew his subjects from historical romances. Mukherji, who had been educated first at the Sanskrit College

[1] *Calcutta Review*, 1871, quoted in Intro. to *Hutom Pyā̃cār Nakśā* (see p. 42, fn. 2), p. vii. [2] Sukumar Sen, *op. cit.*, p. 231.

and later at the Hindu College, was a schoolmaster by profession, and his earlier writings consisted mostly of essays for the classroom. He continued essay writing all his life, and those that he wrote on social and religious topics merit comparison with what was written on similar subjects by Vidyāsāgar and later by Bankimcandra. His *Samājik Prabandha* (Essays on Social Subjects), which were published in a collected form in 1892, were well received by some, not many, critics of his generation. Rājnārāyan Basu wrote, 'This book should be read by all modern writers. It contains an analysis of all the complex problems of India, and statements on deism, patriotism, unity and effort'.[1] Sir Charles Elliot mentioned Mukherji's book in an article published in the Asiatic Society's Journal in 1893. 'No single volume in India contains so much wisdom and none shows such extensive reading. It is the result of the life-long study of a Brahmin of the old class in the formation of whose mind eastern and western philosophy have made an equal share.'[2] It is doubtful however whether Mukherji's essays were ever generally popular during his lifetime. Certainly later critics of Bengali literature seem to find them scarcely worthy of mention.

Whatever literary reputation Mukherji has, and it is not high, rests upon his *Aitihāsik Upanyās* (Historical Novels), which were published together in 1862, though they may have been available in part as early as 1856. The book consists of two separate works: a short prose story, about twelve pages long, and a short novel, about sixty pages long. The former, *Saphal Svapna* (The dream that came true), relates certain incidents in the life of a Turki prince, Savaktāgīn (Amīr Sabuktigīn of Ghaznī), who was the father of Sultan Mahmud of Ghaznī. The prince had left home in search of fortune, and while benighted in a dense forest he dreamed that he would become the ruler of Ghaznī. Various vicissitudes befell him. He was captured by footpads and sold as a slave, but ultimately his dream came true. The short novel, *Angurīyavinimay* (Exchange of Rings), has as its principal characters the Emperor Aurangzeb, his daughter Rośinārā, and the Mahratta chieftain, Sivaji [*sic*].

[1] *Bhūdeb-racanāsambhār*, by Bhūdeb Mukherji, ed. P. N. Biśē, Calcutta, 1957, Intro. p. xvi.
[2] *Ibid.*, p. xvii.

Interest in the history of the second millennium AD grew strongly in the latter half of the nineteenth century. It is usually regarded as having been first awakened by Tod's *Annals and Antiquities of Rajasthan,* which was published in England about 1829. Sukumar Sen's statement is sufficient evidence. 'Tod's *Annals of Rajasthan* was avidly read by the educated Bengalis as it vicariously supplied some solace to their wounded vanity, since India was under the subjugation of the British and the Bengali people had no opening for a military career.'[1] It may well be that the Sepoy Mutiny which on the one hand increased the 'prestige of the British', on the other disposed the hearts of the Bengalis to dwell longer upon the heroes of Rajput lineage and in particular upon their valorous deeds in the defence of Chitor. Hero worship was a congenial soil for the seeds of patriotism. From about the middle of the century, authors writing in both English and Bengali began to take up the theme; and the re-publication of Rām Rām Basu's *Pratāpādityacaritra,* though it owed nothing to Tod, having antedated him by some twenty-six years, was proof of a quickening interest in history and in tales about the exploits of Indian heroes. S. C. Datta's *Tales of Yore,*[2] which was written in English, was perhaps the first product of this new school. Madhusūdan Datta's *Captive Ladie,*[3] a poem in English in the manner of Scott, treats of the rape of Chitor as narrated by Tod. It appeared in Madras in 1848. Rangalāl Banarji's *Padminī Upākhyān* (The Story of Padmini),[4] published in 1858, was the first important narrative poem in Bengali on a Rajput theme; and others from the same author were to follow.

Bhūdeb Mukherji's two prose tales were up to this date unquestionably the most significant contribution to this branch of Bengali literature. One must assume that he knew Tod's *Annals*—it would have been hard for an educated man in the Calcutta of that period to be unaware of them—but he does not mention them. He does however acknowledge indebtedness to another but far less known work, the three volumes entitled *Romance of History* by the Revd Hobart Caunter, which was published in 1836. Mukherji's introductory note to *Aitihāsik Upanyās* contains the following paragraph.

[1] Sukumar Sen, *op. cit.*, p. 208.
[2] *Ibid.*, p. 229.
[3] *Ibid.*, p. 208.
[4] *Ibid.*

'There is a book in English named *Romance of History*. The novel *Saphal Svapna* is based upon the first story in it, and part of my second novel *Angurīyavinimay* is also derived from that book.'[1]

It is interesting to note that Mukherji distinguishes two terms: *upākhyān*, which I have translated *story*, and *upanyās*, which I have translated *novel*. Caunter's work consists of stories; his own of *novels*. He does not define the difference, but he must have intended to indicate that he was aware that one existed. Earlier works of prose fiction had been called *upākhyān*. Bankimcandra refers to his novels as *upanyās*.

Saphal Svapna is based almost entirely on Caunter's first story, *The Traveller's Dream*. It is indeed for the most part little more than a paraphrase of its original, and in some parts it is so close as to be very nearly a literal translation. Passages of free translation are fairly frequent. The two works are not however completely identical. There are differences both of substance and structure. Here and there throughout the narrative Mukherji has sentences which do not occur in Caunter's version. The purpose of these additions is clearly to ensure that the moral of an incident or situation is fully drawn. The moral of a tale was important and had to be stated in such a way that none could fail to understand. This attitude is in keeping with the didactic propensity which underlies so much prose writing of the time. The change in structure which Mukherji introduces is a small one, but it is significant. After Savaktāgīn had married the king's daughter and was firmly established as his heir, Caunter devotes two or three pages to the narration of his further military exploits. Presumably they were part of the historical material on which he was drawing, and he included them for that reason. Artistically they have nothing to commend them. The story has a plot, namely a dream and its fulfilment; and once the dream had been fulfilled there would seem to be no necessity to produce more evidence of the hero's prowess. Mukherji omitted them altogether, and by doing so imparts to his work a greater structural coherence than his original has. As the omission must have been deliberate, it can be inferred that Mukherji realized something of the

[1] *Bhūdeb-racanāsambhār*, p. 258.

need for structural unity in the art form he was trying to create. It may be speculated whether the presence or absence of such structural considerations was for him the criterion which distinguished *upanyās* (novel) from *upākhyān* (story). It is probable that this is too sweeping an inference to draw from such little data, but the repetition in his second work of a similar though more highly developed organization of his plot within a predetermined mould does lend it credibility. Even in so embryonic a work as *Saphal Svapna*, Mukherji showed that he appreciated the importance of the ending. Caunter stopped when the tale ran out; Mukherji stopped when the tale had reached a point which in his view was a satisfactory rounding-off of the whole. This understanding of the difference between the two is, in my view, a landmark in the history of the novel in Bengal.

Angurīyavinimay is a longer piece and gives the author greater scope for his artistic originality. Though it is, as Mukherji admits, based on Caunter's tale *The Mahratta Chief*, it is far less of a copy than *Saphal Svapna*. It contains much more original matter, and is significantly different in structure. Caunter's narrative runs as follows. Sevajee [*sic*] is at war with the armies of Aurungzebe [*sic*], which from time to time he either defeats or outwits. In one of his forays he seizes a valuable prize, the emperor's daughter Roshinara [*sic*]. The two fall in love, take a pledge of marriage and the princess falls pregnant. Later Sevajee is betrayed by one of his generals and Roshinara is recaptured by Aurungzebe, who is furious that she has become the wife of his enemy. Sevajee is at last defeated and captured. The victorious Muslim commander in the field assures him that the emperor will receive him with the honour and dignity due to his rank and courage. The promise is not honoured by Aurungzebe who insults Sevajee and places him in confinement. Meanwhile a son is born to Roshinara. The child is taken away from its mother, and as he grows up he is trained to be a soldier. He shows exceptional prowess and powers of leadership. When Sevajee contrives to escape with Roshinara and regain his own country, the son is sent with an army against him. Father and son confront one another in battle, and a fierce combat ensues. The son is grievously wounded but not fatally. He is recognized, recovers, and joins his parents.

When death comes to Sevajee and Roshinara after a happy married life together, the son succeeds to his father's throne.

Such in brief was the raw material that Mukherji took over. In the early chapters, which are devoted to an account of Śivājī's exploits against the armies of Aurangzeb and the capture of Rośinārā, he follows his original fairly closely. The descriptive passages in particular are taken almost whole from Caunter, either by paraphrase or in some cases by translation. This section of the book however is not without charm, for both Caunter and Mukherji had a sense of the picturesque. The treatment of the characters however, even at this early stage in the book, shows quite a difference of approach. Mukherji devotes more attention to detail, and in consequence his characters are more alive. Caunter's personae are never more than the agents of his story, and at no time is the reader emotionally involved in what happens to them. Mukherji's Śivājī and Rośinārā are not fairy tale persons but man and woman, and his sympathetic delineation of them lifts his work on to a different artistic plane.

Mukherji also shows far greater sensitiveness, especially when differences of religion arise. The fact that he was himself an Indian would account for his having a deeper understanding of one side at any rate, but his sympathy and delicacy where the personal feelings of either Muslim or Hindu could have been involved is a tribute to his own broad and fair attitude. Throughout he is scrupulously respectful to both religions. The following quotations show with what insight and courtesy he could tread on difficult ground. They describe the preparations the Chief has made for the entertainment of his enforced guest.

(Caunter)

'One of her women, who was an adept at story-telling, and had made herself acquainted with many of the singular legends of Hindoo history, entertained her mistress by relating some of those monstrous fictions which abound in those two poetical depositories of the marvellous, the Mahabharat and Ramayana.'

(Mukherji)

'Getting up at dawn the next morning, the princess went on a tour of inspection of the house which was to be her dwelling place. As she did so she came across a pile of books, romantic works, written in a beautiful hand in the Persian language, Phardausi, Hāphej, Sekh Sādi,[1] and others. From a child she had learned to read in her own language . . . and was charmed to find all these books in such a place.'[2]

How much more courtly the one is than the other!

Both books narrate an incident in which the princess is insulted by one of the Mahratta generals. The Chief at once challenges him to mortal combat to avenge the lady's honour, and leaves him for dead on the ground. The general however does not die, but revives and in his anger makes a pact with the Moghul commander to betray his master. He leads a detachment of troops by a secret way into the Mahratta fortress. The fortress falls and the princess is released and sent back to her father. Here the similarity between the two accounts ends. Caunter's traitor dies a traitor's death while trying to apprehend his master and hand him over to the foe. In Mukherji's version both come out of the conflict unscathed, Śivajī to rally his scattered forces, the general to return to the Moghul camp. They meet again in a later battle, when the general, stricken with remorse that he has betrayed his master and his people to the enemy, dies a death of expiation trying to save Śivājī from capture. The matter is not important, but it does show that in affording a man who had once held a position of trust an opportunity to rehabilitate himself Mukherji was sensitive enough to try to find the goodness in one who had not always been a traitor.

A more important feature of the treatment of the main theme is that Mukherji's Śivājī and Rośinārā though in love do not enter into a marital relationship while they are together in the Mahratta fortress. Śivājī respects the religion of the princess, but he does not lose sight of the obligation which his own religion imposes on him. His acceptance of his religious duty and his steadfastness in the performance of it are sustained by the advice of his guru, Rāmdās Svāmī. Śivājī remains a good Hindu to the end, and Rośinārā a good Muslim. Much of the nobility of *Angurīyavinimay* arises from Mukherji's delicate handling of the relationship between his two main characters. In spite of the tempting vicissitudes through which they pass,

[1] *Bhūdeb-racanāsambhār*, p. 276.

[2] Properly, Firdausī, Hāfiz, Shai*kh* Sordī, all Persian classics.

the book comes to an end without even the suspicion of a slur on the religious faith of either of them. Mukherji has succeeded in making a noble Hindu meet an equally noble Muslim, and he makes them part in sorrow but with clear consciences.

It is in the latter part of the book, when the scene has shifted to Delhi, that the measure of Mukherji's creative originality becomes manifest. From now on the book has a dramatic quality. The three principal characters are together in Delhi, and the action is concentrated on them by the employment of the dramatic convention of the three unities. There is a central scene which is the turning point of the action, the point at which the problem is posed. Aurangzeb receives Śivājī in audience, and treats him with hostility and intolerable disrespect. Rośinārā from behind the screen that separates the women's quarters from the audience chamber, sees and hears all that takes place. She knows that Śivājī will not suffer in silence or inaction such an insult to his dignity and his honour; and is prepared for a tragic *dénouement*. Śivājī is determined to escape and take up the war with his enemy, whom he knows now he cannot any longer trust; but he hopes to be able to take Rośinārā with him. He gets into communication with her by a device which has a long history in Bengali literature. He sends a message and his ring to her by hand of a flower woman who is also a pedlar of trifles. Rośinārā makes a last plea to her father and promises to marry anybody he names if he will pardon and release Śivājī. Aurangzeb promises, but without any intention of keeping his word. Meanwhile Śivājī has escaped from his prison house and is awaiting Rośinārā at the appointed place. Here begins the final scene of the play. A woman arrives, but it is the flower woman, not Rośinārā. She hands to Śivājī a ring which Rośinārā has sent in exchange for his own to serve as a pledge of life-long fidelity, and with it a letter to explain why she cannot escape with him. Rāmdās Svāmī is with Śivājī at the time. He has been worried lest in the vehemence of his love for the Muslim princess, Śivājī should forget his duty as a Hindu monarch and marry her. Śivājī passes him the letter to read. He is so moved by the nobility of the message that he gives Śivājī permission to accept the ring as a symbol of spiritual union. It is a well-conceived, well-executed and very dramatic ending. I quote the last two paragraphs which contain the letter and Rāmdās's valediction.

'"O Mahratta King! O beloved! How am I to address you? I hardly know what to write either. I cannot be sure that you understand what I have in my mind, but I know what you have in yours; but if I explain why I cannot join you as your companion, I am sure you will understand and not be angry with me. More I cannot say. You are my husband. Today is our marriage consummated. But if I join you and live with you, the real ideal of your spirit will fail of fulfilment. This is why I deny myself the bliss of living with you as my husband. You may say that you are content to forsake your kingdom for my sake—I should not disbelieve you if you did—but I would bid you look into your heart which will tell you that kingship is not the only ideal that your spirit holds dear. So just as I deny myself companionship with you because I know the grief of spirit that will torture you as my husband, so you must go away without me, your wife, because of your devotion to your race and faith. I cannot write more. Your slave, Rośinārā."

'Rāmdās read the letter with astonishment and exclaimed, "Maharaj! I did not know that so noble a lady was living on the earth today. There are some who are prepared to kill themselves to preserve their fidelity to their lords; but even such devotion is not as great as this. I consent to your accepting her ring. If the Scriptures are true, this daughter of the Emperor will be born again to be your duly wedded spouse."'[1]

The method by which Mukherji contrived the climax and the *dénouement* is not the only debt that he owes to the art of the drama. The scene of the climax is followed by one in which he makes effective use of dramatic soliloquy. Aurangzeb is sitting alone.

'"The night is dark. At this hour all my subjects, even the poor and the unhappy, have shed all their cares and are sleeping peacefully, but I their emperor, have not a single moment in which to sleep. The fever of anxious thought burns my spirit

[1] *Bhūdeb-racanāsambhār*, p. 330.

endlessly. My cares have no end, they know no respite; and even if they did what would it avail me? If all need to worry about the future were taken from me, the memory of all my past misdeeds would still be with me. Nevertheless it is right that I should remain for ever thoughtful. Let those who have never travelled the slippery road of sin strive to shake off anxious thought. Man's life is like a game of chess: the more one studies it the greater the pleasure; and the more cautious one remains the higher the hope of victory. Why, look! Even the cunning Śivājī has been caught in my net. He thinks that because Jayasiṃha has testified on his behalf I shall receive him with honour and let him depart. What a fool! Jayasiṃha! Jayasiṃha! The very name scorches my ears. He has served me well, it is true; but a man who renders service is not incapable of rendering disservice also. Besides, once a task has been successfully completed, what need is there to retain the services of the agent who accomplished it? There is no need of a fruit hook once the fruit has fallen. But will it serve my purpose to destroy Jayasiṃha? Whom did my father not destroy?—And then, there is my son too. But he is completely under my control. Yet I must be cautious. I must find out first who my enemies are and who my friends." He paused from his reflections for a while, and then an inspiration came to him from heaven. "Jayasiṃha! Let him beware! If he fails this test he will be destroyed. Neither will it be my fault. And you, my son! I have cut you off from your friends, so never try to fly from me." The emperor at this point began with great care to write a letter to his son. The gist of it was as follows. "My son, you are utterly in my power, and for that reason I am confident that I can trust you with a most dangerous undertaking. I have no such confidence in any of my other sons. From your childhood I have trained you to be obedient. Not long ago to test your courage and obedience I made you fight a tiger single-handed, and you did it. It is with great labour that I have won dominion in India, and you may be sure that I shall bequeath it only to a son who proves obedient in all things. Your eldest brother, Mahomed, has great talent but he ignored my commands, and in consequence he is spending the rest of his life in the fort at Gwalior. So beware lest a similar plight befalls you. As soon as you receive this letter summon

Jayasiṃha and all the other generals to a secret conference. Inform them that you have rebelled against your father and have assumed the sovereignty. Make a note of the names of all those who agree to support you and send them to me without delay. If you carry this task through successfully you may be sure that you yourself will in due course enjoy the fruits of all my toil."

'The emperor read the letter to himself two or three times, and pondered it. "If my son consents to do what I want, I shall know for certain the names of all my enemies; and if he himself ever plots a rebellion on his own account, I shall know whom I cannot trust. But if he feels that he is in a strong position and does rebel, what ought I to do? The great problem for kings is that they must trust somebody. They cannot do anything if they do not. Alas, if only I could do all that has to be done by my own hand alone, and if the world were on one side and I on the other, I could be confident of victory." Here he thought for a little while, and then called a very trustworthy servant. "Take this letter and go quickly to Vijaypur. Place it with the utmost secrecy in the hands of my son. Ask him to allow you to stay near him when Jayasiṃha and the other generals come to his conference. If my son lets you stay assume the role of attendant in his tent. Listen to all that is said and if Jayasiṃha agrees to rebel as my son will propose, give him something to drink. Here is the spice for that drink." So saying Aurangzeb placed a paper packet in the servant's hand. "If you are not permitted to stay, get into conversation with the attendant who works in Jayasiṃha's tent. Do you understand?" The servant smiled, and talking the letter and some money for the journey set off.'[1]

This soliloquy renders unnecessary any further attempt on the part of the author to portray the character of Aurangzeb. At the same time it permits the author, without violating the unities his dramatic purpose required, to describe the state of affairs in the country at the time, the precariousness, real or simulated, of Aurangzeb's hold on his vast empire, and the fiendish cunning he was prepared to employ in securing it. We also know his intentions with regard to Śivājī. It is hard

[1] *Bhūdeb-racanāsambhār*, pp. 31–6.

to see how all this could have been achieved with greater economy. The soliloquy is brief, but brilliantly vivid. It fills in the whole canvas of contemporary political life to serve as a back-screen against which the principal characters are to act out their parts.

The climax scene, the soliloquy and the *dénouement* owe nothing to Caunter. Another innovation of Mukherji's is the figure of the guru. The device of the holy man, so often employed by Bankimcandra, may well have been suggested to him by Rāmdās Svāmī. Yet there is a difference between the use the two authors make of this type of character. Rāmdās is primarily the embodiment of Śivājī's conscience, ever present to remind him of the duties required of him as a Hindu king. Mukherji never attempts, as Bankim was to do, to make him assume the role of a *deus ex machina,* whose function it is to disentangle knots of circumstance in which the human characters are caught up and from which they cannot escape without supernatural assistance. Rāmdās Svāmī is a holy man, but he is still a man; he is not an enigmatic being, half man and half god, as Bankim's are.

Angurīyavinimay is short but it is without question the first historical novel to be written in Bengali. The only previous work which is in any way comparable with it, *Pratāpādityacaritra,* was a work of historical fiction, it is true, but it is not a novel. It is surprising that in this first essay into so difficult a field, Mukherji should have developed such a command over his material and his technique and should have realized so clearly the difficulties involved in combining history with fiction. *Angurīyavinimay,* which strangely enough is almost unknown in Bengal, achieved so much and promised so much more; but it was at the same time a beginning and an end, for Mukherji did not attempt to write another historical novel.

At this stage it may be useful to pause and attempt an assessment of literary achievement so far. By 1862, with the publication of *Ālāler Gharer Dulāl, Hutom Pyẫcār Nakśā* and *Angurīyavinimay,* the writing of prose narrative in Bengali had advanced to a point at which it can be said that the novel had begun to emerge. It was not yet fully formed but it was ready for a birth.

Very great progress had been made since the beginning of

the century when the authors of the Fort William school commenced their struggle with the elements of their linguistic material and strove to shape them into a language suitable for the writing of prose. Spelling had been standardized, or almost so, by the compiling of dictionaries. The range of literary vocabulary had been explored, from the high preponderance of Sanskrit words and phrases at one extreme to the colloquialisms of Siṃha at the other; and words of foreign origin, including Persian and English, were settling into use in their appropriate contexts. Grammatical analysis and statement had made considerable progress in the labours of Rām Mohan Rāy and Carey. Punctuation on the English model was being adapted to the requirements of the Bengali sentence and paragraph; and phrase, clause and sentence structure had acquired a greater formal diversity and stylistic potentiality.

Literary prose style analysed on the basis of vocabulary preferences and a dichotomy of verbal and pronominal forms was beginning to be classified in two categories, *sādhu bhāṣā* and *calit bhāṣā*. These categories have not yet been fully analysed or defined. They are imprecise, and lead easily to an oversimplification when applied to different styles, particularly those of a later period. They have at this period in the history of literature however, a certain general usefulness. *Sādhu bhāṣā* implied a preference for the Sanskritic elements in the vocabulary and the use of the longer verbal and pronominal forms; *calit bhāṣā* implied a preference for the more colloquial elements and the use of the shorter verbal and pronominal forms, which as written corresponded fairly closely with those current in the spoken language. Vidyāsāgar and Bhūdeb Mukherji employed *sādhu bhāṣā*, Siṃha *calit bhāṣā*, and Mitra used both but in different contexts. What is important from the historical point of view is that by this time literary style had been practised and studied to such an extent that this dichotomy was consciously realized. Authors were now in a position, indeed were required, to make a choice between the two. Failure to keep them apart was subject to unfavourable criticism. Mixed diction was dubbed *gurucaṇḍālī* (brahmin and outcaste). The term itself is interesting, implying, as it seems to do, a preference for *sādhu* as against *calit bhāṣā*.

In the course of the six decades three types of subject had

established themselves as suitable for prose narrative. The first, drawing on Bengali social life, had been popular for forty years, from the unknown writer of the *upākhyān* in the *Samācar Darpan* in 1821, to *Hutom Pyãcār Nakśā* in 1862. The second, which chose its subjects from Hindu mythology, had reached its highest peak of excellence at the hands of Vidyāsāgar, particularly in his *Sītār Banabās*. The third category was historical or quasi-historical. It began with *Pratāpādityacaritra* in 1801, and received its most modern exposition up to date in *Angurīyavinimay* in 1862.

In 1865, Bankimcandra Chatterji's novel, *Durgeśnandinī*, appeared, and like all but his very last works of fiction was published in serial form in magazines, the most important of which was his own *Bangadarśan*, which commenced publication in 1872. *Durgeśnandinī* was followed at regular intervals by other novels until 1887 when the last of them, *Sītārām*, was published. Bankim wrote no new novel after 1887, but he did much revision for re-publication. A number of his novels were revised more than once, some of them being almost completely rewritten. Bankim wrote fourteen novels in all, though two were so short as to be more like short stories. He also wrote a book of sketches entitled *Kamalākānter Daptar*, published in 1875, and though it is not a novel or even primarily narrative, it does contain some fictional narrative, part of which is very good indeed. The many other prose works of Bankim will not be examined here as they fall outside the scope of our present inquiry. He contributed to his own and other magazines a large number of articles on social, religious, historical and educational topics, and wrote two long dissertations on religious and philosophical themes. He attempted poetry also, but with little distinction. His novels however represent his most important contribution to Bengali literature. In point of time Bankim was the first Bengali novelist. What had gone before was preparatory stuff, at best the novel in embryo. Bankim's novels were really novels.

This is not the time, neither is there space in a short monograph, to attempt a critical appraisal of Bankim's novels; but it is important for our purpose to remember that their appearance created a furore of excitement, first in Calcutta, and later in other parts of India. Contemporary and later critics bear clear testimony to his great and immediate popularity. An article in the *Calcutta Review* of 1873 contains the following sentence: 'This novel [*Biṣbṛkṣa*] was to be found in the *baithak-khana* [sitting room] of every Bengali Babu throughout the whole of last year.'[1] Tagore in his autobiographies describes the impatient eagerness with which he and others waited for the next instalment. The first quotation is from *Jībansmṛti*, the second from *Chelebelā*.

'Then came Bankim's *Bangadarśan*, taking the Bengali heart by storm. It was bad enough to have to wait till the next monthly number was out, but to be kept waiting further till my elders had done with it was simply intolerable. Now he who will may swallow at a mouthful the whole of *Chandraśekhar* or *Bishabriksha*, but the process of longing and anticipating, month after month; or spreading over the long intervals the concentrated joy of each short reading, revolving every instalment over and over in the mind while watching and waiting for the next: the combination of satisfaction with unsatisfied craving, of burning curiosity with its appeasement; these long-drawn-out delights of going through the original serial none will ever taste again.'[2]

'*Bangadarśan* was like a comet in the sky. Sūryamukhī and Kundanandinī (from *Biṣbṛkṣa*) went to and fro in every house as if they were members of the family. The whole country was on edge with anxiety to know what had happened now, and what was going to happen next. When *Bangadarśan* arrived nobody in our part of Calcutta had their afternoon nap that day.'[3]

Modern opinion is well represented by Sukumar Sen. 'No Bengali writer before or since has enjoyed such spontaneous and universal popularity as Chatterji. His novels have been

[1] Quoted by Brajendranāth Bandyopādhyāy in his Introduction to the Baṅgīya Sāhitya Pariṣad edn. of *Biṣbṛkṣa*, p. vi.

[2] Quoted from the English version of *Jībansmṛti* entitled *Reminiscences*, pub. Macmillan, 1954, p. 115.

[3] *Chelebelā*, pub. Viśvabhāratī, Calcutta, 10th edn., 1957, pp. 61–2. Trans. by Marjorie Sykes.

translated into almost all the major languages of India, and have helped to stimulate literary impulses in those languages.'[1] Whatever conclusion posterity may reach about the intrinsic merits of his work, no critic may safely ignore the extraordinary enthusiasm his novels created in his own and subsequent generations.

Durgeśnandini, the first of the fourteen, is a historical novel. In his prefatory note the author described it as *itibṛttamūlak upanyās* (novel based on history). Like Bhūdeb Mukherji before him, Bankim drew his inspiration from the material made popular by Tod's *Annals and Antiquities of Rajasthan*. The hero in *Durgeśnandinī* is a Rajput in the service of the Moghul emperor, and the co-hero a Paṭhān general in the service of the Paṭhān sultan of Bengal. It is a tale of warlike deeds and courage with a double love interest, one between Jagat Siṃha, the Rajput hero, and the daughter of a Hindu chieftain, the other a triangular affair involving Jagat Siṃha, Osmān, the Paṭhān general, and Āyeṣā, daughter of the sultan. *Durgeśnandinī* differs in one significant respect from *Angurīyavinimay:* the action is placed in Bengal and the heroine is a Bengali princess, an innovation which did not fail to stir the emotions of its Bengali readers. Like Mukherji also, Bankim includes in his characters a holy man, Abhirām Svāmī, the first of a number of such semi-supernatural beings he was to employ. Contemporary critics were quick to suggest a resemblance between *Durgeśnandinī* and some of Scott's novels. They claimed that the unreturned love of the Muslim princess, Āyeṣā, for Jagat Siṃha, is similar to Rebecca's love for Ivanhoe. Be that as it may, Bankim according to his own statement had not read *Ivanhoe* at the time.[2]

Bankim's third novel, *Mṛṇālinī*, was described in the prefaces to the first and second editions as *aitihāsik upanyās* (historical novel). The action takes place in Bengal at the time of Lakṣmaṇ Sen during the first Muslim invasion of Bengal. Against this background is set a love affair between a prince of Magadha and a merchant's daughter from Mathurā. They are in fact man and wife, but had become separated in the confusion of the times. The story for this pair ends happily, but the secon-

[1] Sukumar Sen, *op. cit.*, p. 238.

[2] Intro. to Baṅgīya Sāhitya Pariṣad edn. of *Durgeśnandinī*, p. xvi.

dary love affair, also to do with a man and his separated wife, ends in *satī*. Other historical novels followed: *Candraśekhar* (1875), set in the British period when Mīr Kasim was Navāb; *Rājsiṃha* (1882), a story of the time of Aurangzeb; *Ānandamaṭh* (1882), probably Bankim's most famous novel, set in the British period and having as its main subject the revolt of the Sannyāsīs; *Debīcaudhurāṇī* (1884) also set in the British period and portraying from a somewhat romantic angle the banditry which was prevalent in the late eighteenth century; and finally *Sītārām* (1887), set in Bengal in the early eighteenth century before the British assumption of power.

Two general features in Bankim's novels are noteworthy. The first is the shifting of the scene in some of them from Rajputana, Maharastra and Delhi to Bengal, with Bengali heroes and heroines in certain of the leading roles. Thus heroism came to Bengal, at first vicariously it is true, but soon it began to naturalize its domicile there, and this was not without effect on the political stirrings that were beginning to be felt at this time. The second feature, also of consequence politically, is the shift of Bankim's sympathy with regard to the communal problem during his career as a novelist. In *Durgeśnandinī*, Osmān, though a Muslim, is presented as a hero, noble of sentiment and brave in action. In the later novels, Bankim's attitude towards Muslims is hostile. In *Ānandamaṭh* and *Sītārām* particularly they are *par excellence* the enemy. They are portrayed as cowardly and cruel, rapacious and tyrannical. The heroes were Hindu, the villains Muslim. Patriotism was unequivocally identified with Hinduism. The hymn *Bande Mātaram*, the marching song of the Santāns in *Ānandamaṭh*, became the first rallying song of Hindu patriots, and, as Arobindo Ghoṣ later called it, the *mantra* of Nationalism.[1]

It would be unjust to Bankim, I feel, to leave the present brief consideration of his historical novels without examination of his mature opinion on the nature of the historical novel and in particular of the relation between the novel and history. He called *Durgeśnandinī* and *Mṛṇālinī*, written at the beginning

[1] 'The Role of Bankimcandra in the Development of Nationalism', by T. W. Clark, in *Historians of India, Pakistan and Ceylon*, ed. C. H. Philips, pub. OUP, 1961, pp. 438–9.

of his career, historical novels, but later he changed his mind and requested that they should not be so regarded. His views are set out in the preface to the fourth edition of *Rājsiṃha*,[1] which he wrote only a few years before his death and several years after the publication of his last novel, *Sītārām*. 'I have never written a historical novel before [i.e. before *Rājsiṃha*]. *Durgeśnandinī*, *Candraśekhar* and *Sītārām* cannot be called historical novels. This [i.e. *Rājsiṃha*] is the first historical novel I have written. Hitherto no author has been successful in writing a historical novel. It goes without saying that I have not been successful either.' In the preface to *Debīcaudhurāṇī*,[2] there is something of an emotional note in his plea. 'I shall be obliged, reader, if you will please not regard *Ānandamaṭh* and *Debīcaudhurāṇī* as historical novels.' The reasons for this curious change of opinion are, so far as I am aware, nowhere fully expounded, but references in various places make it possible for us to detect in part at any rate the direction of his thinking. 'Since the publication of *Ānandamaṭh* many people have asked me to tell them whether the book is founded on history or not.'[3] It is possible that he found these questions embarrassing, not, I think, because he could not answer them, but because his readers seemed to be too ready to take all that he wrote in these novels as historical truth, thereby raising doubts in his mind as to whether the novel could be a suitable vehicle for history. 'Occasionally', he wrote, 'the purposes of history can be accomplished in a novel. The novelist is not always bound by the chains of truth. He can when he wants to resort to the use of his imagination to achieve the effects he desires; for this reason the novel cannot always take the place of history. . . . To ensure that my novel is a novel I have had to introduce many matters which are imaginary. . . . There is no need for everything in a novel to be historical.'[4] And then finally, 'A novel is a novel; it is not history'.[5] Bankim wrote a number of essays on historiology and urged that the study of history was essential if India was to develop politically. Great

[1] Baṅgīya Sāhitya Pariṣad edn. of *Rājsiṃha*, Intro., pp. 26–8.
[2] Baṅgīya Sāhitya Pariṣad edn. of *Debīcaudhurāṇī*, preface, p. i.
[3] *Ibid.*
[4] Baṅgīya Sāhitya Pariṣad edn. of *Rājsiṃha*, Intro., pp. 26–8.
[5] Baṅgīya Sāhitya Pariṣad edn. of *Indirā*, Intro., pp. v–vii.

nations, he said, had great historians. Much of India's weakness could be ascribed to the fact that it had had no sense of history and that in consequence it had lost all connection with, and knowledge of, the greatness of its past. There is no need here to examine the logic of these arguments, but it is important to know that Bankim was convinced by them. He felt that India needed history, scientific history, not history so mixed up with mythology, as it had been in the past, that no one could tell the true from the fanciful. It is therefore feasible that his disclaimers about the historical status of some of his novels were based on a conviction that history cannot consort with fiction without diminution of its value as history. Hence *Durgeśnandinī* and the rest, except *Rājsiṃha*, were to be classified as novels, but not as historical novels, or even as novels based on history.

An author has a right to be heard when he is discussing his own work, but when every consideration has been paid to the problem Bankim was trying to solve, one cannot but feel that if the degree of historicity which he implies a historical novel must possess is accepted, there could be no historical novels. On the same argument Shakespeare's historical plays should not be called historical. A novel which has a historical setting may not be reliable as a source of accurate historical information, but it can have a place in literature as a novel, and there seems no harm in calling it a historical novel. *Durgeśnandinī* and the other six novels which have the same type of historical background must be called historical novels. It is hard to know how else to classify them. This conclusion is at any rate convenient, even though Bankim would not concede that it is correct. If it is accepted, then seven of Bankim's fourteen novels are historical novels. One, *Rājsiṃha*, deals with the early Muslim period; two, *Durgeśnandinī* and *Mṛṇālinī*, with Rajput and other heroes in the period of established Muslim power; and four, *Candraśekhar*, *Ānandamaṭh*, *Debīcaudhurāṇī* and *Sītārām*, with eighteenth-century history before and after the coming of the British.

The remaining seven of Bankim's novels cannot be so easily classified. They do not form a single homogeneous group. In some the story is told for its own sake, in others it is told for an ulterior didactic purpose. Like some of his predecessors,

Bankim wrote about the society in which he lived; but his approach, unlike theirs, was seldom that of a satirist. He tended to treat human relationships and social problems seriously, as problems to be solved. Satire was only an occasional weapon. He was capable of caustic and humorous condemnation, but he indulged it sparingly. Hīrālāl in *Rajanī* is said to be a caricature of a certain journalist, a high-talking, wine-drinking, very westernized Babu. Amarnāth in the same novel, who is presented as typical of his class, is chided for being self-centred. He is shown as totally unconcerned with the pressing problems of the day, such as the marriage of widows, kulin polygamy, juvenile marriage, the improvement of social conditions and the emancipation of women. The list, which is Bankim's, is interesting. A current scandal is referred to in the preface to *Indirā*. The method is characteristic.

'I have been criticized because I have expanded *Indirā* and also put up its price. If a man is promoted by favour of government or society he puts up his fees. The standard bribe for a police officer is one rupee, but when he becomes an inspector the rate goes up to two rupees. He has been promoted, so has his fee. Poor *Indirā* is entitled to say, "I have become a big book, so why should not my price go up?" '[1]

All Bankim's novels, including the historical novels, have a love theme as their principal human interest. The nature of the theme varies. In *Rādhārānī*, the heroine chooses her own mate, and pursues him to the happy conclusion of marriage. The blind Rajanī falls in love and after numerous difficulties is happily married; and, to add greater happiness to her married life, Bankim arranges somewhat miraculously for her sight to be restored by a holy man. Another aspect of the love theme is the temporary separation or alienation of husband and wife. In *Indirā*, the hero and heroine had married young and been separated. The husband has forgotten what his wife looks like, but she recognizes him when they meet in Calcutta, and is able with the help of friends to arrange a happy reunion. Nāgendranāth and his wife Sūryamukhī, in the tragic story *Biṣbṛkṣa*, are finally brought together again. The ending

[1] Baṅgīya Sāhitya Pariṣad edn. of *Indirā*, Intro. pp. v–vii.

however is not always happy: the love of Nabakumār and Kapālkundalā ends in a fatal accident just when the difficulties which have beset the path of their married love are beginning to be resolved; and there is the sad plight of Pratāp and Śaibalinī, in *Candraśekhar*. They are childhood sweethearts but cannot marry because their relationship falls under the interdiction imposed by the Hindu law of affinity. Two of Bankim's lovers are widows. One of them, Kundanandinī, in *Biṣbṛkṣa*, marries the hero and temporarily estranges him from his lawful wife, Sūryamukhī; but the estrangement does not last and the unfortunate Kundanandinī poisons herself. The other widow is Rohinī in *Kṛṣṇakānter Uil*. She lures the hero Gobindalāl away from his wife, but towards the end of a tortuous story he murders her. Polygamy also features in his marital pictures. Brajeśvar of *Debīcaudhurāṇī* and Sītārām of the novel which bears his name both had three legal wives. In neither case is any condemnation of multiple marriage implied, though in *Rajinī* Bankim does express disapproval of multiple marriages of the type entered into by kulin brahmins.

In certain cases Bankim's attitude to the love theme is that of a story teller. He is in them primarily concerned with his lovers as men and women and with the evolution of the action in which they participate. Yet in some of his later novels Bankim had a didactic purpose. His subject was the sanctity of orthodox Hindu marriage and in particular the nobility of wives who saw their highest duty in devotion and service to their husbands. *Debīcaudhurāṇī* is brought to an unconvincing end because Bankim was determined that Praphulla should be made to conform to his image of the perfect wife. She surrenders the excitement and benefits of her Robin Hood-like career to return to her husband, who at best is a colourless person. He had allowed her to be driven away from home by his father, who is a coward and a despicable rogue. Nor does it stop here. In the final paragraph she is apotheosized and invoked as the divine embodiment of Hindu wifehood. 'Come, come, Praphulla! Stand once more in the world of men and let us behold you. Stand in the society of this world and proclaim yourself, "I am not new; I am from everlasting. I am the divine word. However often I come to you you forget me; yet I am here once more—

"From age to age I am born to save the good, to destroy the wicked, and establish true religion." '[1]

The social life of Bankim's novels is pitched at different levels, according to the status of his principal characters. He himself came of a middle-class family, and it is only when dealing with characters of this class that he is at home and that his descriptions are realistic and convincing.

Of the domestic and social life of princes and the very wealthy he knew little from first-hand experience, and what he says of them is from the outside. The best part of *Kṛṣṇakānter Uil,* which Bankim said was his favourite among the novels, is not its unhappy story and the vagaries of its main characters, but the picture it presents of middle class life in a Bengal village. Life in a Calcutta home is sketched in some detail in *Indirā.* Yet interested as he was in the problems thrown up by contemporary social life, Bankim had not an eye for the details of human behaviour and social situations the faithful delineation of which constitutes the greatest charm of at least two Bengali novelists of a later generation.[2] He was a story teller rather than an observer of men and of their ways with one another.

Bankim's religious beliefs cannot be described adequately by reference to his novels alone. He studied the subject deeply in later life, but his conclusions are to be found in his essays *Dharmatattva* and *Kṛṣṇacarit,* which lie outside the purview of the present inquiry. Nevertheless it is clear from his novels that his position is that of an orthodox Hindu. He took his stand with the defenders of the ancient faith. He has nothing to say of Christianity and Islam as religions, though believers in these faiths occur frequently as characters in his stories, particularly Muslims. In the early novel *Kapālkundalā,* one of the characters is a kapālik, a sect whose unsavoury, esoteric rites included sexual orgies and human sacrifice; but though he speaks of these rites with distaste and makes the kapālik an unpleasant character, the teacher in Bankim had not yet

[1] *Bhagavadgītā,* 4.8:
paritrāṇāyś sādhūnām vināśāya ca duṣkṛtām,
dharmasaṃsthāpanārthāy asambhavāmi yuge yuge.

[2] I.e. Saratcandra Chatterji and Bibhutibhūṣaṇ Banerji.

come uppermost, and he does not attempt to develop his views on Tantricism. Of the Brāhmo Samāj too he says very little, though it was probably at its most powerful in the Calcutta of his day. He preached two deities, Kṛṣṇa and Śakti, the latter under different names, Caṇḍī, Kālī and Durgā. Bankim's Kṛṣṇa is not the deity of Caitanya; he is the heroic, kingly deity of the *Gītā*. Kālī and Caṇḍī respectively are the divine supporters and inspirers of the Hindu armies in *Ānandamaṭh* and *Sītārām*. Bankim attempts to make a unity of Kṛṣṇa and Śakti in *Ānandamaṭh*. The Santāns are Vaiṣṇavas, but they also worship Kālī. Their marching song, *Bande Mātaram*, invokes the female goddess as the Mother. Presumably the purpose behind this attempted synthesis was to bring together the two main sects in Hinduism, the Vaiṣṇavas and the Śāktas (or Śaivas), by supplying them with a unified concept of the deity. In practice the attempt did not succeed, and its theological justification was not convincing; but the enthusiasm with which *Ānandamaṭh* was received owed much to the attempt it made to justify Hinduism and promote the pride of Hindus in their creed. Judged as a novel, *Ānandamaṭh* is faultily conceived and constructed, but as a prophetic utterance it was the most powerful word spoken in Bengal in the nineteenth century.

Bankim's art as a novelist owes certain debts to some British writers. Similarities to Scott are discernible, though they can be overstated, as has been indicated earlier. Both tell a good fast-moving story, and both are emotionally attracted to heroism in men and self-sacrifice in beautiful women. Hero worship and admiration for good women, particularly good wives, lie near the heart of most of Bankim's stories, and constitute an important legacy to Bengali literature and thought. Contemporary readers were quick to notice similarities between Bankim's novels and Scott's. They were soon to call him the 'Scott of Bengal', though the bestowing of this title may also have been occasioned by a desire to give their distinguished compatriot status among the writers of the world. In his preface to *Rajanī*, Bankim admitted that in writing that novel he was indebted to two other British authors. 'In that excellent novel by Lord Lytton, *The Last Days of Pompeii*, there is a blind flower girl named Nydia. . . . The character of Rajanī is built on this foundation.' And later on in the same preface he wrote, 'It is not common in the construction of a popular novel to make the hero and heroine speak for themselves, but it is not new. It was done first by Wilkie Collins in his *Woman in White*.'[1] He goes on to say, with a naïveté I find hard to understand, that one of the advantages of letting the characters speak for themselves is that the author cannot be held responsible for any peculiar or unnatural things they may say. Can an author so easily shrug off the responsibilities of creation? In *Indirā* the narrative is in the first person, the speaker being the heroine herself. This device had been used before him by both Defoe and Dickens whom Bankim had possibly read. There is no doubt that he gave much thought to the structure of his novels, and it is no detraction from his originality that he read the novels of British writers as part of that discipline and borrowed from them what seemed suitable to his purposes.

Certain other devices however which he may have borrowed Bankim clearly overworks. The first is that of the holy man. This character was first introduced into fiction by Bhūdeb Mukherji, and he on the whole handled him with discretion. Bankim used him excessively. No fewer than five of his novels have one. Furthermore he tended to use the holy man as a *deus ex machina* to intervene in the natural sequence of events when they seemed to have got out of hand, thereby casting doubts on the ability of the author to control the course of the action he himself had set in train. Divine or semi-divine intervention in the lives of men had had a long history before Bankim, particularly in the mythological ballads known as *maṅgalkāvya*, but there it could be justified as it involved no violation of the reader's willingness to believe. In a novel which deals with men and women in real life situations such intervention runs the danger of making the action seem incredible. Another type of *deus ex machina* by which Bankim strains the credibility of his plot is the frequent introduction of chance accidents. The evolution of the story in *Debīcaudhurānī*, to cite the most notable instance, is almost entirely directed by accidents. One might have been acceptable, as accidents do happen in everyday life, but four is too many; and in any case two of them go far beyond what is probable. They belong to the realm of romance, not to that of the realistic

[1] Preface to *Rajanī*, Baṅgīya Sāhitya Pariṣad edn., p. 8.

novel. Praphulla, the heroine, as the result of a fortunate but not incredible accident, finds herself alone in a forest at night. She wanders on blindly and eventually comes to a derelict house which she enters in search of shelter. There she finds an old man who is dying. She ministers to him, and before he dies he bequeathes all his possessions to her. They include a large hoard of gold coins. Having money but no food, she goes out to look for a village market. On the way she meets the leader of a band of robbers, who discovers the whereabouts of her fortune, but instead of appropriating it, he arranges for her to undergo a course of instruction in Sanskrit usually reserved for young brahmins. On completing the course she takes over from him as a sort of female Robin Hood. Success attends all her campaigns until the forces of government are massed against her and she is surrounded. At this moment a cyclonic storm descends on the area and the police party is scattered. A third device which Bankim overworks is that of disguise. He probably inherited it from the popular literature of the past, and within reason it is unexceptionable; but he uses it in no fewer than seven novels, and in some more than once.

'With regard to language also something needs to be said. Nowadays writers and students of language fall into two classes. The first of these is of the opinion that Bengali grammar should in every respect conform to that of Sanskrit. The other group, which includes a very large number of excellent Sanskrit scholars, thinks that what has now passed into current use should continue to be used even if it violates the rules of Sanskrit grammar. I myself incline to the views of the second group, but I am not prepared to support them in all cases and without reservation.'

This passage forms part of the last paragraph in the preface to the fourth edition of *Rājsiṃha*, which has already been referred to in other connections. It was written only a year or two before his death, and may therefore be presumed to be a statement of his mature opinion. The two types of language which the protagonists groups support are *sādhu bhāṣā* and *calit bhāṣā*. Bankim's position, according to his own declaration, falls somewhere between the two extremes. He inclines towards *calit bhāṣā* but has reservations, and his inability to commit himself wholly to it is reflected in the language he used. It is neither one nor the other; and his choice which is neither *sādhu* nor *calit* is important in the history of written Bengali. It is no longer defensible to analyse Bengali prose into these two categories, as though the language of all prose composition were either *sādhu bhāṣā* or *calit bhāṣā*. Bankim took up an intermediate position; and many followed his precept without copying his practice, with the result that by the end of the century there were not two types of language, but many.

In the course of his career Bankim's style changed. To begin with he was nearer the Sanskritic extreme, but later he moved more and more in the direction of the colloquial; yet to the end he disliked and refused to adopt the fully colloquial style and vocabulary of *Hutom Pyā̃cār Nakśa*. The first paragraph of his first novel is very Sanskritized. It is a short paragraph but it contains five Sanskrit compounds (samās), one having four constituents. Moreover he used a number of Sanskrit loan words for which acceptable Bengali equivalents were available. The first four lines contain no fewer than six of them. The proportion of Sanskrit words and compounds diminished with the years, and the vocabulary of his later novels is less heavy as a result. Bankim however was not able to bring himself to use the shorter verb and pronoun forms, which corresponded to those of the spoken language. In consequence his conversational passages are never natural: they are done in book language and so cannot be spoken. The otherwise excellent conversational opening to *Debīcaudhurānī* is perhaps the best example of the difficulty he was in but could not resolve. In it he lapses into short forms, but not often. The short forms in 'yeman adṛṣṭa *kare esechili*!' (what an unfortunate life you were born to!) are so right in the context; whereas 'upas *kariyā* kay din *bā̃cibi*?' (how long do you expect to live if you eat nothing?), strikes an artificial note. One could wish that Bankim had followed the example of Pyāricā̃d Mitra, who used the short verbs and pronouns in his conversations and the long ones in his narrative and descriptive passages, as did some of the greatest successors of Bankim in the art of novel writing.

To say so little about Bankim's style and language is to be unfair to him. He was a great writer, and his works represent a high-water mark in the history of Bengali prose. In his maturer compositions his sentences have a pleasant and easy flow. He has power, clarity and the feel of the artist for the right word; and in spite of some conservatism in his approach to the language problem, his work represents a great advance on the turgid and often difficult compositions of the orthodox school, many of whom still regarded Bengali as a 'barbaric vernacular'.

It is far easier to find faults in Bankim's novels, than it is to give adequate expression to the extent of his achievement and the services he rendered to Bengali literature. When he died, prose in Bengali was firmly established as a literary mode, and the reading public, which not many years before had complained that there was hardly anything worth reading in their own language, had a library of books and articles which they read avidly and with pride and enjoyment. In less than ninety years, from 1801 to 1887, Bengali prose fiction had climbed from nothing to a pinnacle whence it could claim recognition both in India and abroad; and it was not to stop there, for some ten years before Bankim ceased to write, the pen of his younger and far greater contemporary, Rabindranāth Tagore, was already at work.

EARLY PROSE FICTION IN MARATHI[1]

by IAN RAESIDE

Literary prose is a late developer in the history of any language and in Marathi, as for most other Indian languages, it does not appear in any significant quantity until the middle of the nineteenth century when the influence of English was beginning to transform a hitherto almost exclusively verse tradition. Before this the use of prose is limited to commentaries, to a few hagiographical works of the Mahānubhāv sect written in the late thirteenth and early fourteenth centuries, to historical narratives from the time of Maratha independence and to private and diplomatic correspondence of the same period. Of course, there must always have been a flourishing popular oral literature of fables and ghost stories, adaptations of episodes from the Puranas and the Epics, but these were never written down. Even among the well known Sanskrit story collections, only the *Pancatantra* is found in an early prose version in Marathi.[2]

This amount of prose is already considerably more than can be found in many of Marathi's neighbouring languages. However, very little of it can be treated as literature, and none at all, apart from the isolated example of *Pancatantra*, as fiction. The style of the early Mahānubhāv works is exceptionally colourless and dessicated, resolving itself into a series of short, staccato sentences, the form of which is obviously derived from verse forms such as the *ovi* couplet where the sense and the syntactical group rarely overrun the end of the line. Without rhyme or metre the effect is jerky and repetitive:

'Then Mahādāisā said, "Nāgdev, let us go to the Gosāvī." Bhaṭobās said, "Where is the Gosāvī?" Mahādāisā said, "Is he not in Ritpur? Śrīprabhu Gosāvī has sent for us". . . . And

[1] This paper was originally contributed to a seminar held at the School of Oriental and African Studies in 1960 and was published in the *Journal of Asian Studies*, XXVII, 4 (August 1968), pp. 791–808. It is reprinted here by permission and has been slightly revised to take account of subsequent publications. Chief among these is Part IV of *Marāṭhi Vāñmayācā Itihās*, ed. R. S. Jog, Poona (Mahārāṣtra Sāhitya Pariṣad), 1965, which contains a valuable chapter on the story and the novel (kathākādambarī) by L. M. Bhingāre.

[2] An excerpt is given in S. G. Tulpule, *An Old Marathi Reader*, Poona, 1960, p. 117.

Mahādāisā came with Bhaṭobās. Seeing the Gosāvī they said, "Alas, he is gone. Śrīcāngdev Rāul is no more." Bhaṭobās and Mahādāisā were very sorrowful. Śrīprabhu Gosāvī comforted them. They kept on saying, "He has gone! He has gone!" Then they remained fourteen years in the company of Śrīprabhu Gosāvī. Mhāimbhaṭ also came. And all the other disciples came. They remained with him and began to serve him.'[1]

The historical *bakhars* of the seventeenth and eighteenth centuries, though naturally more modern in language, are in a similarly uninspiring style that seems inseparable from the narration of predominantly military events and which can be found in an almost identical form in the minor chronicles of most languages. Nevertheless, occasionally in the description of some climax—a battle, a murder or a tragic death—they may include a telling phrase or two and give a piece of dialogue that has an authentic flavour. It is noticeable that there is still no trace of any developed sentence structure. All this early prose is essentially an affair of short phrases, rarely linked by conjunctions and without puctuation except for the occasional vertical stroke used in poetry. Such effectiveness as this style has is cumulative, like certain passages of Rabelais or Saint-Simon.

'Then next day Dattājī Sinde set out and came to the camp of Durānī. Then he saw a mound of heads; and it brought tears to his eyes. In one moment fifteen thousand picked soldiers had died. It was such that scarce one could be recognized. Such carnage of our men! There was lamentation throughout the army. Such carnage! Somājībābā Bhosle was standing in the ranks only a little while. He was a holy man pure and simple. That day he did a warrior's duty for a moment only; but it was his hour! His head too was cut off and carried away. With great trouble his body at least was sought out. That body was offered to the flames'.[2]

This then was the stage that prose had reached at the time of the collapse of the Maratha empire. Its subsequent develop-

[1] V. N. Deśpaṇḍe, ed., *Smṛtisthaḷa,* 2nd ed., Poona, 1960, p. 4. Further examples of Mahānubhāv prose are given in Tulpule, *op. cit.*, pp. 94–116.

[2] S. N. Jośī, ed., *Bhāūsāhebāncī bakhar*, 7th edn., Poona, 1959, p. 63.

ment as a form and style was almost entirely due to the stimulus of Western, predominantly English, culture. Prose fiction was created as fables, stories, novels, essays, prose drama—all were imitated and often directly translated or adapted from English sources. Books of fables and moral tales were among the first printed books in Marathi, and in this category Aesop, the Sanskrit *Pancatantra* and *Chambers' Moral Classbook* existed happily side by side. The stimulus may have come from the West, but it soon began to operate on indigenous material. Before trying their hands at original works of fiction. Marathi writers began with prose versions of familiar Puranic tales such as *Bakāsurācī bakhar* or *Nandarājācī goṣṭ*, and numerous collections of *Arabian Nights* type stories from Persian, although even these were usually translated via English.[1]

The characteristic of this early period is that all these types of prose were given equal weight, and indeed some of the best and most influential Marathi writers of the time seem to have produced practically no original work of fiction. It was a pioneering age in many ways. The population of Maharashtra, or rather it would be truer to say the high-cast élite of Poona and Bombay, had been pitchforked into the nineteenth century from the somewhat decayed medieval splendours of the Peshwa's court, and after a short period of utter bewilderment had avidly accepted a kind of Samuel Smiles philosophy. Marathi people decided that they were backward and ignorant of the workings of the material world and that they must set about bettering themselves. It became more virtuous to write a school textbook on geography or hygiene than to produce a work of the imagination, and even imaginative works were put out under a smoke screen of reformist propaganda and attached to resounding moral homilies. This is perhaps the case with early prose fiction in any language. The overt excuse for Richardson's *Pamela* is that it is a moral tale for the edification of young girls, exhorting them with a wealth of titillating detail to fight for their virtue against all odds. There are close parallels to *Pamela* in early Marathi romances, in theme if not in execution.

It is necessary to make this equipollence of literary forms

[1] For example, *Bakhatyāranāmā*, 1855, from Ouseley's translation from Persian; *Bāgobahāra*, 1869–72, from Duncan Forbes' Urdu translation.

clear because we shall inevitably be concentrating here on original works of prose fiction. They are more important to us as being part of a productive genre. In succeeding periods of Marathi literature, say after the first novel of Hari Nārāyaṇ Āpṭe in 1885,[1] prose fiction means roughly what one would expect—the novel and the short story. In this first, experimental period, if one were to ask what was the most outstanding work of prose literature one would probably be told by the majority of Marathi critics that it was Cipaḷūṇkar's *Ārabī bhāṣetīl suras va camatkārik goṣṭī*, a translation of the *Arabian Nights* from English. Originality and invention only began to be appreciated after a kind of flood of unsophisticated story telling which immediately followed the beginnings of printing and early educational reforms.

Before dealing with original works, therefore, it would be as well if we described briefly the other brands of fiction and also said something about the earliest printed works in Marathi.

The first printed book in Marathi was almost inevitably the result of missionary activity. In 1805 William Carey produced a grammar and a translation of Matthew's Gospel into Marathi at his Serampore press with the aid of a Marathi pandit, Vaijanātha Śarmā.[2] Some time later, 1814–15, Carey published his first collections of tales in Marathi—*Siṃhāsana-battīsī*, *Pancatantra* and *Hitopadeśa*. The credit for the first printed book of fables, however, goes to Sarphojī, the ruler of Tanjore, who again with missionary help printed the *Bālbodha-muktāvali* in 1806—the first of the many versions of Aesop's fables to be done into Marathi. For some time after this nothing was done in Maharashtra itself, but after the end of the Peshwa's rule in 1814 missionary activity increased rapidly in Bombay and the surrounding districts. Schools were established and printing presses set up, but at first nothing emerged but Bible translations. In 1820 the Bombay Native School-book and School Society was set up under the patronage of Elphinstone, the Governor. In 1821 the Poona Pāṭhaśālā was founded, and

[1] The end of the 'ingrajī avatār' of Marathi literature is usually taken to be in 1874, when the first number of Kṛṣṇaśāstri Cipaḷūṇkar's *Nibandhamālā* appeared. Stylistically this may be valid, but in the field of prose fiction I can detect no natural break until the advent of H. N. Āpṭe.

[2] On Carey's Serampore press see T. W. Clark, *The languages of Calcutta, 1760–1840*, BSOAS, XVIII, 3, 1956, pp. 459–60.

later various other schools, high schools and societies for the dissemination of knowledge of one kind and another. These institutions demanded books, but there were no examples of simple Marathi prose for the students to read. As a result prizes were offered for suitable works as early as 1825, but it was not until three years later that these brought any result. In 1828 Sadāśiv Kāśināth Chatre, a founder member of the Bombay Education Society, produced two translated works: *Isāpanitikathā* (Aesop again) and *Bālmitra*. The second merits some attention because it is a fine example of the odd works of 'literature' that turn up in India in the nineteenth century. It is a translation of an English version of a kind of early children's newspaper called *L'Ami des Enfans*. The original was by Arnaud Berquin and was published in monthly parts in London and Paris simultaneously from January 1782 for several years. It consists mainly of one-act plays and stories of a crushingly moral character. One, for instance, entitled 'Le Lit de Mort' concerns the deathbed conversation of an old woman who gathers her grandchildren around her and encourages them to lead exemplary lives. Numerous selections from this seminal work were made in English in the early nineteenth century and it must have been introduced to India quite early for it can be found translated into most of the modern Indian languages. I am not sure if the Marathi translation was the first, for it may have crept into Bengali earlier, but a Gujarati translation of Chatre's original was republished in Bombay as late as 1933—one hopes as a centenary edition only. Chatre's introduction has an interesting passage bewailing the translator's lot at this epoch. It is only the first of many similar complaints:

'This book Bāḷmitra was first in French, and then came into English and from there into Marathi. If you consider the French and English languages, which have been polished and improved for hundreds of years, in which are written books on every subject, in which there are words to express every kind of thought and meaning and which are used and understood by men of great learning, then how can the achievements of such languages be repeated in Marathi?—in a language which even now has no grammars or dictionaries, which has no attraction for learned men, the vocabulary of which is small and the manner of speaking immature.'[1]

Production of similar moral tales for school children went on throughout the period. Sardār's book[2] which is an invaluable bibliographical aid for the period up to 1874, lists twenty-four of them. Another group of early works consists of prose versions of Puranic stories, of which a dozen or so were published between 1845 and 1869. Sardār's list is probably incomplete,[3] for this sort of thing is being turned out regularly even today. Versions of Persian and English tales began in the following decade, in 1854, which saw the appearance of *Hātimatāī*, from the translation of Duncan Forbes, and Barthoḍ.[4] I have already mentioned Cipaḷūṇkar's translation of the *Arabian Nights*, which came out between 1861 and 1865. From the West came various stories from Shakespeare (through the medium of Lamb's Tales), *Robinson Crusoe*, the first part of *Gil Blas* (via Smollet's translation), Scott's *Ivanhoe* and Johnson's *Rasselas*. This last is also the work of Kṛṣṇaśāstrī Cipaḷūṇkar and is considered a model of its kind. It is certainly a very careful and faithful translation, aided no doubt by the classical, 'general' nature of *Rasselas* itself. *Gil Blas* obviously caused more trouble, but the exotic names have been transcribed with commendable fidelity and the translation is reasonably accurate, although there is a considerable amount of simplification and shortening where strange foreign manners and materials are concerned.

Some of the Persian stories were blamed for dealing too much with love and sensuality, and thereby as tending to corrupt the morals of pure Maharashtrian youth. There is certainly plenty of love in them, but to a modern reader it

[1] S. K. Chatre, *Bāḷmitra*, Bombay, 1828, intro. The first grammars of Marathi in Marathi, notably that of Dādobā Pāṇḍurang, were not published until 1836. Carey published a Marathi-English dictionary in 1810 and Vans Kennedy another in 1824, but the first monolingual dictionary, sponsored by the Bombay Education Society, came out in 1829, the year after Chatre's complaint.

[2] G. B. Sardār, *Arvācīn Marāṭhi gadyācī pūrvapīṭhikā, 1800–1874*, 2nd edn., Poona, 1956.

[3] *Ibid.*, pp. 67–8.

[4] This work was taken from an obscure English translation of a once famous Italian original. Cf. I. Raeside, 'Bertoldo', *Rivista degli Studi Orientali*, XXXVII, 1962, pp. 105–13.

seems that the Marathi has usually paraphrased or sidestepped the already faint traces of licentiousness left by the English translators.

In 1854 also, a few more original works began to be written with a collection of stories for and about women known as *Strīcaritra*. Written by 'Ramjee Gunnojee, First Hospital Assistant Pensioner', the English subtitle gives a good idea of its contents: 'Streechuritra or Female Narration, comprizing their course of life, BEHAVIOUR and undertaking in four parts with Moral reprimands checking Obscenity to secure Chastity'. The tales themselves are patently imitated from the *Arabian Nights*, with the hero generally replaced by a heroine. A work on similar lines, *Suśikṣit Strīcaritra*, was written much later, 1872–73, and on the evidence of the titles alone these two are generally classed together with a third, *Vidagdha Strīcaritra*, which came out in 1871.[1] This, however, is a horse of quite a different colour. Its plot would make it eminently suitable for inclusion in the *Decameron*. Two young men set out to see the world. One finds a lucrative job at a prince's court and settles down while the other continues seeking adventures. After four years they meet again and while the rolling stone recounts his adventures, mainly amorous, the unenterprising one wryly laments his choice. The principal story concerns Vasantakalikā who deceives her husband and contrives to give most of her jewellery to her lover by seducing her husband while disguised as another woman (her lover's nonexistent wife), and then forcing the husband to hand over the jewels as hush-money. This is preceded by a short episode reminiscent of the Miller's Tale and a ribald anecdote about a holy man on a pilgrimage who climbs into the bullock cart where a widow is sleeping, tips up the cart and is found by the other pilgrims lying on top of the widow under a pile of luggage on the ground. Hardly a 'Moral Tale'! It is unfortunately rather tediously written and is quite untypical of the rather strait-laced tone of Marathi literature at that time and even now.

The cunning of Vasantakalikā brings in another very popular type of story produced at this time—that illustrating the

[1] Bhingāre, however, has described this work in detail and sees it as a direct descendant of the mildly pornographic tradition of Sanskrit tales. R. S. Jog, *Marāṭhi Vāñmayācā Itihās*, IV, p. 186.

quick wit or cunning of the main protagonist. Many of these were again adapted from Sanskrit or Persian sources, but some of the later ones may contain stories of the author's own invention, or more likely traditional oral tales that had not before appeared in print. Such are K. R. Conce's *Mahārāṣṭra bhāṣet manoranjak goṣṭī*, 1870–73, and *Barthoḍ*, which I have already mentioned and consists largely of tales of rustic wit attributed to the boorish Italian folk-hero Bertoldo. Such tales are the nearest approach to short stories to be written during this period, but they do not of course qualify for such a description. There is little depiction of character in them and no trace of any structure. They are merely anecdotes.

One representative of this genre which is still fairly well known, by reputation at least, to Marathi readers is Morobā Kānhobā's *Ghāśīrām Kotvāl*, written in 1863. There are twenty-eight chapters all built around the central character of Ghāśīrām, who was a notorious police chief under the Peshwas, and many of these are not even anecdotes but merely a list of *faits divers* in the form of conversations between Ghāśīrām and better informed persons (and almost anyone is better informed than Ghāśīrām) on such subjects as sword-swallowers, diamond mines and bearded women. Mixed with this, however, are many of these cunning-trick stories, and Ghāśīrām, who is a sublime mixture of ignorance, cupidity, superstition and vice, is frequently the victim. The whole work is written with considerable vigour and humour, and the dialogue is often vivid. Here is one of the shorter stories in which Ghāśīrām is not the main protagonist:

'Every evening after his meal Ghāśīrām used to sit in his house chewing betel or tobacco, and at that time a crowd of flatterers would gather round him praising his judgement and power of swift action. On one occasion a man from Bijapur was there and began to sing the praises of a magistrate of his own city, telling the following story: Last year in the month of āṣāḍha a perfumier of our city called Rāmdīn had made up about 25 maunds of scented powder, packed it into fifty sacks and was going to send it by ox-cart next day to Pandharpur to sell at the big festival. Meanwhile the sacks were left in the yard behind his shop. In the morning Rāmdīn got up early and went into the yard. No sacks! But there were bits of powder scattered around and signs that the sacks had been dragged over the wall. So he set up a cry of "Thief! Thief", the neighbours came running and he told them what had happened and then went and complained to the city kotvāl, Samśerkhān. The latter immediately sent messengers to close all the gates and instituted a search, but there was no trace of the sacks.

'Thereupon he summoned all the scent-shop keepers and their workmen and began an interrogation that lasted till midday. Still no result! Then Samśerkhan stood them together in a bunch, walked round them slowly three times and finally came to a halt in front of them. He laughed aloud and said, "Well, you're a brazen lot. Stealing the stuff is one thing, but then to come along here with a spot of it on your forehead!" As soon as he said this four of the men in front of him whipped their hands up to their foreheads and then sniffed their fingers surreptitiously. They were immediately singled out and questioned and it turned out that two were brothers and the other two were their servants. Their shops and cellars were searched with the help of torches and the fifty stolen sacks were found in a dark corner. And so all four were punished and everyone praised Samśerkhān Kotvāl for his shrewdness.

'After hearing the Bijapur merchant's story Ghāśīrām said, "If this Tarvārkhān or whatever his name was was such a genius why did the kingdom of Bijapur collapse? Now if a theft like that had happened in this city we wouldn't have taken half a day to catch the thieves. We'd have slung the whole lot into a dungeon and then stood four or five of them on a red-hot grid-iron. We'd soon have known who the thief was." At this all Ghāśīrām's toadies applauded furiously and began to make fun of the merchant from Bijapur. So the poor fellow took himself off.'[1]

This then is the stage that the 'short story' had reached—either translations or adaptations of foreign works or these 'clever trick' tales which are told with a considerable verve at times but which are basically traditional, a carrying over into

[1] Morobā Kānhobā Vijaykar, *Ghāśīrām Kotvāl*, ed. N. R. Phāṭak, Bombay (Mumbaī Marāṭhi granthasangrahālaya), 1961, pp. 10–11.

print of the sort of storyteller's tale that might delight a village audience to this day.

Having cleared the ground to some extent, we now come to the beginnings of the novel; that is, as a minimum definition, a longish connected prose tale with a range of named protagonists, distinguishably characterized, a judicious mixture of dialogue, narrative and description and some sort of structure. At the very least the characters must be introduced, must undergo various *péripéties* either physically or psychologically and finally come to a position of rest—death or resignation or tranquillity, according to whether the story has a happy ending or not.

It is usually said that the first two original novels in Marathi were both Christian works. They are Bābā Padmanjī's *Yamunā-paryaṭaṇ* published in 1857, and *Phulmunī āṇī Karuṇā* published in 1859. The latter, however, is a translation of a story published in English in Calcutta and has no claim to be considered as an original work in Marathi. Fortunately, *Yamunā* is more readily available than many other works of this period, having been reprinted in 1937 when the 'ingrajī avatār' (English incarnation) of Marathi literature was included in the B.A. syllabus at Bombay University.[1]

Bengali normally lays claim to the first Indian novel with one that came out in 1858. *Yamunā* antedates this by a year, but I am not sure if its is sufficiently novel-like in form to dispute the point. The plot, in brief, is that Yamunā, who is secretly a Christian, is married to an enlightened young man who shares her ideals without openly accepting her religion. They travel around Maharashtra on some unspecified business of the husband's, and finally he is mortally injured by a bullock cart while saving a child's life. Before dying he persuades Yamunā to baptize him informally, and also makes his father promise not to subject her to the usual harsh treatment reserved for widows in India. However, the mother-in-law is incensed by this and with the backing of the family priest they prepare the head-shaving, jewellery stripping and so on, but Yamunā forestalls them by running away to the house of a Christian couple. And that is all, except that it is mentioned

[1] The phrase 'ingrajī avatār' seems to have been coined by D. V. Potdār in his book *Marāṭhi gadyācā ingrajī avatār*, Poona, 1922.

casually in the last line that she subsequently marries again—an overt Christian this time.

The main plot, therefore, is tenuous in the extreme, but in fact two-thirds of the book is taken up with widow-remarriage propaganda, sometimes in the form of direct exhortation by the author but more usually by means of horrific stories. Yamunā and her husband in their travels keep meeting widows, or staying in a house where some widow is leading a miserable life, and these individuals then tell their story at length to the sympathetic audience. This episodic form is scarcely that of a novel and is rather similar to didactic works such as Johnson's *Rasselas*, which were undoubtedly popular at the time with those who could read English—and indeed *Rasselas* was later translated into Marathi in full as has been mentioned.

There are some characteristics of the novel all the same. Yamunā and her husband are cardboard figures, but some of the minor protagonists—the rather feeble father-in-law and the family priest for instance—are fairly sharply characterized. There is plenty of dialogue, much of it of a rather expository kind between husband and wife. A technical point is that dialogue is normally printed in dramatic form, with the abbreviated name of the speaker given first, thus avoiding a repetition of 'he said', 'she said', etc. This technique may possibly have been imitated from plays, of which a handful had been published at this time, or it may well have been adopted spontaneously as a convenient device. It remained in vogue throughout the period we are discussing, although not all authors used it. There are some descriptions, although few are striking. However, in one place there is an attempt to convey the essence of the interior of a simple village hut (with moral overtones of the superiority of simple village life which are somewhat discordant with the main theme) which does seem to have something of the *chose vue* about it:

'Yamunā and Vināyak went inside and found a little room in which two banana-leaf plates were set out, each with its heap of salt. The room itself filled them with delight. Everything in it spoke of village life. The room had only one door made of jack-tree wood, very thick and heavy with a massive iron bar to shut it. The cow-dung floor was smooth and beautifully clean. On it the sun's rays, coming through tiny holes in the roof, lay scattered like bright gold coins, while specks of dust danced within the rays themselves which gave the only light there was in the room. All four walls were smeared with red ochre and overhead ran great twisted beams which carried baskets of rice and firewood and dried *palas* leaves for platters, all tied on with thick grass rope. On Yamunā's left hand was a huge quern for grinding rice and near it, lying against the wall, was a pestle the handle of which gleamed like gold in a stray beam of sunlight which fell upon it. On Vināyak's right was a pile of jars stacked one on top of the other. All this stuff was neatly and carefully arranged so that there was no suggestion of disorder in the room, but rather of beauty.'[1]

That is quite vivid, especially when you take into account the early date and the fact that there was no tradition of realistic description then or for a long time afterwards. By contrast here is another description from the same chapter of *Yamunā* in which the beauties of the dawn—an infinitely more conventional theme—are described in the form of a dialogue of incredible triteness and implausibility:

'Yam. Ah! What a lovely cool breeze is blowing!

'Vin. Look, beloved, what a beautiful golden light shines in the East. Could man ever make such splendour? Before such beauty how drab and wearisome would seem an emperor's palace adorned at the expense of thousands of rupees!

'Yam. How variegated are the colours! I can see red and yellow and purple and pink. And look where the sun is rising, what a glorious light is there as if a goldsmith had poured out his crucible of liquid gold. . . .'[2]

And so on, with long digressions on the lilies of the field and God giving heed to every sparrow.

Yamunā-paryaṭaṇ is basically a work of Christian and social propaganda and is scarcely typical of the original works of fiction which follow. It is four years before the first really indigenous romance appears with *Muktāmālā* in 1861, and this

[1] Bābā Padmanjī, *Yamunā-paryaṭaṇ*, 4th edn., Bombay, 1937, p. 74.
[2] *Ibid.*, pp. 60–1.

set a pattern for a number of works in the same genre—a score or so in the thirteen years before 1874. The author states in his preface that he is writing to create rather than to satisfy a demand for this type of literature:

'Formerly our people thought that it was rather a joke that they should have to learn the Marathi language, but now many have realized that it is not so easy to learn a language properly and to write books in it. However, it seems to me that our people have not taken as much pleasure as they should in reading books and newspapers in their own language, and so I have written this book with the intention of furthering such an interest. . . .'[1]

In *Muktāmālā* there is no attempt at any kind of realistic setting. The plot unfolds in a kind of Indian Illyria 'in olden time' and is not worth describing in detail. It concerns a wicked king and his evil counsellors. The one virtuous courtier, Muktāmālā's husband, is thrown into prison on a trumped-up charge by his wife's stepbrother who is after the inheritance. Muktāmālā escapes and wanders around from one city to another, at one point disguised as a man. Her life and her virtue are constantly in danger, but something always turns up to save her at the last minute and all ends happily with the wicked destroyed, the good restored to power and the virtuous younger brother of the bad king established on the throne. The book, more than 200 pages long, is practically all narrative and is better written and more swiftly moving than many later examples of the genre. The plot bristles with coincidences, but most of them are at least plausibly led up to and explained, and there are signs of construction in the switching of emphasis from one character to another. Characterization is minimal, with everyone either very black or very white. The dialogue is rather literary, and much of the direct speech consists of soliloquies in which the various oppressed characters lament their cruel fate. Direct speech is distinguished only sporadically by inverted commas and is lost among the enormous paragraphs in which books of this era are printed. There is a certain amount of description, and one rather interesting feature is

[1] Lakṣmaṇ Moreśvar Haḷbe, *Muktāmālā*, Bombay, 1851, intro.

that many of the chapters, seven out of nine, begin with a descriptive set-piece which only exceptionally has any relevance to the succeeding action. The descriptions themselves are of the most classical, that is to say generalized, nature. Here are the opening paragraphs of *Muktāmālā*:

'When the rainy season ends and winter begins and you look upon the earth in the early morning from the top of some hill, it is delightful and wonderful to behold. You see fields of various kinds of grain, some in flower and some ready for harvesting, groves of mangoes, coconuts, areca palms and so on, gardens, pasture, and on each side of the roads rows of trees; so that whatever part of the earth you look at seems to be bursting with life, and it seems as if a many-coloured carpet has been thrown over the earth. The winding thread of the river, brimming over both its banks, looks very beautiful. Here and there are lakes which give joy to the mind of the beholder more than anything else because of the many coloured flowers that bloom in them. In the towns and villages there is more to see. The houses and palaces seem to be wrapped in a mixture of mist and foliage and smoke from the newly-lit fires, and the temples and towers seem to lift their heads above the trees to see the delights of the world for themselves.

'And if you look closer there are more things to take the eye. You see people starting their daily work. Travellers, some on horseback, some on foot and some in carts are coming and going by various roads. Farmers and cowherds driving their cows and bullocks are leaving the villages in all directions. Some have set out to sell corn, hay, wood, vegetables and such things as these. Some are going to the river and some to the well. They call out one to another and the song of the different kinds of bird mingles with these sounds so that a constant noise comes to the ear. Wherever you turn your gaze you see something else to delight you. If you look towards the hills, some near and some far, the eye has a further pleasure. In some places there are valleys and in others great and small cliffs are cut in the hillsides; in some places thick and awesome woods and in other scattered trees; in some places only grass and in others bare rock. . . .'[1]

[1] *Muktāmālā*, pp. 1–3.

This is all thrown in without any kind of selection or organization, and also without any particularization. It is a landscape with figures like a Breughel, but there is no point in it, for the leg of Icarus is missing. The city of Jaypur, which is the centre of the action which follows, is not localized in this scene in any way.

This criticism applies to most of the scenic descriptions which occur in the romances of this early period of Marathi literature. They are all, in a way, set pieces, although they may not be set apart so explicitly as in *Muktāmālā*. There are certain points in any narrative where you can say with confidence, 'Here comes a description'. For instance, people are constantly setting out on journeys and after a few miles they leave the inhabited area near the town and come into the wilds. And then it comes! various sorts of trees and bushes with various kinds of birds singing in them, all sorts of wild beasts roaring and grunting and screeching in the middle distance. These set themes seem to be characteristic of unsophisticated, often bardic, literature; of works written for the ear rather than the eye. In the *chansons de geste* there is a list of objects that qualify for a descriptive interlude that you could count on your fingers: shields, armour, tents, feasts and so on. You have the feasts in Marathi also, as well as gardens and palaces. Every king seems to have a palace right in the middle of his city, set in the exact centre of a beautiful garden which has a lofty 'pleasure dome' in each corner, with gilded and painted walls and superb views over the garden. Clearly this is inherited from earlier verse works and from the Sanskrit prose tales such as *Pancatantra*, and at this early stage in prose fiction the conventions are adopted unthinkingly. It is less perhaps a positive influence than a negative thing; an absence of interest in the detail of everyday life and surroundings which it never occurred to anyone might be worth talking about until prose fiction, which is essentially a realist genre whatever the age in which it is written, had got properly under way. A passage from the introduction to another romance, *Manjughoṣā*, written in 1868, brings this out very clearly:

'The basic aim of works like "novels" is to show how in this world a virtuous man attains happiness after suffering various setbacks at the hands of evil men. . . . Because of our attitude to marriage and for several other reasons one finds in the lives of us Hindus neither interesting vices nor virtues, and this is the difficulty which we find in trying to write novels. If we write about the things that we experience daily there would be nothing enthralling about them, so that if we set out to write an entertaining book we are forced to take up with the marvellous. . . .'[1]

Here of course the author is talking more about plot and defending his own liberal use of magic and supernatural devices, but the attitude is the same. That is why the little descriptive passage quoted from *Yamunā-paryaṭaṇ* strikes one so favourably.

There is little more to say about *Manjughoṣā*, which is excessively tedious and implausible, and which is also written in a laborious archaic style bristling with Sanskrit borrowings and *alankārs*. The style was deliberate, since the author considered it more fitting to some vague bygone age in which romantic adventures between the sexes were possible. As a sample of the remaining romances we may take *Rājā Madan* and *Suhāsyavadanā*.

Rājā Madan[2] was the second of these early romances to appear, in 1865, and has always earned special mention in the histories of Marathi literature because it is the only one without a happy ending. In fact this is only partly true. The principal hero and heroine live happily ever after just like everyone else, and it is only the secondary characters who are eliminated. On the whole I am somewhat prejudiced against *Rājā Madan* because it has been consistently overpraised (or rather less despised, for until very recently Marathi critics have taken a thoroughly jaundiced view of all this literature). Justice Rānaḍe once wrote a short article in English on these early works, which unfortunately I have been unable to trace, in which he gave the opinion that '*Muktāmālā* and *Rājā Madan* are probably the best', and this has been dutifully repeated ever since. It would seem that Rānaḍe must have been playing

[1] Nāro Sadāśiv Risbuḍ, *Manjughoṣā*, Poona, 1868, intro., pp. 3–4.

[2] Bābājī Kṛṣṇa Gokhale, *Rājā Madan, duhkhaparyavasāyī kathā*, Bombay, 1865.

safe by picking the two earliest works, for *Rājā Madan* seems to be one of the feeblest of the genre. It is nothing but a long 'virtue in danger' story of astonishing implausibility, concerning wicked kings and ministers and their designs on the virtuous wives of absent colleagues. Some of the methods they use for getting the poor women into their clutches are quite delightfully elaborate, such as digging an underground tunnel for miles and laying a kind of camouflaged elephant trap over the end of it. The eponymous Rājā Madan is absent throughout, and so devoted is the author to his titillating episodes that he does not even bother to finish off the main plot properly. When the last oppressed female has jumped out of a window rather than submit to the advances of the last villain, the final sentence is: 'Next day the Raja returned to the city and punished all the evildoers and began to rule again in peace and prosperity.' The End!

The 'virtue in danger' theme mentioned here recurs constantly in Marathi romances of this and later periods. It seems to be mainly an indigenous preoccupation, for there is very little of it in the Persian tales, but it must have received a powerful boost from Western novels such as those of Reynolds[1] and even Scott. It is hard to say how soon the influence of such novels was felt. There is no definite evidence of it before the eighteen seventies, when we know that the young Hari Nārāyaṇ Āpte was an assiduous reader of Reynolds, and *The Seamstress* was translated or rather adapted in 1877, but they may equally well have been read by the preceding generation. In any case the popularity of these English writers was doubtless due in part to the fact that they struck a sympathetic chord in their Indian readers.

Suhāsyavadanā[2] too has its share of attempted seductions, but not to any wearisome extent. Its plot is more elaborate than the romances so far discussed. There is much to-ing and fro-ing of the characters and numerous conspiracies, stratagems and confused adventures. There is also a rather daring episode where the hero rescues the heroine from drowning in a lonely

[1] The novelist G. W. M. Reynolds, who is not worthy apparently of an individual entry in the encyclopaedias, had more influence in India than almost any other nineteenth-century Western writer.

[2] Vāman Kṛṣṇa Deśmukh, *Suhāsyavadanā*, Bombay, 1870.

spot and proceeds, chastely, to put her into some dry clothes that he is conveniently carrying in his saddle bag. But this is passed over very gingerly. The characterization is of the usual black and white variety, except that there appears here for the first time a character who turns up continually in later novels, and particularly in the historical novels by H. N. Āpṭe. This is the smart young lad who is always a faithful servant of the hero, who spies out the land, collects information, hoodwinks the sentries and so forth. Indeed in *Suhāsyavadanā* the happy ending is almost entirely brought about by this admirable person, for the hero, though brave and worthy, is more than a little obtuse. His origin may perhaps be in the Sanskrit 'dūta', who filled a similar role of messenger and confidant. Altogether this novel is quite readable, of its kind, mainly because it is fast-moving and not too verbose. Still it has most of the faults that have already been mentioned: conventional descriptions, lack of realistic dialogue (although there is an attempt to convey rustic speech by means of mixed Marathi and Hindi), and a special kind of repetitiveness which is due to a rather primitive technique, in that events already described are narrated with scarcely any abbreviation to some third party in the story.

We have dealt with only a few of the numerous romantic novels that are characteristic of this period, but it is enough to give a fair idea of them all. They are all more or less timeless and placeless and make no attempt to reflect any specific *milieu*, whether historical or contemporary. A few extraneous touches, such as the introduction of widow-remarriage into Halbe's second novel *Ratnaprabhā*[1] or a character in *Vicitrapurī* who wears shoes and socks and is an M.A. of Calcutta University,[2] have no real effect on the plot. It should also be remembered that this type of romantic tale continued to be written until the end of the century, and some of them were still being reprinted in the nineteen twenties, so that the later ones were able to borrow a few historical or social frills from their more modern contemporaries. On the whole, though, the *genre* was astonishingly homogeneous, with plots, characters and descriptive interludes that seem freely interchangeable. To end

[1] L. M. Halbe, *Ratnaprabhā*, Bombay, 1866.

[2] Keśav Lakṣmaṇ Jorvekar, *Vicitrapurī*, Bombay, 1870.

with K. B. Marathe's often quoted words: 'Every hero is the God of Love incarnate, every heroine is a Tilottamā. In every tragic episode the sorrow is a deathly sorrow and in every joyful one the joy is heavenly rapture—nothing less.'[1]

Despite these exaggerations, the origins of a different kind of novel are also to be found within our period. *Bodhasudhā* is usually listed among the romances, but in fact it has as much claim to be called a social or realist novel as *Yamunā-paryaṭaṇ*, and is equally didactic in tone.[2] The framework of the plot is that a rich man is spending the hot season at Mahabaleshwar, the hill-station south-west of Poona, with his two sons who both have bad characters and cause their father much concern. While out walking they meet a distinguished old man whom they eventually invite home and who proceeds to tell them the story of his life. This, of course, is of a very edifying nature. He was once rich, wasted his father's fortune, deserted his wife for a beautiful temptress and ran away with her. In the village he is boycotted, so he moves to the anonymity of Poona, gets a job, sinks lower and lower and finally, when he is lying ill, he discovers that his mistress has found a new rich lover and is planning to poison him off.

The story is not told with any great distinction, and is frequently interrupted by the two youths asking questions which give the old man an excuse for long diatribes on ethical and social topics. The dialogue is stilted and unreal, the descriptions of nature in the linking passages are as generalized as ever—the story takes nearly a week in the telling and the narrator stays as a guest until he has finished it, and every morning they all get up early and stroll round Mahabaleshwar and see the birds and the trees and the industrious peasants. However the interest of the work is that it seems to be the first hostile reaction *in fiction* to British rule and Western ideas. The time is the present. The hero at one point is brought up before an English magistrate's court and takes the oppor-

[1] Quoted from Potdār, *op. cit.*, 2nd edn., Poona, 1957, p. 83. K. B. Marāṭhe's 'Nāval va nāṭak hyāviṣayī nibandh', a paper first read before the Marāṭhi Jñānaprasārak Sabhā in 1872 and subsequently published as a pamphlet, was one of the first and harshest criticisms of the Romances. Although quoted in every history of Marathi literature, the original is hard to come by and I have not seen it.

[2] Keśav Baḷavant Keḷkar, *Bodhasudhā*, Bombay, 1871.

tunity to make a few cynical remarks about corruption and how you cannot cure it simply by paying magistrates a decent salary as the British seem to think. The author also takes a few sly digs at the missionaries. Talking about conversions the narrator says, 'Well, we won't inquire too closely why a lot of people embrace Christianity', and he goes on to contrast *dharma*, the doing of one's duty here on earth, with the 'pie in the sky' motive. He is not entirely reactionary, for he attacks early marriage on purely practical grounds, but has nothing to say on more controversial topics like widow-remarriage and the education of women. Indeed he takes a very traditional view of women—they should not be oppressed unduly, but they ought to be firmly deterred from the vices to which they are naturally prone.

In short, this Hindu counterblast to reformist ideas has some slight claim to be considered the first social realist novel. The characters may still be incredible, but at least the plot is contemporary and is not entirely outweighed by moralizing or by a string of independent tales as in *Yamunā*.

Nārāyaṇrāv āṇi Godāvarī, which was not written until 1879, is usually said to be the first social novel. Clearly the author, M. V. Rahāḷkar, envisaged himself as striking out into a new field.

'All the novels published in our language, with very few exceptions, have situations, settings and characters of one and the same kind. The heroes and heroines are always princes and princesses, or at least are enormously rich. Their wealth is the wealth of Kuber, their beauty like that of Madan and Rati . . . compared with their love the love of Rām and Sitā is derisory'.[1]

He himself, he says, wants to write about ordinary people and to be released from the bondage of the happy ending. He certainly achieves his second aim. The book begins with a most respectable social theme. Godāvarī, the heroine, is about to be sold by her miserly father to be the second wife of a drunken lecher. However she avoids this fate quite early by

[1] Mahādev Vyankateś Rahāḷkar, *Nārāyaṇrāv āṇi Godāvarī, duhkha-pariṇāmī kalpit kādambarī*, Poona, 1879, intro., p. 2. The echo of Marāṭhe's words is probably not coincidental.

her own efforts and marries Nārāyaṇ, an enlightened young schoolteacher, and at this point the social question is lost sight of and the plot becomes a simple melodrama. Godāvarī is entangled in the snares of her disappointed fiancé, and finally Nārāyaṇ is persuaded that she has betrayed him. The idea is that once Godāvarī has been turned out by her husband she may be collected off the street for the asking, but Nārāyaṇ is a man of action and exceeds all expectations by killing Godāvarī in a fit of jealousy. Immediately afterwards he learns the truth, and from the melodrama we pass to *grand guignol*. Nārāyaṇ finds all his enemies conveniently gathered together in one of those garden 'pleasure domes' that I have already mentioned, and as they are incapacitated with drink and debauchery he proceeds to carve them up slowly and methodically with a sharp sword, starting with the minor offenders and working up. And so perish one lecher, one pimp, one corrupt priest, one venal mameledar and one libidinous school inspector. Nārāyaṇ ends the evening by blowing his head off with his own shotgun.

This bloodthirsty story is told with considerable gusto and the dialogue is much livelier and more credible than anything we have met so far. But Rahāḷkar cannot take the credit for innovating here. The historical novel, the best novel written before the emergence of Āpṭe, had preceded him by eight years.

Rāmcandra Bhikājī. Gunjīkar's *Mocangaḍ* opens with a few introductory sentences setting the scene in historical time and in time of day. Various kinds of birds twitter in the bushes and a pale light grows in the East, and there is nothing to show that one is not in for a long, rambling and possibly irrelevant introduction in the *Muktāmālā* style. And then, abruptly, one is plunged into the narrative in a very effective and quite new way:

'On the slopes of a hill in the Sahyādrī mountains two men came out of some bushes. They seemed about twenty-five years old. They were handsome and strongly built, and although their faces were lined with misery and suffering, you could still see that they were men of high rank. They were dressed only in ragged jackets, short dhotis of coarse cloth and another wisp of cloth wound around their heads, and these few clothes were dirty and tattered. Their hair and beards were long, and on their legs were heavy fetters so that they took each step with precaution, but as quickly as they could so as to make no noise.'[1]

That, I think, is an excellent beginning to an adventure story. It is still rather stimulating to be plunged into the story in an effective way like this, and in an age of tedious introductions it must have been a lot more so. Undoubtedly a technical revolution of this kind is due to the influence of Western models such as Scott but it is none the worse for that, and Gunjīkar was not only the first to use it but the first by a long way.

It is not necessary to go into the plot of *Mocangaḍ* except to say that it sets a pattern for many a Marathi historical novel to come. It is centred around a fort, one of the Deccan hill forts which can only be compared to an iron-age camp reinforced with Mediaeval masonry, and the action is terminated and the happy ending finally brought about by the capture of the fort by the national hero and founder of the independent Maratha state, Shivaji.

Apart from the way in which it opens, this novel represents a great step forward in other ways. It has a plot which has evidently been constructed with care and deliberation. Actions are motivated and reasonably logical, although it must be allowed that coincidence is somewhat overworked. Up until now there had been little attempt at plausibility or a well-ordered plot. Biographical tales like *Yamunā* or *Bodhasudhā* simply ran along from start to finish like any other unsophisticated story, with constant repetition of 'and then . . . , and then. . . .' A romance like *Suhāsyavadanā*, written only one year earlier, had more pretensions. It says such things as: 'And now we must leave this subject for a time and see what Suhāsyavadanā's parents were doing back in Kīrtipūr', but when you get back to Kīrtipūr you find that they are not doing anything much except wringing their hands or deciding to send a messenger to find out what is happening. There are no real sub-plots. At the most you have two rival gangs surging

[1] Rāmcandra Bhikājī Gunjīkar, *Mocangaḍ*, Bombay, 1871, p. 2.

backwards and forwards from one city to another and occasionally colliding in some intermediate desert, but it is all rather meaningless and is obviously designed solely to keep the hero separated from the heroine for as long as the reader can stand.

Mocangaḍ has no real sub-plot either, and the final capture of the fort by Shivaji is quite extraneous, but one thing it *has* got is a kind of unity of time. The whole affair takes place in about a fortnight. Without giving undue weight to the French classical ideal, it seems to me that this is in itself an advance in the development of an artistic form like the novel out of an earlier tradition of long rambling stories. Almost anything can be a novel no doubt, but at some point in its development in any one language some sort of unity has to crystallize out of the stories and fables and fairy-tales or whatever it was that flourished earlier, and one way of achieving such a unity is by restricting the time scale as is done here.

To return to the constructon of *Mocangaḍ*, the plot is developed by leaps, and the leaps are made to some purpose. As we have seen it begins with the two escaped prisoners and we follow their fortunes in a couple of palpitating chapters during which they jump over the cliff surrounding the fort, fetters and all, and begin to stagger down the hill with one man carrying the other, wounded, on his back. The following chapter begins in a village at the foot of the hill on the opposite side. A soldier comes riding down with a message from the governor of the fort to tell the village *pāṭīl* about the escape and instruct him to keep an eye on the prisoners' families in case they try to contact them. The action is immediately carried forward and at the same time you are still left in suspense about the fugitives. The suspense element is very important, for this must be one of the first novels to be published in serial form in Marathi.[1]

Altogether the first half of *Mocangaḍ* is extremely well done, but then it goes off rather badly, to my taste at least, with a long piece of 'virtue in danger' business. Even this, however, is rather more plausible than usual, and certainly more exciting. The heroine, after protracted argument with her would-be ravisher, succeeds in shooting him with his own

[1] In *Vividha-jñāna-vistāra*, a monthly started in Bombay in 1867, only four years earlier.

pistol. But only by accident I regret to say. Women are still expected to take a very passive role.

The descriptive passages are of specific scenes and places which have some connection with the action, and are, therefore, much more factual and more relevant than we have come to expect. The dialogue is good, and at last shows signs of becoming colloquial and alive. At one point a Shiledar from the fort—one of the minor villains—comes down to his home village to show off his horse and his sword and his new glory. All the villagers twit him at first: 'Oh, it's old Saṭhvyā, the one who ran away from home because he'd been caught stealing coconuts. Wonder how long he's been a soldier? Rām Rām, Saṭhvājī. Have you given up your old job yet?' Saṭhvājī bridles somewhat and lets them all known how prosperous he has become.

'As soon as money was mentioned everyone moved up a bit to let him sit down and somebody said that of course it wasn't true that childish vices always remained and men improved enormously through travel, "so come and sit down, Saṭhvājī!"

'But Nimbājī said, "And why should such a rascal be short of money? He's only got to raid some money-lender's shop and take all he wants. . . . He's a real hero, he is."

' "What do you mean? You don't become a shiledar for nothing you know. You have to go into battle with your life in your hand."

' "With your nose in your hand you mean, in case someone catches you thieving and cuts it off."

' "What? Look here at this sword, still stained with blood!"

' "Oh yes! Looks as if you must have overpowered some goat or hen just around dinner-time." '[1]

Not very subtle humour perhaps, but it is lively and it makes a change. It is not an isolated example. Even when the heroine is fending off the villain she manages some very spirited retorts.

One should not, of course, exaggerate the virtues of this novel. There are still numerous implausibilities in the plot and the contemporary taste for oppressed females is fully catered

[1] *Mocangaḍ*, p. 46.

to. There are also many of those long, boring soliloquies where the characters commune with their consciences or lament their fate *ad nauseam*. Nevertheless, such things remained popular for long after *Mocangaḍ*, and proliferate in the historical novels of Āpṭe for instance. When you consider that *Mocangaḍ* is the very first historical novel in Marathi, it really is surprisingly better as a novel than any of its predecessors. It matters very little that Gunjīkar has imitated Western models, for he has succeeded in recreating something in Marathi and in terms of Maharashtrian life and history, and in laying the foundations of many things that a later writer such as Āpṭe had only to develop. It is a very respectable achievement.

There are only two other historical novels that were written in the pre-Āpṭe period. *Sambhājī* by V. N. Bapat represents no advance on *Mocangaḍ*.[1] It is more 'historical' in that it introduces a number of real historical personages into the action. For that very reason it is less of a novel, combining as it does undigested lumps of history with a thin romantic sub-plot. The same criticism can be made of V. J. Paṭvardhan's *Hambīrrāv āṇi Putalābāī*,[2] which is an attempt to write a historical novel around much more recent events—the mutiny of 1857. Again it is not a very successful attempt, since a large part of it consists of a purely domestic story about a young wife being estranged from her husband by the machinations of her co-wife, interspersed with solid historical narrative of the main events of the mutiny—the two being entirely unrelated until the last third of the book when the wife, driven from home, is abducted by a band of rebellious sepoys. There is a great deal of dialogue, much of it superfluous since the weak construction leaves laboriously prepared situations unfinished and hanging in the air. One interesting feature, however, is that the speech of some of the 'low-life' characters is given in a vulgar, rustic brand of Marathi, and this is conveyed by typographical devices which have since become standard for colloquial forms. In 1875 they must have been fairly new. At least this is the first example of such conventions that I am acquainted with.

Finally Raṇdive's *Śikṣak* might be mentioned briefly as a kind

[1] Nageś Vināyak Bāpaṭ, *Sambhājī*, Bombay, 1884.
[2] Viṣṇu Janārdan Paṭvardhan, *Hambīrrāv āṇi Putalābāī*, Bombay, 1875.

of politico-historico-romantic amalgam.[1] Here the romantic adventures of the hero, always accompanied by the mentor who gives the novel its title, take place against a background of pre-mutiny events reminiscent of those in Jhansi. The hero is an adopted son whose inheritance of a minor princely state is disallowed by the harsh Dalhousie government. In spite of the political implications of this theme, the pervading atmosphere is nonrealistic and there is no reason to suppose that Part Two would have been any different.

Mocangaḍ remains outstanding not only against this very feeble competition in the historical field, but among all the novels written before the advent of Āpṭe.

In the period before 1885 prose fiction in Marathi developed, largely under the influence of Western writing, from practically nothing to a point where all the ingredients of a major novel were at hand but had not yet been assimilated by any one author. After the first simple tales, nearly all of them translated or imitated from English, came the more elaborate romances of which *Muktāmālā* is a better than average example. In these the problems of construction were first tackled but not solved. Dialogue remained literary, descriptions of people and places conventional and lacking in any kind of particularization. Contemporary problems and more realistic settings had been attempted in the very first novel-length work of fiction, *Yamunā-paryaṭaṇ*, but here and in the later *Bodhasudhā* the construction was rudimentary and the plot was overlaid by a great weight of moralizing and didacticism. The first signs of the fruitful influence of Western novels was in the historical *Macangaḍ* which was organized appetizingly for serial publication and which contained lively dialogue and realistic, visual scene painting. The analysis and depiction of individual human beings, however, was still in its very early stages. The short story, so dependent on character in action, had still not arrived.

In technique there had been considerable advances. A livelier dialogue implies the increasing use of colloquial forms, both grammatically and phonetically. Because of this the influence of English sentence structure and of painstaking Sanskritic

[1] Dvārkānāth Nārāyaṇ Raṇdive, *Śikṣak*, Bombay, 1883. (Part I only published.)

literaryness was on the wane during the last decade of the period, and in *Hambīrrāv āṇi Putaḷābāi* there is already established a convention for transcribing phonetic variants from the literary norm. Dialogue was still being printed in dramatic form and continued to be for a good many years with some writers, but this at least had the advantage of separating speech and narrative, and the average page had the same physical appearance as it does today. The conventions of punctuation had been established in conformity with Western usage.

This then was the stage that prose fiction had reached when Hari Nārāyaṇ Āpṭe came on the scene. He took everything that had gone before, shook it up, added the massive reading of Scott, Dickens and Reynolds to which he seems to have devoted his student life, and proceeded to turn out novels of a weight, length and copiousness that was entirely new.

THE DEVELOPMENT OF THE MODERN NOVEL IN URDU

by RALPH RUSSELL

ANTECEDENTS

The history of Urdu literature falls into two almost unconnected parts. It begins in the Deccan—the central plateau of the Indian sub-continent—and from about 1600 grows and flourishes for more than a century. Its achievement was considerable, and though most of the literature of this period is in verse, it includes one outstanding work of prose fiction, the allegory *Sab Ras*, by Mullā Vajhī, written as early as 1635–36.[1] Any comprehensive study of the history of Urdu prose fiction would have to start with this work. However, for reasons which need not be discussed here, the Deccan period comes to an end early in the eighteenth century, and the centre shifts to northern India, where it has ever since remained. And so completely did the new centre displace the old that the greatness of the Deccan's contribution was rapidly forgotten, and had to be largely rediscovered by twentieth-century scholars. The Urdu literature of the Deccan period therefore constitutes (in my view at least) the subject of a separate study, and falls outside the scope of this essay.

In the north, the prevailing language of literary expression had long been Persian, but in poetry Urdu now rapidly gained the ascendancy, first in Delhi, the Mughal capital, and a generation later, to an increasing extent, in Lucknow also. Indeed in some forms, notably the lyric, it had already by the middle of the eighteenth century achieved a standard which many would feel has still not been surpassed. Not least among the reasons why it could do so was that the new Urdu poets were thoroughly familiar with Persian and with Persian poetry, any many of them wrote it with facility. The use of the mother tongue helped them to convey an intensity in their poetry which they could not have expressed in Persian, but they also had ready to hand all the rich tradition of Persian poetry, and of this too they made full use. Narrative fiction is almost

[1] AH 1045, which corresponds to AD 1635–36. See 'Abdul Ḥaq's preface to his 2nd edn. of *Sab Ras*, Anjuman i Taraqqī i Urdū, Karachi, 1953, p. 5.

from the first represented in their work. By convention, its predominant themes are stories of love, and it is written, like Chaucer's *Canterbury Tales*, in rhyming couplets. Broadly speaking, the *masnavī*, as this particular verse form is called, is of two kinds, though love is the theme of both. The first kind, which developed earlier than the second, comprises relatively short poems (one may describe them as being of short-story length) which describe in directly realistic terms the tragic stories of lovers—tragic, because in the society of the day love necessarily *was* a tragedy. Some of these poems are quite clearly accounts of the poets' own experiences. Those of Mīr (?1722/3–1810), the great master of the lyric, are among the earliest and best in this class, while those of Shauq (d. 1871), written probably between 1846 and 1862,[1] are the last of real merit. In a society where that most drastic form of segregation of the sexes, the purdah (*parda*) system, is still widely prevalent, and where love is therefore by definition scandalous, orthodox opinion still frowns upon poems of this kind, and they are consequently less widely known and appreciated than they deserve to be. For all that, the best of them are fine and moving poems, and European taste would appreciate them as such. The other kind of *maṣnavī* is a much longer poem and tells the story of how young lovers, separated from each other by the magic powers of jinns and peris, are ultimately reunited to live happily ever after. By general consent the best of these is Mīr Ḥasan's *Siḥr ul Bayān* (The Enchanting Story), completed in 1785.[2] Its great popularity, which still continues, is well deserved, for within the conventional form Mīr Ḥasan has written an essentially realistic poem in which the experiences of love are beautifully portrayed. It is worth noting in passing that his planning and construction of the story are outstandingly good; this stands in striking contrast to much of Urdu narrative prose fiction, where even to the present day faults of construction are particularly noticeable.

In prose, Urdu had to struggle much longer to supersede Persian. Up to the end of the eighteenth century no prose

[1] 'Aṭāullāh Pālavī, *Taẕkira i Shauq*, Maktaba Jadīd, Lahore, 1956, pp. 55, 105.
[2] For a full account see Ralph Russell and Khurshidul Islam, *Three Mughal Poets*, Harvard University Press, 1968, and George Allen and Unwin, 1969. Chapter 3.

work written in Urdu would have been classed as a work of literature, and not until the late 1860s could an Urdu prose which really is quite distinctively Urdu establish itself as the norm. It is a striking indication of the long supremacy of Persian that it long continued even under the British to be the language of administration; thus it was only in 1837 that Urdu took its place in the law courts of those areas of present-day Uttar Pradesh, Bihar, and Madhya Pradesh that were then under British rule.[1] Nevertheless one can say that Urdu began, in effect, to contest its monopoly from about 1800, when works of narrative prose fiction made their appearance, consciously and deliberately written in the spoken idiom of educated native speakers of Urdu. The qualification 'in effect' is necessary because those who made the innovation did not do so with the conscious aim of ousting Persian as the normal medium of literary expression in prose, but for more temporary and mundane motives. By an accident of history the British authorities were closely involved in this. Shāista Akhtar Bānu Suhrawardy, in her book *The Development of the Urdu Novel and Short Story* (London, 1945) has described how.[2]

'In order to enable the employees of the East India Company to learn the vernaculars, the Fort William College, Calcutta, was founded in 1800, and Dr John Gilchrist placed at the head of it. . . . He travelled in the regions where the choicest Urdu was spoken, and from Delhi, Lucknow, Cawnpore and Agra he collected a band of men who were masters of Urdu idiom. He set them to translate[3] into Urdu prose stories from Persian and Sanskrit. As the object was to get as quickly as possible books which could be used as textbooks for teaching young Englishmen Urdu, he had them written in easy flowing prose. . . .'

The best of these productions is generally held to be Mīr Amman's *Bāgh o Bahār*, which was written in 1801.[4] It is a

[1] Ram Gopal, *Linguistic Affairs of India*, Asia Publishing House, London, 1966, pp. 163–4.

[2] Shāista Akhtar Bānu Suhrawardy, *The Development of the Urdu Novel and Short Story*, Longmans Green and Co., London, 1945, pp. 14–15.

[3] 'Translate' is perhaps too precise a word for what they did.

[4] The title means 'The Garden and Spring'. As very frequently with Urdu works, it gives no indication of what the book is about. It is chosen because, read as a chronogram, it gives the date of composition of the book.

story—or rather, five stories set within a single frame-story—very much in the style made familiar to the English reader by the *Arabian Nights*. Those who wish to acquaint themselves with it can do so through the rather literal, but quite readable translation of Duncan Forbes, published in London in 1862.[1] Nearly all the Fort William productions are stories of this kind.

It is significant that though these books were primarily intended as texts for English students, they did in the course of time reach a wider public. The process by which this happened has not been investigated as it deserves to be. The fact that Fort William College had a press which printed and published these works was doubtless an important factor. Nevertheless, judging by the India Office Library Catalogue of Hindustani [i.e. Urdu] Books, *Bāgh o Bahār* seems to have taken nearly thirty years to acquire sufficient popularity in the real homeland of Urdu—the Delhi–U.P. area—to warrant publication there.[2] The reception accorded to these Fort William works was by no means one of unmixed enthusiasm, and in Lucknow in particular they were the target of much ridicule—not on account of their subject-matter, but because of the language in which they were written. Every gentleman of taste, asserted the Lucknow critics, knew that this was not the way to write literary prose; and to show how it should be done they pointed to Rajab 'Alī Beg Sarūr's *Fasāna i 'Ajāib* (A Tale of Wonders).[3] It is not known when Sarūr wrote this book, but according to his own statement it attracted little attention when it first appeared, and it was not until many years later that its popularity suddenly began to grow rapidly, and to such an extent that it was decided to print it. (This, it can be established, was between 1838 and 1842.) Sarūr himself tells us that his literary ambitions first led him to attempt writing in Arabic and Persian, and only when he was regretfully forced to conclude that he would never excel in either of these languages did he turn to Urdu. It is clear that he consoled himself by making his Urdu prose as close as he possibly could to the ornate Persian prose style then in fashion. *The Tale of*

[1] W. H. Allen, London, 1862.

[2] See p. 106, fn. 1. below.

[3] The information about *Fasāna i 'Ajāib* is taken from Sayyid Maṣ'ūd Ḥasan Rizvī Adīb's edition of Sarūr's *Fasāna i'Ibrat*, Kitāb Nagar, Lucknow, 1st edn., December 1957.

Wonders is written in rhythmical, often rhyming, prose. The closest parallel to his prose style in English literature is perhaps Lyly's *Euphues*, but a closer parallel still is provided by those passages of rhyming prose in the *Arabian Nights* which Burton was at such pains to imitate in his translation, and which he has done as well as perhaps it can be done in English.

This then was the style which for decades together contested with that of Mīr Amman for acceptance as the norm, and the volume of support which it could command is amply attested by the number of editions of the book which continued to appear.[1]

Obviously this contest is of great importance in the history of the prose narrative in Urdu, but the accounts of it occupy what is, in my view, a disproportionate place in the histories of Urdu literature. For the main form of Urdu prose narrative before the modern period is neither that of Mīr Amman nor that of Sarūr, but that of what in Urdu is called the *dāstān*. (Indeed, Sarūr's book itself is only a special kind of *dāstān*.) The word, which comes into Urdu from Persian, means simply 'story' or 'tale', but it is used primarily of enormous cycles of medieval romance, closely comparable to those of medieval Europe which Cervantes parodied in *Don Quixote*. The most

[1] The catalogue of Hindustani books in the India Office Library, published in 1900, lists an edition of *Fasāna i 'Ajāib* published in Lucknow in 1845. There is then a gap until 1866, but between that date and 1889 sixteen different editions are listed, of which, however, only the last was published outside the Delhi–U.P. area (from Bombay).

But, significantly, the editions of Mīr Amman's *Bāgh o Bahār* are even more numerous; and its popularity clearly starts earlier and spreads further afield. Most of the early editions were published outside the Delhi–U.P. area. Then, from 1850, it clearly becomes very popular in the Delhi–U.P. area also. Finally, in the 1870s, its popularity spreads to Bombay and the South. Precise figures are as follows:

From 1804 to 1847—eight editions, of which only two (Cawnpore, 1832 and 'Delhi, 1845?') are from the Delhi–U.P. area.

From 1850 to 1871—twelve editions, *all* from the Delhi–U.P. area.

From 1872 to 1879—sixteen editions, of which eleven are from the Delhi–U.P. area, the other five being from Bangalore (1872), Bombay (1874, and two in 1877), and Madras (1876).

An edition in Devanagari (Hindi) characters appeared as early as 1847, and there are other Devanagari editions in 1852, 1869, 1870 and 1879. There is also one in Gujarati characters published from Bombay in 1877.

I have left out of account editions and translations by English scholars—mostly published in London—clearly intended for the use of English students; also a translation into French published in Paris.

famous is that which relates the exploits of the legendary champion of Islam, Amīr Ḥamza,[1] the uncle of the Prophet, who, like the Christian knight of medieval European romance, rides through the pages of the tale fighting for the true faith against unbelievers, witches and sorcerers, and emerging triumphant over seemingly insuperable difficulties. Most popular in India was one part of this enormous cycle entitled *Ṭilism i Hoshrubā* ('the enchantment which steals away one's senses') which itself comprises seven tall, bulky volumes, totalling more than 7,500 pages. (The totals for the complete *Tale of Amīr Ḥamza* are 18 volumes and nearly 16,500 pages.) The stories on which the *dāstān* is based seem almost certainly traditional in origin and go back several centuries. One Indian tradition was that the *Tale of Amīr Ḥamza* was written in Persian by Faiẓī,[2] the great courtier of the Mughal emperor Akbar (1556–1605), while some add that its purpose was to divert the Emperor's attention from the great Hindu epic, the *Mahābhārata*.[3] But there is no evidence that this tradition is correct. As to content, the stories are almost certainly much older, while as to form, the most reliable writer on the subject[4] argues convincingly that the *dāstān* assumed its present shape in the second half of the eighteenth century. The *dāstāns* were originally recited at the courts of the nobles, but also before more plebeian audiences, in very much the same way as their Arabic counterparts were once recited in Egypt. In fact the chapters headed 'Public Recitations of Romances' in E. W. Lane's classic *Manners and Customs of the Modern Egyptians*, first published in 1836, will serve also as a generally accurate description of the way the Urdu *dāstāns* were recited in India.[5]

[1] The account of the *dāstān* of Amīr Ḥamza derives mainly from Rāz Yazdānī's article *Urdū dāstānoṉ par kām kā tajziya aur tabṣira*, published in the Indian government periodical *Ājkal*, Delhi, issue dated July 1960.

See also 'Abdul Ḥalīm Sharar's account in Chapter 12 of his *Guzashta Lakhnaū*. (Many editions. The best is perhaps that which comprises a volume of *Maẓāmīn i Sharar*, in the collected edition published from Lahore, Sayyid Mubārak 'Alī Shāh Gīlānī, n.d.)

[2] The Newal Kishore Press (see below) itself made this claim. See, for example, the announcement on p. 2 of the cover of the second volume in the series, *Nausherwān Nāma*, Daftar i Awwal, Jild i Duwam, Lucknow, 3rd edn., 1915.

[3] Cf. Fīroz Ḥusain, *Life and Works of Ratan Nāth Sarshār*, 1964 (unpublished Ph.D. thesis, University of London), p. 99.

[4] Rāz Yazdānī. See Note 1 above.

[5] Cf. also Sharar's account referred to in Note 1 above.

(The rhythmical prose, with its rhyming phrases surely owes much of its origin to this tradition of recitation.) The *dāstāns* had been widely popular as oral literature long before the present version—or more accurately, the most substantial of the present versions—were written down, at the instance of Newal Kishore, the founder of a press which still exists in Lucknow and has performed inestimable services to Urdu literature. The present versions are in part the work of two of the most famous *dāstān*-reciters of old Lucknow, Mīr Muḥammad Ḥusain Jāh and Aḥmad Ḥusain Qamar. In publishing them Newal Kishore stated that they were translated from Persian originals, but this is somewhat too large a claim. Persian versions of some parts of the story do indeed exist, but there is no known Persian original for the greater part of the work, and in at least one instance the 'translator' himself notes that he has departed from the Persian version he has before him because it does not accord with the story in the tradition with which he is familiar. An inquiry recently made on this point to the successor of the Newal Kishore Press brought the reply that 'No trace of Persian originals (of the *dāstāns* in their present form) can be found. The truth is that there certainly were one or two books on which they were based, but the *dāstān*-reciters employed by the Press used to come every day and recite the stories, and the scribes would write them down. . . . And this is how they came into existence.' There is no reason to doubt that the facts are substantially as here stated.[1]

The *dāstāns* are therefore, in the main, original Urdu works,

[1] Rāz Yazdānī's statement, and that of the letter which he elicited from the successor of the Newal Kishore Press, is not accurate in every detail. Ghālib, in a letter to Nawwāb Kalb i 'Alī Khān of Rampur dated August 21, 1865 (see *Makātīb i Ghālib*, ed. Imtiyāz 'Ālī 'Arshī, Rampur, 1937) speaks of a Persian work *Rumūz i Ḥamza*, and says that it was written in the days of Shāh 'Abbas II (1642–66).

In 1965 Qāẓī 'Abdul Vadūd of Patna showed me detailed notes which he had made on this work. It is a relatively short single volume. He told me that *Ṭilism i Hoshrubā*, which is in his view indeed the best part of the Indian *Dāstān i Amīr Ḥamza*, owes little or nothing to *Rumūz i Ḥamza*. The remark of the 'translator' who departed from his Persian original was drawn to my attention by Miss Fīroz Ḥusain (see fn. 3, p. 107 above); but, regrettably, I failed to note the reference. Cf. also Muḥammad Ḥasan 'Askarī's introduction (p. 20) to his selection from *Ṭilism i Hoshrubā*, Maktaba Jadīd, Lahore, 1953, on new material avowedly introduced by the *dāstān-go*.

and even so brief an account of them makes it clear that the importance of Sarūr's *Fasāna i 'Ajāib* should not be exaggerated. In both language and content it is entirely within the *dāstān* tradition, and the most that can be claimed for it, considered as a step towards the development of the modern novel, is that its material is presented within the compass of a single short volume.

The *dāstāns* can quite justly be called propagandist literature of a highly tendentious kind. Everything is in black and white—the virtuous are all virtue and the vicious all vice. It follows that there are no three-dimensional characters, and very little realism of any kind. Neither is there anything that can really be called a plot, nothing but a succession of episodes following one upon another in endless profusion. It is noteworthy that the *dāstāns* flowered in the second half of the eighteenth century, when the Mughal Empire was in headlong decline and where every principle of conduct in the medieval code was everywhere and every day being violated. Men who knew no other code, including those who were daily offending against it, could escape from the sordid reality around them into the world of the *dāstāns* where everything was splendidly simple and where the true Muslim warrior not only behaved unfailingly as a true Muslim should, but by doing so achieved the most eminently satisfactory results. Moreover, the authors of the *dāstāns* had made provision for pleasing changes of diet. In the *Tale of Amīr Ḥamza* the hero is accompanied and supported in his exploits by his trusty friend 'Amar 'Ayyār—'Amar the Artful, who possesses magic powers and uses them to reinforce Amīr Ḥamza's valour. He does this mainly through the use of his magic bag Zanbīl into which he can cause almost anything to disappear and out of which he can cause almost anything to emerge. Very often he uses his magic to make his enemies look ridiculous, and his function in the tale is thus, to a large extent, to give comic relief from the prevailing atmosphere of high seriousness. Relief of another kind is provided by episodes with a love interest, in which the Islamic warriors' amorous adventures are related, often in circumstantial and titillating detail. (Their conduct in these scenes is not quite perhaps that which strict adherence to Islam would permit; but everyone seems to have been too absorbed to notice this.)

Thus the *dāstāns* provided a rich banquet of good and varied fare.

THE TRANSITION TO THE NOVEL

(*a*) *Ratan Nāth Sarshār* (*1846–1902*)

The elements of the modern novel come into Urdu literature piecemeal, and the development is most clearly seen if one follows a logical, rather than a strictly chronological, order, beginning with the work which is closest to the *dāstān*, namely, Ratan Nāth Sarshār's[1] *Fasāna i Āzād* (The Tale of Āzād). Sarshār himself was at pains to emphasize that *Fasāna i Āzād* was something quite new in Urdu fiction, and, as we shall see, there are good grounds for his claim. But for all that, its points of resemblance to the *dāstān* are striking. The most obvious resemblance is in sheer length; its four larger-than-quarto volumes contain about 3,000 pages in all, with two columns of print to the page. (A rough word-count gives a total of two and a quarter million as against about 700,000 words for the Maudes' English translation of Tolstoy's *War and Peace*.) But this is only the first resemblance of many. Āzād, its hero, is a typical, two-dimensional *dāstān* hero—handsome, brave, intelligent, talented, a great lover (though at the same time, of course, purity itself), and a great champion of the right. There is the same absence of plot, the same endless succession of loosely connected episodes, the same pattern of innumerable difficulties triumphantly surmounted, and the same black and white tendentiousness. Just as Amīr Ḥamza has his faithful companion 'Amar the Artful, so does Āzād have *his* faithful companion K͟hojī, and K͟hojī's main function is, like 'Amar's, to provide comic relief. Finally there is a marked resemblance even in style and language, for Sarshār is almost as fond of rhyming prose as the *dāstān* writers were. Thus it would not be hard to defend the statement that *The Tale of Āzād* is in the direct line of descent from the *dāstān*.

Nevertheless, in *The Tale of Āzād* the *dāstān* form is adapted to what is in one major respect a new content. Āzād is the champion of the New Light against the Old, the champion of modernism (which, in this context, means the values and

[1] For a full account of Sarshār see Fīroz Ḥusain, *op. cit.*

outlook of Victorian England) against every form of medievalism. Very conveniently, historical circumstances enabled him to be at the same time the champion of Islam, in true *dāstān* tradition; for the framework story tells how Āzād falls in love with a beautiful, pure, and above all *educated* lady named Ḥusn Ārā ('Beauty-adorning') and is commanded by her to go off to the Crimean War and fight alongside the British and his fellow-Muslims, the Turks, in their struggle with the Russians. He does so, and returning victorious after countless adventures, wins Ḥusn Ārā's hand. (Had Sarshār been writing a few decades later, when the expansion of the European powers brought them into conflict with the Muslim states in the Near and Middle East, he would have been denied this happy chance of combining his hero's new role with the old. But in fairness to him it must be added that when at the end of the last volume the British authorities in India ask Āzād's help in their war against Muslim Afghanistan, he gives it without hesitation. It is the fight for modernity which is his real mission.) Another major difference from the *dāstāns* is that *The Tale of Āzād* is virtually free of supernatural incident, and its setting is in the contemporary world. In the earlier part the scene is laid in nineteenth-century Lucknow, which is vividly and realistically described.

Thus there is a certain parallel between *The Tale of Āzād* and *Don Quixote*, and we know that *Don Quixote* did in fact directly influence Sarshār.[1] His later book *Khudāī Faujdār* (The Godly Warrior) *is Don Quixote*, though considerably abridged and freely adapted. In *The Tale of Āzād* itself, the character of Khoji, Āzād's ignorant, uncultured, cowardly, blustering, but faithful friend, owes at least as much to Sancho Panza as it does to 'Amar the Artful. But in other respects Sarshār's characters are, of course, the reverse of Cervantes'. Whereas Don Quixote is the deluded champion of the old, Āzād is the clear-thinking, self-confident champion of the new. Whereas Sancho Panza is, in one of his aspects, the expression of down-to-earth common sense, Khojī is, especially in the earlier part of the book, little more than a buffoon, the personification of everything ridiculous and outmoded in the

[1] Cakbast, *Maẓāmīn i Cakbast*, Shaikh Mubārak 'Alī, Lahore, n.d., Essay on Paṇḍit Ratan Nāth Sarshār, p. 24.

traditional Indian way of life. True, as the story progresses he becomes a more complex figure, embodying also, especially in his complete loyalty to Āzād, much that was admirable in the old order; and here there is a certain parallel between him and Don Quixote. Other differences between the two writers go deeper. Sarshār has nothing of Cervantes' mature wisdom, or of his intellectual and artistic power. His modernism is of the most crude and uncritical kind. The values and the way of life of Victorian England are to him the last word in human wisdom, and all that is 'old-fashioned' in Indian life (with the one significant exception of the *parda* system) is condemned in an equally wholesale way. Once again one is reminded of the *dāstāns*, where good is unalloyed good and evil unalloyed evil, and the struggle between them free of all possible ambiguity. But to say no more on this point would be to do Sarshār an injustice. In his crude extremism Sarshār is the child of his age. In the 1870s the cultural conflict in Muslim India as a whole was all around him being fought out in just these extreme terms. These were the years in which Sir Sayyid Aḥmad K͟hān was bringing about those radical changes in the outlook of the Muslim upper classes which for better or worse (for better *and* worse would perhaps be more accurate) were to determine their course of action for a century to come. Sir Sayyid was perfectly clear about what he was attempting. It was his aim, he said, 'to produce a class of persons, Muslim in religion, Indian in blood and colour, but English in taste, in opinions and in intellect'.[1] (The words, except for 'Muslim in religion', are taken bodily from that most extreme manifesto of British cultural policy in India, Macaulay's Minute on Education of 1835.)[2] And he made equally clear to his compatriots how far he thought they would have to travel to reach this desirable goal. In a letter from London dated October 15, 1869, he wrote: 'The natives of India, high and low, . . . educated and illiterate, when contrasted with the English in education, manners, and uprightness, are as like them as a dirty animal is to an able and handsome

[1] *Addresses and Speeches relating to the Mahomedan Anglo-Oriental College, in Aligarh . . . 1875–1898*, ed. Nawab Mohsin-ul-Mulk, Institute Press, Aligarh, 1898, *Tamhīd*, p. 2.

[2] Cf. *Selected Speeches*, ed. G. M. Young, Oxford University Press, World's Classics series, 1935, p. 359.

man.' (It should be stressed that this is not an opinion confidentially expressed in a private letter; the letter was intended for publication in India and was duly published there.)[1] Not surprisingly, the opponents of the New Light were driven by this kind of thing to a similar extremism and championed the cause of everything traditional simply because it *was* traditional. In any true appreciation of *The Tale of Āzād* all this has to be borne in mind. Not only is Sarshār's own attitude fully typical; his characters too, with their wholesale acceptance or wholesale rejection of the New Light, are portrayed with a greater realism than the present-day reader might at first sight think.

Two extracts will serve to illustrate both the weakness and the strength of Sarshār's work. At one point in the story[2] Āzād runs into an old friend who asks him, quite out of the blue, whether he thinks the Europeans and the Bengalis more advanced than the people of Lucknow. Āzād says that undoubtedly they are, but his friend demands proof, which Āzād promises to give him. Next day as soon as it is light they set off together, and walk until they have left the city proper behind them and reached the cantonment. There they see from the road a fine bungalow standing in well-kept grounds, and inside it, an English gentleman and his wife taking their breakfast. Sarshār's description is interesting. The English gentleman is barely mentioned, but the lady is accorded the full *dāstān* treatment, rhyming prose and all (which, however, I have not attempted to reproduce in my translation). 'There in a fine room was a Sahib seated on a chair, and near him an idol [the standard metaphor for a beautiful woman] with a face like a houri of Paradise—her body as delicate, and her cheeks as red, as a rose—gracing a more delicate chair. Her face was radiant, her black dress was of costly silk, and her perfume so fragrant that gusts of it were wafted to the road outside and permeated all one's senses. Both were conversing sweetly together and making short work of [the expression in the original is equally colloquial] some mutton chops. Āzād's

[1] Urdu text in *Musāfirān i Landan*, ed. Shai<u>kh</u> Muḥammad Ismā'īl Pānīpatī, Majlis i Taraqqī i Adab, Lahore, 1961, pp. 183–4. English translation quoted from G. F. I. Graham, *The Life and Work of Sir Syed Ahmed Khan, K.C.S.I.*, London, Hodder and Stoughton, 1909 edn, pp. 125–6.

[2] *Fasāna i Āzād*, Vol. I, 9th edn., Newal Kishore Press, Lucknow, 1949, pp. 69–70.

friend was lost in admiration and delight.' In other words, the sight of a nondescript Englishman and a highly perfumed Englishwoman eating mutton chops at about seven in the morning[1] is enough to prove the superiority of the English way of life! The narrative continues: 'They pressed on. Five young Bengalis were coming towards them in a carriage—one a barrister, one a civil servant, two M.A.s and one B.A. [Āzād seems to have detected these details at sight.] Āzād knew one of them, and greeted him. He got down and offered Āzād a cigar. Inquiry revealed that all the other four came of a poor family, 'but friends of their learned father had raised the money to send them to England to be educated; and now they held important positions. . . .' And so on and so forth.

This kind of thing is so crude as to be laughable. Yet side by side with it one finds pieces of excellent descriptive and realistic writing. In the first volume,[2] where Āzād has not yet gone off to the war, he and Khoji go on a railway journey from Lucknow. They reach the station in good time, and Āzād finds the refreshment room and goes in. Sarshār continues: 'He was delighted with what he saw: everything was spotlessly clean and in its proper place. From one end of the room to the other were tables with chairs arranged round them, and glasses set out upon them. Lamps were burning brightly on all sides. Āzād sat down. "Bring me something to eat", he said. "But, mind you, no wine, and nothing with pork in it." . . .' The waiter, spick and span in his clean uniform, and with a turban on his head, brought him all manner of English dishes [*sic*] which he served from costly plates of the most expensive kind. Āzād plied his knife and fork with a will, and finished off with lemonade and soda-water. When he came out, there was Khoji, his bedding unrolled on the platform, eating parāthas and kabābs.

'You look as though you're doing all right,' said Āzād, 'the way you're scoffing those kabābs.'

[1] Once again, the picture is perhaps closer to reality than the modern reader might think. Thus Edward Lear comments on 'the enormous meat meals, especially the immense quantities of roast mutton, that English people were accustomed to eat in India at that time. . . .' See Angus Davidson, *Edward Lear*, Penguin Books, Harmondsworth, 1950, p. 212.

[2] Pp. 418–20.

'That's right,' said Khojī, 'some of us like kabābs and some of us like wine.'

'What do you mean, "Some of us like wine"? Do you think I've been drinking wine? I never touch the stuff. I'll swear on the Qurān I haven't touched a drop. You might as well accuse me of eating pork.'

Khojī smiled. 'Right!' he said. 'You wouldn't let *that* chance slip. "You might as well say I've been eating pork!" he says. Well said! You have to think these things forbidden or repulsive to keep off them. But both are allowed to you. You think it's a great thing to have them. Well done, my friend! Today you've really shown your paces!'

'Have you finished? Or do you want to go on abusing me? I tell you, you can put me on oath. I've not so much as put my hand to wine; I've not even looked at pork.'

'You put that well. All right, you haven't put your hand to wine. But it went down your throat, I'll be bound. And anyway, who takes any notice of *your* oaths? An oath means nothing to you. *I* can't make out to this day what your religion is. . . . Oh well, we shall all get the reward of our deeds. Why should I worry about it?'

'You're not going to admit you're wrong, are you?'

'Why should I? Didn't I see you with my own eyes using a knife and fork?'

'Well? Do you think you drink wine with a knife and fork?'

'How do *I* know how you drink wine? Better ask one of your drunken friends about that. But I'm sorry you're so far gone. What a pity! What a shame!'

'Do just one thing for me: just go into the refreshment room and see for yourself.'

'What, *me*? Me, a true Muslim, go into a refreshment room? God forbid! God save us! I leave that to you, and welcome. *Me?* Go into a refreshment room? May God protect me!'

Āzād left Khoji to his kabābs and strolled along the platform. A gentleman with a beard a yard long accosted him, 'Well, sir, may I know your name?'

'Āzād.'

'Āzād.' He smiled. 'Yes, indeed. The name suits you. Freedom and free-thinking [Āzād means free, but its senses range from liberty to licence and 'free-thinking'] are written all over you. And your religion?'

Āzād quoted a Persian verse and then replied, 'Respected sir, your humble servant is a Muslim. Islam is my faith, and I observe the Sharī'at [Muslim religious law]. And *your* name, Maulvi Sahib?'

'Never mind *my* name. Allow me to express my sorrow.'

'Please do. Burst into tears if you like. But remember that Muḥarram [the month when the martyrdom of Ḥusain, the grandson of the Prophet, is mourned] isn't far off. You'll be able to weep then to your heart's content. Why so impatient?'

'You say you are a Muslim and observe the Sharī'at, and yet you go into a restaurant and drink wine. God have mercy on us! My good man, do you never think of Judgement Day?'

'Respected sir, what can I say? I have no more to say to you. God save us!'

'Pardon me if I am rude; but think of yourself when you say "God save us!" Well, you have done Satan's work, but Praise God that your better self reproaches you.'

'Maulana, I swear by God I took only food in the restaurant, and that too only what Islam permits. Be fair! What is wrong with that? After all, in Istambul everybody—including the most eminent doctors of Islam—dine with Christians. Why on earth is it that in India Muslims think it a sin?'

'Listen; I'll explain it all to you. To eat in a restaurant is not creditable to a Muslim. If you'd spread your mat and had the same food brought out to you, that would have been all right. That too would have been open to objection, but not to the same extent. Then again, you may swear as many oaths as you like, with the Qurān raised in your hand, but no one will *believe* that you didn't have pork and wine. If you trade in coals your hands will get black. And don't talk to me about Istambul. The Shah of Persia drinks wine and orders the most expensive brandy. But does that make wine-drinking permissible? Let the Turks eat with Christians as much as they like. That doesn't mean that *we* should. It's against our traditions to do so. Have you got to live in Istambul? Or have you got to live here in India? When you're *in* Istambul, do as they do. But are we talking about Istambul or are we talking about India? After all, there's no lack of food outside the restaurant—kabābs, parāthas, biscuits, everything. So what was to be gained by going there? Why make yourself conspicuous and get yourself laughed at for nothing?'

'My dear sir. First, the food in there is fine and tasty. Secondly, the place is spotlessly clean. Then you can sit and *enjoy* the food. There's a man to pull the fan. The fan is clean. The plates are clean. The tables are clean. There are four waiters standing ready to serve you. Can I get all that outside? God save us!'

'The food may be fine according to *your* taste. As for the fan, out here you can pay a pice [about a farthing] and get yourself fanned for an hour at a time. And what do you want with cleanliness when you are travelling? Besides, it's not as though things out here are filthy dirty. If *you're* over-particular, that's quite another matter. Anyway, it's your business and you can get on with it. But youngsters should listen to what their elders tell them. I've told you. But you must do as you like.'

Āzād thought to himself, 'I shan't do such a stupid thing again. It's up to me whether I eat in a restaurant or not, but I don't have to advertise the fact. From now on I'll be more discreet.'

'Well,' said Khojī, '*now* what about it? You thought you could make a fool of *me*; but now the Maulvi Sahib has told you off. I bet you won't go again in a hurry!'

There is no need to comment in detail on writing of this kind. It is clear that we are here dealing with modern realistic writing of considerable talent, which owes little or nothing to the *dāstān* tradition; and because such writing is not rare in *The Tale of Āzād*, it is, despite its obvious links with the *dāstān*, at the same time a work which brought permanently into Urdu literature some of the major elements of the modern novel.

(b) *Naẕīr Aḥmad (1836–1912)*

Sarshār continued to write prose fiction for nearly twenty years after *The Tale of Āzād* appeared, but none of his subsequent works shows any very great advance upon the best in what he had already achieved, and a rapid and very marked decline soon sets in. To see the advance towards the modern novel carried further, one has to turn to his older contemporary, Naẕīr Aḥmad.

Naẕīr Aḥmad was ten years older than Sarshār, and the first of the series of tales which he wrote between 1869 and 1891[1] pre-dates *The Tale of Āzād* by some years. (Nazīr Ahmad's first tale, *Mirāt ul 'Arūs*, [The Bride's Mirror], was written in 1869. The first instalment of *The Tale of Āzād*—it appeared initially as a serial—came out in 1878, and the last in 1879. It was issued in book form in the following year.) But whereas Sarshār's power as a writer soon wanes, Naẕīr Aḥmad's continues strong throughout at any rate the greater part of his literary life. He was a man of much more vigorous intellect than Sarshār, with a stronger character and a keener sense of realism, and these qualities are reflected in his writings. They have led most modern Urdu critics to regard him as a novelist, and to judge him accordingly. From this standpoint they have either praised him extravagantly or else belittled his achievement—with the majority taking the latter course. But to judge him as a novelist is in itself to do him a serious injustice, and one which is all the less excusable because he himself to the end of his days never made any claim to be one. He wrote to instruct, and he chose a fictional form because in that way he could make his instruction more palatable. That he makes no larger claim than this is clear from a preface written in the year of his death to a little text-book on writing the Urdu script. There he tells us: 'I began writing books at the time when my own children were of an age to start their schooling. I had my own experience both of learning and teaching, and as an employee in the Education Department had also had the occasion to supervise teaching. I knew in every detail all the defects of the educational methods and of the books in use. "Once you have seen the fly in your drink, you cannot swallow it"—and so I began to write books on my own account and to teach from them. This was the motive which first impelled me to write.'[2] This is entirely in keeping with what he had

[1] See p. 121, fn. 2 below.

[2] *Rasm ul Khaṭ*, 5th edn., Delhi, 1919, p. 1. Naẕīr Aḥmad's Preface is dated 1912.

written more than forty years earlier, explaining how his first book, *The Bride's Mirror*, came to be written.[1] And independently of Naẕīr Aḥmad's own statements, we know that it was originally written without even any thought of publication —let alone any pretentious claims to be called a novel—and that only its chance discovery by Kempson, the British Director of Public Instruction in whose department Naẕīr Aḥmad was then employed, led to its being published.[2] Its quite unexpectedly large measure of success[3] encouraged him to write other tales, planned now for a larger audience, but with similar aims in view. An outline account of *The Bride's Mirror*, which is available in an English translation by G. E. Ward (London, Henry Frowde, 1903) illustrates well enough the method of all of them. The aim of the book is to show the young Muslim girl what qualities she must cultivate if she is to meet successfully the problems she will face when she is married. In this case the lesson is taught by a story in two parts—the first a cautionary tale of a girl named Akbarī, and the second (which Naẕīr Aḥmad in fact wrote some eighteen months after his daughter had finished with Akbarī and was clamouring for more)[4] the story of her model sister Asg͟harī. Akbarī has always been spoilt, and the result is that when she is married and goes to her new home (which meant, as in most cases it still means, the home of her husband's parents) she cannot stand the trials to which every new wife is subjected and has a very miserable time of it. The passage in which Naẕīr Aḥmad concludes his account of Akbarī's misadventures and turns to Asg͟harī, sets the tone of the book:[5] 'Now listen to the story of Asg͟harī. This girl was to her family what a rose in full bloom is to a garden, or the eye to a human body. Every kind of acquired excellence, every kind of natural intelligence was hers. Good sense, self-restraint, modesty, consideration for others—all these qualities God had bestowed

[1] Dībāca to *Mirāt ul 'Arūs*.

[2] Iftik͟hār 'Ālam, *Ḥayāt un Naẕīr*, Delhi, Shamsi Press, 1912, pp. 154–5.

[3] Footnotes in the preface to its sequel *Banāt un Na'sh* tell us that by 1888 it had been published in editions totalling more than 100,000 copies, and had been translated into Bengali, Braj, Kashmiri, Panjabi and Gujarati. (*Banāt un Na'sh*, Delhi, 1888 edn., p. 1, footnotes 11 and 12.)

[4] Cf. Dībāca to *Mirāt ul 'Arūs*, and the fuller account in *Ḥayāt un Naẕīr*, p. 154.

[5] P. 51.

upon her. From her childhood she had a distaste for romping and jesting and ill-natured jokes.[1] She loved reading, or doing the work of the house. No one had ever seen her chattering rubbish, or quarrelling with anybody. All the women of the mohulla loved her as they did their own daughters. Blessed indeed was the fate of those parents who owned Asgharī for a daughter! And happy was the lot of that family into which Asgharī was now to be admitted as a bride!'

Asgharī is married at the age of thirteen, and the first period of her life in her new home is well described.[2] 'In the earlier days of her wedded life Asgharī did feel very ill at ease, as was only natural after suddenly quitting her mother's house to live among entire strangers. She had become inured to a life of constant activity and supervision; she could not bear to be without employment for a quarter of an hour. And now she was condemned to sit demurely, confined to one room, with nothing going on, for months together. The liberty which she enjoyed in her parents' home was no longer hers. As soon as she arrived in her mother-in-law's house, everyone was intent on watching her, and scrutinizing her every action. One scans her features; another appraises the length of her hair; another guesses her height; another examines her jewels; and another takes stock of her clothes. If she eats anything, each morsel is observed. What sized bit did she take? How wide did she open her mouth? How did she masticate it? And how did she gulp it down? If she rises from her seat, they look to see how she robes herself in her mantle, how she holds up her skirts. And if she sleeps, they count the hours; what time did she go to sleep? When did she get up? In short, every phase of her deportment was under observation.

'All this was terribly distressing to poor Asgharī; but since she was endowed with common sense and a good education, she emerged with credit even from this ordeal, and her manners in general were approved of by her husband's relations.'

From this good beginning Asgharī proceeds by unfailing tact, a proper humility before her elders, constant hard work, and sheer cold-blooded calculation and intrigue, not only in

[1] 'Ill-natured jokes' is a stronger phrase than the original Urdu warrants: 'teasing' would be a nearer equivalent. (Here and in the passage quoted below, the translation is Ward's.)

[2] Pp. 62–3.

triumphing over all her difficulties, but also in establishing herself as the real ruler of the household.

The Bride's Mirror was followed by *Banāt un N'ash* (literally 'Daughters of the Bier'—one of the names given in Urdu to the constellation of the Plough) which is a sequel to it.[1] It consists mainly of an account of a school set up by Asg͟harī for the girls of the *muhalla*, and details at length the lessons on history, geography and elementary science which she taught in it. Other books were written to counter indifference to religion, to show the evils of polygamy, to ridicule the practice advocated in some advanced modernist circles of adopting English dress and furniture and manners, to expound the application of Islam to modern problems, and to argue (rather cautiously) for widow re-marriage.[2] The didactic aim is well to the fore in all of them, and was intended to be.

But if Naẕīr Aḥmad was not, and never claimed to be, a novelist, it is not difficult to see why he came to be regarded as one. His stories without doubt embody some of the major elements of the modern novel, and these are not only more prominent in his works than in Sarshār's, but show, in general, more talented writing. For reasons of space they must be dealt with rather summarily. As might be expected, Naẕīr Aḥmad's writing owes nothing to the *dāstān* and its world of fantasy, and his prose style reflects that fact. In Sarshār the fondness for rhyming prose and for standard descriptions in vague superlatives is still very much in evidence, and where it intrudes, as it often does, even in the depiction of the everyday contemporary scene, it seems irritatingly out of place. In Naẕīr Aḥmad the *dāstān* style has been banished completely, to be replaced by the vigorous near-colloquial which the Fort William writers had pioneered seventy years earlier, but which acquires in his hands an ease and flexibility which they in their day had not yet been able to impart to it. At the same

[1] It was published in 1872. Cf. *Ḥayāt un Naẕīr*, p. 172.

[2] These are, respectively *Taubat un Naṣūḥ* (1877), *Moḥṣināt* (also known as *Fasāna i Mubtalā*) (1885), *Ibn ul Vaqt* (1888), *Ruyā i Ṣādiqa* (1892), *Ayyāma* (1891). For a brief account of most of them see Suhrawardy (*op. cit.*, p. 104, fn. 2 above), pp. 53–65. For some reason she does not mention *Ruyā i Ṣādiqa*. Nor does she give dates of publication. These are supplied from *Ḥayāt un Naẕīr* where this gives them; otherwise from Bashīr Maḥmūd Ak͟htar, *Naẕīr Aḥmad kī nāval-nigārī kā fan*, Maktaba i 'Ilm, Lyallpur, 1966, pp. 9–10.

time it is a style which can rise to great heights. Naẕīr Aḥmad has a range of descriptive power and an ability to evoke atmosphere which Sarshār cannot match. His description of the cholera epidemic in Delhi,[1] or of a scene in the 'Mutiny' of 1857 where Ibn ul Vaqt (the main character of the story in question) returning to his home at sunset, comes upon the corpses of some of the English shot by the rebels,[2] or of his character Naṣūḥ's dream of the Day of Judgement,[3] a dream so vivid that it marks the turning point in his life—all these are magnificent pieces of writing and make a most powerful impact. His mastery of dialogue is equally outstanding. Every character *speaks* in character as well as acting in character. And finally the characters themselves are portrayed with great realism. This last point is in some ways the most striking of all. In more than one of his tales one sees the realist taking over the reins from the moralist, so that characters created to typify this or that idea then begin to develop according to their own logic, and in a way which damages rather than helps the author's didactic purpose. Asg͟harī, in *The Bride's Mirror*, is a case in point. Naẕīr Aḥmad creates her to show how even a girl of thirteen can develop the qualities to cope successfully with every difficulty. But a girl of thirteen who can do that can also become hard and calculating, acquiring both a keen awareness of her powers and a keen pleasure in exercising them. In *The Bride's Mirror* Asg͟harī does develop in this way, and Naẕīr Aḥmad is instinctively too good a realist not to portray these aspects of her character along with the others, though in so doing he lessens her effectiveness as an exemplar of all wifely virtues. The same sort of thing happens in *Taubat un Naṣūḥ* and in other novels. One is tempted to the no doubt futile, but nonetheless attractive speculation of what Naẕīr Aḥmad might have done if he could have been persuaded to write novels rather than improving tales.

(c) *'Abdul Ḥalīm Sharar (1860–1926)*

Both Sarshār and Naẕīr Aḥmad had already produced their best work when a new writer appeared on the scene, bringing

[1] *Taubat un-Naṣūḥ*, Chapter 1.
[2] *Ibn ul Vaqt*, Chapter 2.
[3] *Taubat un Naṣūḥ*, Chapter 1.

with him fresh themes to diversify the growing stream of prose narrative fiction. This was 'Abdul Ḥalīm Sharar, the pioneer of the historical romance in Urdu. It is in this role that we shall consider him here; but it should be remarked in passing that the historical romance was not his only significant contribution to Urdu literature. He was a strong supporter of Sir Sayyid Aḥmad Khan's ideas, and his prolific writings, which include essays, popular history, and novels on contemporary social themes as well as historical romances, were all intended in one way or another to serve the cause of the New Light. In one striking respect his ideas were more advanced than Sir Sayyid's, for he was a staunch and outspoken opponent of *parda*, and one of his novels is designed to show the disastrous effects which the *parda* system could produce.[1] The day will perhaps come when he will be most valued for his essays, and particularly for the whole series of essays which, taken together, paint a vivid portrait of old Lucknow before the British annexation of 1856. (An English translation of these is likely to be published shortly.) But from his own time to the present day it has been his historical romances which have made the strongest appeal to Urdu speakers. His best known works in this genre appeared between 1887 and 1907,[2] and won immediate acclaim. Stated in the broadest terms, they all have a single theme—the portrayal of the glorious past of Islam and of the great superiority of Islamic civilization in its heyday over that of contemporary non-Muslim (especially Christian) powers. His method may be illustrated by a study of *Florā Florinḍā* which is generally agreed to be one of the best of his books. It was first published serially, from 1893, and appeared in book form in 1899. The story of *Florā Florinḍā* is set in Spain in the third century of the Muslim era (ninth century AD) when Muslim power in Spain was at its zenith. At the time when the story opens, Flora, the heroine, is about eighteen years old. She is the daughter of a Muslim father and a Christian mother and has an elder brother Ziyād. The father had done his best to convert his wife to Islam, but without success. She had

[1] *Badr un Nisā kī muṣībat.* Suhrawardy describes this book on pp. 82–4. Neither she nor Sadiq (see fn. 2 below) gives the date of publication. The earliest edition in the British Museum is dated 1897.

[2] Muhammad Sadiq, *A History of Urdu Literature*, London, Oxford University Press, 1964, p. 339.

never used the Muslim name Zahra which he had given their daughter, but always called her Flora, and in the end the whole family called her by this name. Moreover she had secretly brought Flora up as a Christian, assisted in this, especially after her husband's death, by the organized, secret activities of the Christian Church. The mother too is now dead, but the Christians' secret contacts with Flora have not ceased, and her brother Ziyād, who has all the time been unaware of what was going on, now gets wind of the true situation and like a good Muslim takes steps to correct it. Flora is cut off from all Christian contacts by his command that only visitors who are personally known to him may come to the house. This presents the Christians with a difficult problem, and the Patriarch of the Christian community in Spain personally draws up plans for dealing with it. A nun, Florinda, is sent in the guise of a young Muslim widow to occupy a house in the locality where Flora and her brother live. She is to cultivate their acquaintance, win their confidence, and when opportunity offers, get Flora away to the great cathedral at Cordova, where further arrangements will be made. This she succeeds in doing. Just as the whole Christian Church had been involved in the attempt to get Flora away, so is the whole Muslim machinery of state brought into action to recover her. But no trace of her can be found, and in the end Ziyād disguises himself as a Christian monk and goes out in search of her.

Meanwhile the Patriarch, Florinda and Flora are in hiding in a village in the Pyrenees, and Princess (*sic*) Helen, daughter of Alfonso, Duke (*sic*) of San Sebastian, is soon after sent for to keep her company. She becomes deeply attached to Flora, whose beauty now attracts the unwelcome attentions of the Patriarch. Flora determines to take refuge in a convent, thinking that there she will be safe. Helen and Florinda both try to dissuade her—Helen because she does not want to lose Flora's companionship, and Florinda because she too has grown fond of Flora and as a nun she knows that once in a convent, far from being safe from the Patriarch's attentions, Flora will be compelled as a religious duty to submit to them. Her vows of secrecy forbid her to reveal this to anyone, but after Flora's departure for the convent, in her emotional distress she tells Helen. Helen reacts with anger and contempt both for Florinda and the Patriarch and for nuns and priests in general, and stays on alone in the village when they have gone—Florinda to stay for a while in the same convent as Flora. Some days later a young monk (Ziyād) appears, having traced the fugitives to the village. He and Helen fall in love; he reveals his true identity to her, and she persuades him to take her along with him in his search for Flora.

Flora, now a nun, is raped by the Patriarch and becomes pregnant. Helen marries Ziyād, and though he makes not the slightest attempt to convert her, she of her own accord grows steadily more sympathetic to Islam. Ultimately, after several months they succeed in tracing Flora, Florinda and the Patriarch to the convent where, for the moment, all three of them are. The place is surrounded by Muslim forces and thoroughly searched, but without success; for only an hour or so earlier, dramatic events had taken place there.

Flora, now seven to eight months pregnant, had been summoned at night by the Patriarch to the comfortable outlying room at the nunnery set aside for the satisfaction of the carnal lusts of the monks, priests and dignitaries of the Church; she had submitted to him with apparent complaisance and then, when he was sunk in sleep, attacked him with a knife she had concealed in her robes, and taking advantage of the uproar resulting from his discovery, had escaped leaving him for dead. The Patriarch had been removed to the home of a poor Christian layman, where he could be tended without fear of discovery until he should recover.

Flora flees blindly from the city and ultimately finds herself in a cave. By a remarkable coincidence this turns out to be the very cave in which Ziyād, on assuming Christian dress, had left his clothes and his sword. Flora recognizes them, and assuming for some reason that he has been killed by the Christians, determines there and then to disguise herself in his clothes, to discover his murderers and to revenge his death with his own sword. Without informing us how a girl in such an advanced state of pregnancy achieves this remarkable feat, Sharar assures us that in Ziyād's clothes she is taken for a strikingly handsome young Muslim man, and in this guise she is taken into the service of a Muslim traveller named Abū Muslim, and eventually reaches the outskirts of Cordova in his company. Here she takes leave of him, and again assuming Christian dress, takes a house in an obscure quarter and settles down to wait until an opportunity for revenge should offer itself.

We are now in the 30th and final chapter, and Sharar having written 340 pages[1] seems all of a sudden to feel that all this has gone on long enough and it is time to end. In no more than 13 pages, therefore, he resolves all his outstanding problems, and the story comes to an end in a welter of blood, tears, improbabilities and striking coincidences which take the reader's breath away. Flora realizes that the birth of her child cannot now be far off, and that her condition is so obvious that only by the utmost care can she continue to make her male disguise plausible. For the next few days, therefore, she goes out as little as possible, and that too only after nightfall. One evening as she returns from the bazaar she is approached by a Christian priest who even at close quarters notices nothing to suggest that she is anything but the young man she wishes to be taken for, and asks if he can be of service, for he has observed that 'he' is a newcomer and is alone. Flora (to the reader's astonishment) says she would be obliged if he would occasionally visit her, and gratefully accepts his suggestion that he should call in every morning as he returns home from church. He pays his first call the next morning and sits talking to Flora at length without any untoward suspicion arising. (The problem of concealing her pregnancy seems to have disappeared.) From the conversation she learns that the Patriarch, whom she had left for dead, has recovered, that he is in hiding in Cordova, that her visitor knows his whereabouts and has been to see him several times, and finally that he is willing to grant Flora's wish that he should take her to see him; and he goes to get the Patriarch's formal consent to this, saying that he will then be able to take her to him that very evening. Flora rejoices at this unexpected opportunity of taking her revenge on him and decides to do this first and pursue Ziyād's murderers afterwards if she survives to do so. Between her visitor's departure

[1] There have been numerous editions of *Florā Florinḍā*, as of most of Sharar's novels. That which I have used was published by 'Maktaba i Urdū', but bears no date or place of publication. I obtained it from Pakistan in about 1960. Occasional page references are to this edition.

and his return the same evening Sharar conveniently arranges for Flora to be delivered of her baby and make herself presentable for her interview with the Patriarch. She realizes that to conceal the child as she takes it along with her will be 'a little difficult'—which the reader may feel to be a considerable understatement—but this too is managed. She puts the child in a sort of bag improvised from a sheet and carries this on her arm, puts on a flowing robe which conceals the bag, and accompanies her guide to the Patriarch's hiding place. All this while the child makes no sound. At length she is conducted to a small room where the Patriarch awaits her. She bows before him, and at the same time lays the child on the ground and draws the sword (which she has also concealed under her flowing robe); with this she half-severs his neck, and then plunges it into his breast, calling upon him as he dies (and, as we shall see, he is allowed more than enough time for this) to see the fruit of his evil-doing lying on the ground at his feet. The Patriarch now recognizes her, and calls on someone to revenge him on her while he still lives to see it. At this a door opens and a man springs upon her and stabs her in the side. She falls dying to the ground, and she and her assailant then recognize each other. He is Abū Muslim, the man in whose employment she had come to Cordova. She is asking how he, a Muslim, comes to be where he is when three others burst into the room. These are none other than Ziyād, Helen and Florinda. (Ziyād had by a lucky chance caught Florinda and a monk red-handed in a plot to murder Helen: he had killed the monk on the spot, and Florinda had later been compelled on pain of death to guide Ziyād and Helen to the Patriarch's hiding-place.) Ziyād asks the dying girl who she is, and she tells him she is Flora. At this Helen runs to her and embraces her. Flora calls her by name and Abū Muslim no sooner hears it than he turns his wrathful gaze upon her and leaps upon her with dagger drawn; but Ziyād intervenes in time, and strikes his head off with his sword at the same moment as Helen recognizes him as her father. The Patriarch now calls out in a feeble voice telling Ziyād to kill Florinda, but he refuses to sully his sword with her blood. But the priest who had guided Flora here, and has been standing in astonishment all this time, now picks up 'Abū Muslim's' dagger and buries it in

Florinda's breast. The Patriarch urges him to kill Flora and Helen too, but dies as he speaks the words, and Ziyād seizes the man, wrests the dagger from him, and binds him fast. Flora now has time to give Helen a concise account of all that had befallen her since they parted in the Pyrenees, and having done so, turns to her brother, declares herself a convinced Muslim and asks his forgiveness. Ziyād is now weeping uncontrollably, and Helen, in the double grief of Flora's and her father's loss, is in even greater distress. But she takes Flora's baby in her arms and weeping copiously, promises, despite Ziyād's initial objection, to bring it up as her own son. At this Flora bursts into tears and in the same moment dies. Ziyād and Helen continue weeping for a long time; then Ziyād asks her forgiveness for killing her father. She recognizes that he could hardly have done otherwise, and forgives him readily. We are now on the last page of the book. Helen goes on to say that now her father is dead there is no longer any reason why she should not openly embrace Islam, and she thereupon does so. And so all ends satisfactorily.

It hardly needs saying that a tale of this kind takes us right back to the world of the *dāstān,* although Sharar himself boldly calls his book a '*nāval*' (novel). The opening sentence of *Florā Florinḍā* reads, 'Our interesting novel begins about the year AH 230' (i.e. about AD 845). There are indeed significant differences. It does not exceed the length which the use of the word 'novel' would lead one to expect, and the narrative is well-constructed (albeit full of improbabilities), moves at a rapid pace and is, in general, written in simple but vigorous Urdu. Its dialogue too, where the themes are those of everyday occurrences, is natural and convincing. Yet the overall atmosphere is unmistakably that of the *dāstān.* There is the same evocation of the heroic age of Islam, the same battle of unalloyed virtue against unalloyed vice, the same dependence on exciting episodes following one upon another to maintain the reader's interest, and the same spicing of the story with erotic detail. Faiẓ Aḥmad Faiẓ, in an excellent article on Sharar, writes of him,[1] 'It is rather a harsh thing to say, but all the same it must be said that when in his moral and religious zeal he depicts the evils of the churches and the monasteries . . .

[1] Faiẓ Aḥmad Faiẓ, *Mīzān*, Nāshirīn, Lahore, 1962, p. 229.

his writing borders on the pornographic'. This judgement is fully justified. Sexual lust, allied with religious fanaticism, is portrayed as the dominant motive of the Christian characters. Sharar sets the tone on page 10, where Christians first make their appearance. A small number of monks and nuns are depicted as they assemble at a desolate spot in the mountains outside Toledo. Sharar writes, 'But it is impossible to tell why they have come here in this way, and with what object they have assembled in this desolate and awe-inspiring place.' He goes on, quite gratuitously, 'Incidents arising from the carnal desires and illicit lusts of nuns and priests are so well-known throughout the country that everyone will at first surmise that they have come here to this wild and lonely place to give full vent to their uncontrolled desires and allow full freedom to their lusts. But no, that is not the case.' Similarly, Ziyād, in his first serious talk to Flora warning her of the dangers of too tolerant an attitude towards Christians tells her,[1] 'Their monks, who pretend to have abandoned the world, are the worldliest of men—in fact, they worship worldly things and more than anyone else in the world they are the slaves of their own desires. In the same measure nuns, who are dedicated to the Church to live out their lives as virgins, are almost without exception addicted in the highest degree to fornication. And the association of these lustful monks and abandoned nuns has resulted in a situation where the church has generally become a place of fornication. Thousands of abortions are carried out, and thousands of babies are secretly buried alive in the precincts of the church.' And such immorality is not confined to the monks and nuns; the institution of confession spreads it amongst the laity as well. We are told in a footnote (in Chapter 18): 'In the Roman Catholic religion it is obligatory for every man and woman once a week to go before the priest and confess all his or her sins of the week, and to ask forgiveness. On these occasions the priests receive the right to ask respectable women all manner of shameless questions. and to express freely to them their lustful desires. This is what is called confession. In former days, under the cloak of this confession, priests have depraved thousands of chaste women—not to speak of the fact that, since the priests become fully acquainted

[1] Chapter 4, p. 38.

with all the women's secrets, they can bring such pressure to bear on respectable women that, from fear that their secrets may be revealed, they are in no position to refuse any of the priests' desires.'

Examples could be multiplied. More characteristic still of the *dāstān*-like atmosphere is the whole chapter in which Florinda step by step arouses Ziyād's passion until he escapes the sin of fornication by a hair's breadth, saved by his strong devotion to Islam, but constrained by the violence of his feelings to press Florinda to marry him without delay.

The only Christian character portrayed from the start with any sympathy is that of Princess Helen, and here the fervour with which Sharar describes her beauty as good as tells us at once that she is destined to become a Muslim—which, as we have seen, she ultimately does on the very last page of the book.

Sharar makes full use of her as his most effective propagandist for Islam. At one point she interrupts Florinda to tell her forcefully:[1] 'It was you people who had impressed the idea upon me that the Muslims are cruel and bigoted. But since I came here it has become crystal clear to me that it is you nuns and monks that go around slandering them and fanning the flames of prejudice against them. In fact they are people who prize justice, and there is no trace of deceit or hypocrisy in them. They respect and honour any man who lives a sincere and honest life, no matter what his religion may be. My own example is there to prove it.' It is indeed; but readers will recall another example which leads perhaps to a less flattering conclusion. In Chapter 2, Ziyād is explaining his family history in a gathering adorned by numbers of the most distinguished and admirable figures of Muslim Spain. He tells how his mother had from the outset secretly brought Flora up as a Christian, and how in spite of all his efforts to cut her off from all contact with Christians he is only too bitterly aware that he has not been able to bring about a change of heart. He turns to his host—the most holy and most distinguished Muslim in Cordova—and asks him what he should do. His host replies:[2] 'You should make it clear to Flora that if she adopts the Christian religion she will be put to death; for in Islam the penalty for apostasy is death. Probably this threat will be effective.' The

[1] Pp. 326–7 (towards the end of Chapter 28).

[2] P. 24.

non-Muslim reader and, indeed, one hopes many Muslim readers too, will be bound to conclude that a man who can give such advice may have many virtues, but that tolerance is not among them; for leaving aside the question of whether tolerance and the death penalty for apostasy can go together, to regard as an apostate a girl who from earliest childhood has been taught Christian doctrines by her mother is, to say the least of it, going rather far. But Sharar was writing for an audience which took such things in its stride.

As in the *dāstāns*, the love-interest is as strongly in evidence in the Muslim camp as in that of its adversaries—though here, of course, nothing in the least reprehensible occurs. The portrayal is again in *dāstān* terms—terms which, incidentally, are common to the *dāstān* and the *ghazal*, the traditional Urdu lyric. Love at first sight, or nearly at first sight, expresses itself in an immediate, complete, and absolute devotion to the beloved, and in a declaration of willingness to sacrifice even life itself in her cause. And here both the depiction of the lover's feelings and the dialogue between lover and beloved are completely stylized in marked contrast to the dialogue elsewhere. Sharar is clearly aware of the appeal which such scenes made to his audience, for they recur throughout the book, and often in contexts where they are of little or no relevance to the development of the story.[1] It is commonly said that another feature which Sharar's tales share with the *dāstān* is his interruption of the narrative to display his skill in depicting the scenes in which the action is set. But in *Florā Florinḍā* at any rate this is not much in evidence.

Sharar's tales have played an ambiguous role from the time they made their first appearance right up to the present day. The popularity which he won is, I think, largely explained by the same sort of combination of historical circumstances that favoured Sarshār. The apostles of the New Light had found that one effective way of appealing to their fellow-Muslims was to remind them of their glorious past—the argument being that the civilization of Islam had once been far in advance of the Christian world, and that the Muslims therefore had it in them to emulate, and even overtake, the advanced nations of the West. Sharar himself belonged to this school of thought.

[1] Cf. Chapter 20, p. 202, and Chapter 24, pp. 264–5.

But by the end of the nineteenth century the argument had tended to boomerang. The recollection of the glorious past of Islam was used to justify the argument that Muslims had nothing of importance to learn from the British and that the awe and respect with which the New Light regarded them was entirely misplaced. Sharar's books must, I think, have appealed to both audiences. Faiẓ, in the article already quoted, writes,[1] 'Sharar's age is . . . an age when the Muslims had just awoken to a consciousness of their decline. These romantic tales in the first place helped them to forget the bitterness of everyday life. Secondly, the recital of past conquest partly inspired them with self-respect and partly with emotional solace, with the thought that even if *they* were not heroes at least their forefathers had been. And thirdly the description of the vices of other peoples provided them with a way of taking mental revenge for their present subjection. . . . This is why Sharar's novels are so popular. . . . Sharar is not a novelist, but a teller of tales, and one of considerable skill. . . . In general, all children and a good many among the young and not so young expect nothing more of a story-writer, and Sharar is still the novelist most popular with these young and not-so-young children.'

THE FIRST TRUE NOVEL: RUSVĀ'S 'UMRĀO JĀN ADĀ'

If Sharar's work, as compared with Naẕīr Aḥmad's and even with Sarshār's, represents in some measure a reversion to the *dāstān*, his contemporary Mirzā Muḥammad Hādī Rusvā (1858–1931) took the next major step forward, and that too a step of such significance that one can truly say of his greatest work *Umrāo Jān Adā* (1899) that with it a real novel, in the internationally accepted modern sense of the term, at last makes its appearance in Urdu literature. In the preface to another book[2] he sets out his views on the writing of fiction, criticizing in passing both Naẕīr Aḥmad and Sharar, although without actually naming either. On Naẕīr Aḥmad he expresses himself quite mildly: 'It is the practice of some contemporary

[1] P. 229.

[2] *Ẕāt i Sharīf*, Ashrafi Book Depot, Lucknow, n.d. (?1963), pp. 3–4.

writers to frame a plot in order to prove a particular point and then fill in the details accordingly. I make no objection against them, but I shall not be at fault if I simply say that my method is the opposite of theirs. I aim simply at a faithful portrayal of actual happenings and am not concerned with recording the conclusions to be drawn from them.' On Sharar his tone is more sarcastic; after saying that he (Rusvā) writes of what he knows, he goes on: 'I have not the inventive power to portray events that happened thousands of years ago, and moreover I consider it a fault to produce a picture which tallies neither with present-day conditions nor with those of the past—which, if you study the matter carefully, is what usually happens. Great ability and much labour is required to write a historical novel, and I have neither the ability nor the leisure to do it.' He gives his own view of fiction at some length, saying that the fiction-writer is a kind of historian, and in a way his fiction is of greater value than histories are, because historians write the history of individuals (*sic*) and cannot give an overall picture of reality. The novelist generally gives a picture of what he has seen in his own time—that is, the novelist who makes Nature his teacher; for this is what a novelist should do. Aristotle well said that poetry is the imitation of Nature. 'Understanding these things,' Rusvā continues, 'I have made it a principle in my own writing to record in my novels those things which I have myself seen, and which have made an impression upon me, believing that these things will make an impression on others also.' He goes on to apologize, perhaps with his tongue in his cheek, for the fact that 'the scene of most of my novels is my birthplace, Lucknow', but excuses himself on the ground that this is the only place that he knows well—after which follows the hit at Sharar already quoted. Elsewhere[1] he reinforces his earlier point: 'My novels should be regarded as a history of our times, and I hope it will be found a useful one.'

In *Umrāo Jān Adā* he showed that he could not only enunciate these principles but also apply them in practice (though at the same time it must be said that his other novels fall short of the standards he set himself). The book is the life-story of a Lucknow courtesan, whose name forms the title

[1] The concluding sentence of *Ẕāt i Sharīf*.

of the novel, and the story covers, roughly, the years 1840–70—that is the decades spanning the great watershed of the 'Indian Mutiny' of 1857. In those years courtesans of Umrāo Jān's class—beautiful women, who besides being expert singers and dancers were also highly educated in the traditional culture of their day and were quite often poets, as Umrāo Jān herself was—played a role in Lucknow society closely comparable to that of the *hetaerae* in ancient Athens, and through her experiences one really does see something of the social and cultural history of the times. The story is beautifully told and extraordinarily well constructed. Not only are the characterization and the dialogue excellent; the story has a proper plot, and real development, with 'a beginning, a middle, and an end'. Rusvā begins with an account of how it came to be written. He had a friend from Delhi, who was very fond of Lucknow and frequently came to stay there for long periods. On these occasions he would rent a small house, and would often invite his friends there to spend the evening with him. The room where they used to sit together, talking and reciting their verses to one another, was separated by only a thin partition wall from the house next door. In it was a sort of hatch, the shutters of which were, however, always kept closed. They had been given to understand that the occupant of the house on the other side of the wall was an elderly courtesan, but had often noticed how quiet and unobtrusive a neighbour she was. One evening the host arranged a small informal *mushā'ira,* that is a gathering at which the guests, turn by turn, recite their verses. (This is still a popular institution with educated Urdu-speakers, amongst whom almost every other person seems to be a poet.) On these occasions the expression of appreciation is loud and uninhibited, and on this particular evening Rusvā has just recited a verse when the company is surprised to hear an exclamation of approval coming from the other side of the partition wall. The host smiles and calls out, 'Come in and join us. It's not proper to call out from there.' But there is no reply. A few minutes later a maid-servant appears and asks 'Which of you is Mirzā Rusvā?' Rusvā identifies himself, and the maid says that her mistress is asking to see him. The other guests are quick to note that the lady next door knows Rusvā well enough to recognize him from the sound of his voice,[1] and there is some chaffing at his expense. He excuses himself, goes out with the maidservant, and is taken in to see her mistress, whom he at once recognizes as Umrāo Jān. Knowing her accomplishments as a poet, he urges her to return with him and take part in the *mushā'ira*, and after some demur, she does so. Her verses are much appreciated, and after that evening she frequently visits the house to take part in gatherings of this kind. One evening she and Rusvā are talking with their host after the other guests have gone, and they tell her how interesting it would be if she would relate to them the story of her life. Rusvā is particularly persistent; and in the end she agrees to do as they ask. The rest of the book is an account of the successive meetings with Rusvā in which she tells him her story. After each occasion, unbeknown to her, Rusvā writes it all down, including the occasional exchanges between them with which her narrative is interrupted—a device which very effectively enhances the illusion of reality. Space does not allow even a summary account of her adventures, beginning with her childhood recollections, until at the age of seven she is kidnapped by a sworn enemy of her father and taken to Lucknow to be sold into a brothel, and recounting all her changing fortunes during thirty years until she retires quietly to spend her old age alone in the house she now occupies. When her story is complete Rusvā hands her his manuscript and aks her to read it through and correct any mistakes he may have made. She later describes to him her reaction.[2] 'Mirzā Rusvā Sahib, when you first handed me the manuscript of my life-story and asked me to revise it, I was so angry that I felt like tearing it into little pieces. I kept thinking to myself, "Have I not suffered enough shame in my own lifetime that now my story should be written down, so that people will read it and curse me even after I am dead?" But my own dilatory nature, and a regard for the labour you had spent on it, restrained me.

'Last night at about twelve o'clock I was dropping off to sleep when suddenly I felt wide awake. As usual, I was alone in the room. The servants were all asleep downstairs. The lamp

[1] Or, perhaps, she recognizes the verse.

[2] Mirza Rusvā, *Umrāo Jān Adā*, ed. Ẕahīr Fateḥpūrī, Majlis i Taraqqī I Adab, Lahore, 1963, pp. 321–3.

was burning at the head of the bed. For a long time I kept tossing and turning, trying to get to sleep; but sleep would not come, and in the end I got up and made myself a *pān* and called the maidservant to come and get the hookah ready. I lay down again on the bed and began to smoke. I thought I might read a story. There were plenty of books on the shelves at the head of the bed, and one by one I picked them up and turned the pages. But I had read them all before several times, and could not arouse any interest in any of them. Then my hand fell upon your manuscript. I again felt deeply agitated, and, I tell you truly, I had quite made up my mind to tear it up when it seemed as though some unseen voice said to me, "Very well, Umrāo. Suppose you tear it up, throw it away, burn it. What difference will it make? The recording angels of God—a just and mighty God—have by His command written down in every detail a clear account of all the deeds of your life. And who can destroy *that* record?" I felt myself trembling in every limb, so that the manuscript nearly fell from my hand, but I managed to rally myself. Now all idea of destroying it had left me, and I wanted to put it down again and leave it as it was. But as though without my own volition, I began to read. I read the first page and turned over, and before I had finished the next half-dozen lines I was seized with so consuming an interest in my story that the more I read the more I wanted to. No other tale had ever engrossed me so completely. When you read other stories the thought is always with you that all this is invented, and did not really happen; and this thought lessens the pleasure you feel. But your whole narrative was made up of things which I myself had experienced, and it was as though they were all returning to pass before my eyes. Every experience seemed as real to me as it had been at the time, and I felt more vividly than words can describe all the emotions which it had aroused in me. If anyone could have seen me then, he would have thought me mad. Sometimes I would burst out laughing; at other times the tears would overflow and drop on to the page. You had asked me to make corrections as I read, but I was too absorbed even to think of it. I read on and on until daybreak. Then I performed my ablutions, said the morning prayer, and slept for a while. I woke again at about eight o'clock, washed my hands and face, and again began to read. By sunset I had finished the whole manuscript.'

The book concludes with the account of a final session together in which Umrāo tells Rusvā her own reflections on the experience of her life.

We are not left in any doubt that Rusvā's deepest sympathies are with Umrāo Jān, whom he sees as the victim of others' sins against her; and a striking passage in the novel shows how passionately he feels about such things. He tells her,[1] 'Wise men have divided sins into two kinds. The first are those which affect only the sinner, and the second those whose effect extends to others. In my humble opinion the first are minor sins and the second are major sins (although others may think otherwise); and sins that affect others can be forgiven only by those whom they have harmed. You know what Hāfiz[2] says: Drink wine; burn the Qurān; set fire to the Kaba, and dwell in the house of idols: but do not harm your fellow men! Remember this, Umrāo Jān: to harm one's fellow men is the worst of sins. This is a sin for which there is no forgiveness, and if there is, then God preserve me, His godhead is in vain.' Characteristically, the words are spoken in a context where they do not apply directly to Umrāo Jān. (Whenever Rusvā talks to her about herself it is always in a half-serious, half-bantering tone.) But their application to her own case is clear. Yet Rusvā's approach to her is entirely unsentimental, and he can speak to her with a bluntness which is almost cruel. At one point in the story Umrāo is living in hiding at the house of a lawyer, who is defending her in a long-drawn-out lawsuit. One day when he is away, his wife, feeling the need of someone to talk to, comes across to the outhouse where she has her quarters and invites her into the house. While they are talking quite amicably together, an old woman comes in. She completely ignores Umrāo, but speaks contemptuously about her to the wife, and when she remonstrates with her a heated quarrel develops, which ends in the wife beating the old woman with her slipper. By this time the wife's mother-in-law and her old maidservant have appeared on the scene, and these two, who also treat Umrāo as though she were not there, proceed

[1] P. 263.
[2] The great Persian poet.

to discuss the rights and wrongs of the wife's conduct. As a result the old woman is ordered out, but they agree that in the first place it was the wife who was at fault. Umrāo, seeing that she is not wanted, returns to her own room. As she relates the incident to Rusvā she expresses the anger which after the lapse of all these years she still feels at the contempt with which she had been treated. Rusvā cuts her short and tells her bluntly that in his opinion the old women had been quite right to behave as they did, that the wife was indeed to blame, and that if *his* wife should ever do such a thing he would send her packing back to her parents and not allow her to set foot in his home again for six months. Umrāo demands to know why, and Rusvā replies:[1] 'I will tell you why. There are three kinds of women—good women, depraved women and prostitutes. And depraved women are of two kinds—those who keep their depravity secret, and those who openly lead a wicked and immoral life. Haven't you the sense to see that only women whose character is unstained can associate with good women? Think of their position. Poor women, they spend their whole lives imprisoned within their own four walls, and have troubles without end to endure. When times are good anyone will stand by a man, but these stand by him in good times and bad alike. While their husbands are young and have plenty of money, it is usually other women who get the benefit of it. But when they grow old and have nothing, no one else so much as asks after them; and it is the wives who go through all manner of distress, and trust in fate to revenge them on the others. Don't you think they are right to pride themselves on all this? And it is this pride which makes them look upon immoral women with utter loathing and abhorrence. God will forgive a sinner who repents, but these women will never forgive her. And there is another thing. You often find that no matter how beautiful his wife may be, or how admirable her character, or how adequate in all her duties, her fool of a husband will get an infatuation for prostitutes who cannot so much as compare with her on any score, and will desert his wife, sometimes temporarily, and sometimes for life. That is why they get the idea—or rather the conviction—that prostitutes practise witchcraft which dulls their husbands' senses. And that too, in a

[1] Pp. 280–1.

way, testifies to their goodness; because even in these circumstances it is not their husbands that they blame, but the immoral women who lead them astray. And what greater proof of their loyalty could there be than that?'

Umrāo's own attitude towards herself is equally unsentimental. She tells Rusvā at the end of her story that a woman like herself who has been a courtesan is deluding herself if she thinks that marriage or love or security, or indeed any relationship which demands of others that they love and trust her, is possible for her. She must live her own life and rely on no one but herself to see her through. She obviously regrets that this should be so, and says she now shares the deep admiration and respect for purdah women which Rusvā had expressed earlier, and wishes that their lot could have been hers (though she adds, with characteristic realism, that the suffocating atmosphere of purdah would now be unbearable to her). But all this is said in a dry, matter-of-fact way, and with a complete absence of any maudlin self-pity.

Much more could be written about this novel, which in my view has nothing to fear from comparison with its English and European contemporaries. It is unfortunate that the only English translation is that of Khushwant Singh and M. A. Husaini, published in India in 1961.[1] The translators have failed to do justice to the original, and so have given a very inadequate impression of its true worth.

CONCLUSION

Umrāo Jān Adā has remained in many respects an isolated achievement. Even Rusvā himself never wrote anything to compare with it. His other two major novels are more closely comparable with Nazīr Aḥmad's tales than with his own masterpiece. They deal with two contrasted themes. In one[2] the central character is a member of the old decadent Lucknow aristocracy whose complacent persistence in an outmoded way of life brings him to inevitable ruin. In the other[3] the hero is also a man of aristocratic family, but one who is thrown entirely upon his own resources early in his life and makes his

[1] By Orient Longmans Ltd.

[2] *Ẕāt i Sharīf.*

[3] *Sharīfzāda.*

way in the world through sheer hard work and determination to adapt himself to the new conditions around him. The moral is in both cases made as crystal clear as in anything that Naẕīr Aḥmad ever wrote.

The strong moral didactic trend continues in Urdu prose narrative to the present day. The propaganda for western ways began to be met early in the twentieth century by counter-propaganda for the traditional Islamic way of life which stressed the danger to religion and morals which the western outlook brought in its train. (Very little writing of this kind—and there is a good deal of it—reaches any worthwhile standard.) In the twenties themes of nationalism and Gandhism appear, especially in the work of Prem Cand (1880–1936); and from the thirties socialist and communist trends emerge strongly, to continue up to the present day. The development of prose narrative in the twentieth century has been not so much towards a greater realism as towards an extension of the range of themes. The one really important novelist of the period is Prem Cand, who wrote both Hindi and Urdu versions of all his works and is thus a major figure in both literatures. His Gandhian message is expressed mainly in tales of peasant life. He knew the life of the peasantry intimately, and his best work portrays it extremely well. His numerous short stories are generally agreed to contain his best work, and the situation has not changed in this respect since his death, for while a few novels of some merit have been written, the short story has been developed to an appreciably higher standard, and Urdu can now show work in this field which, even judged by international standards, is in the highest class. Some of the factors that hold back the development of the novel are undoubtedly economic. Urdu writers work in a community where the standard of living is low and the percentage of illiteracy is still very high. A collection of short stories by a popular writer who has already established his reputation will rarely be published in an edition of more than 1,000 copies, and, at a price of somewhere about three rupees (that is, roughly four shillings) is beyond the reach of very many of his would-be readers. No Urdu writer can depend solely on writing for a livelihood, and few can devote even a substantial part of their time to it. (This is one of the reasons why the short story has flourished more than the novel.) Another factor is that of cultural tradition. Poetry still enjoys a higher prestige than prose literature, and men who feel that they have creative talent tend to apply it accordingly. Nevertheless, the achievement in the field of prose narrative is substantial enough, and forms a firm basis on which present and future writers will continue to build.

THE RISE OF STANDARD HINDI, AND EARLY HINDI PROSE FICTION[1]

by R. S. McGREGOR

PRE-NINETEENTH-CENTURY PROSE AND PROSE FICTION IN HINDI DIALECTS

Before the nineteenth century there seems to have been comparatively little literary prose written in the Devanāgarī script in any of the dialects of the modern Hindi language area. This is the area within which standard Hindi is now the dominant cultural language, embracing roughly the part of northern India extending from the Punjab and Rajasthan, north and west of Delhi, eastwards across the Ganges plain and the northern part of Madhya Pradesh to Bihar. The established literary figures of this tract had all been poets, and we know that many poetical works were very widely recited and popular. Poetry was mainly devotional or rhetorical in character, or dealt in conventionalized ways with the topic of *śṛṅgāra*, passionate love; many themes and motifs can be traced back to traditional Sanskrit sources.

It is very probable that alongside this poetry prose tales or fables based on the same sources or on the prose story cycles of early Urdu literature, or on everyday life, came to be circulated orally in some sort of standardized form, but little such material has come down to us in writing from this period. One tale in rhymed prose and verse, possibly dating from about 1500, may point towards the emergence of a prose narrative tradition,[2] and the Rājasthānī *vātas* offer further hints of the existence of such a tradition at a later period. These *vātas* are prose texts, usually quite short and in fairly colloquial language, chiefly historical in subject matter but liable to be expanded with fictional material; some are purely fictional, and a few are translations of Sanskrit tales.[3] They can have had no

[1] A shortened version of this essay appeared in the *Journal of the Royal Asiatic Society* (*JRAS*), October 1967.

[2] See M. P. Gupta, 'Purānī khaṛī bolī kā ek navprāpt sūfī kāvya "Kutuba-śataka" ', *Śrī Candrabhānu Gupta abhinandangranth*, Delhi, 1966, 354–65.

[3] See L. P. Tessitori's descriptions in *A descriptive catalogue of bardic and historical manuscripts* I (Bardic and Historical Survey of Rajputana, Bibliotheca Indica, N.S. 1409), Calcutta, 1917, especially Pt. II (Bikaner), Nos. 9a, b; 15a, b; 20a; 22a; xiv (collections of *kahāniyāṁ*); 15y, z, A (translations).

influence on the development of written prose fiction as a genre in the nineteenth century, but it is interesting that a description of the magic deeds of a yogi which one of them[1] contains is typical of the subject matter of the late-nineteenth-century Hindi prose romances, and the fact that three manuscript copies of the text are preserved suggests that this sort of tale enjoyed some popularity.

Apart from the above material we are left in the field of prose with a variety of texts: sectarian chronicles, mostly of uncertain date and authorship; historical or quasi-historical chronicles of Rājasthānī royal families; academic works, chiefly commentaries on Sanskrit texts, with a few Hindi translations of Sanskrit texts; and some miscellaneous compositions. These works are chiefly in Rājasthānī dialects and the Braj Bhāṣā dialect spoken around Agra and Mathura, which held a literary ascendancy over the other western dialects as the vehicle of traditions of the Krishna cult. There are also a few early prose works extant in the Khaṛī Bolī dialect, spoken around Delhi and Meerut; the earliest dates from the late seventeenth century. Prose translations of two Sanskrit texts are recorded in this same dialect from the middle of the eighteenth century.[2] The existence of this material makes it clear that before the nineteenth century there had existed a long, if fairly limited tradition of prose-writing in dialects of the Hindi language area, and that within this tradition it was quite customary to borrow words from Sanskrit to eke out the vocabulary of one's own dialect, and to write in the Devanāgarī rather than the Perso-Arabic script.

URDU AND HINDUSTANI

Other traditions of script and language were flourishing at this time all across the Hindi language area. A distinct style of Persian- and Arabic-influenced language had early developed out of the contact of the Muslim rulers of northern India with the Indian dialects spoken around their first main settlement,

[1] *Nāpai Sāṁkhalai rī vāta*, *Descriptive catalogue*, Pt. II, 39, 50, 69.

[2] L. S. Vārṣṇey, *Ādhunik hindī sāhitya kī bhūmikā*, Allahabad, 1952, surveys most of the early prose material; see also H. Śrīvāstav, *Madhyakālīn hindī gadya*, Delhi, 1959, 38 ff.

at Delhi. Of these dialects a pre-eminent place was held by a form of Khaṛī Bolī. The cultural and literary languages of the Muslims being Persian and Arabic, they fell back on these languages to supply the shortcomings of Khaṛī Bolī as they made wider use of it, and the Hindus with whom they came in contact learned for their part numerous Persian and Arabic words and expressions, and began to use them habitually. They likewise became acquainted with a modified form of the Perso-Arabic script.

In these circumstances Persian- and Arabic-oriented Khaṛī Bolī underwent a twofold development during the Muslim period. On the one hand, it evolved in the early eighteenth century into a refined and subtle literary style which was adopted quickly by educated Muslims everwhere in north India; to this style, one in which only persons versed in Islamic culture could hope to feel fully at home, the name Urdu came to be given.[1] At a lower level, the basic grammar of Khaṛī Bolī and many Persian and Arabic words and expressions had earlier become widely known all over northern India, and beyond, to those who came in contact with Muslims, or the Muslim government. Khaṛī Bolī as used in this way often came to be called Hindustani, the language of Hindustan, or northern India.

As a lingua franca Hindustani was admirable, particularly for the Hindi language area, because of the closeness to Khaṛī Bolī of many of the dialects spoken in the area. Its use across the eastern part of the Hindi language area and in Rajasthan, where the dialects spoken were least similar to Khaṛī Bolī, must have been furthered by the wide popularity of the Krishnaite verse in the closely cognate Braj Bhāṣā, and by that of certain sectarian verse, such as that of the poet Kabīr, in whose mixed language Khaṛī Bolī forms are quite well represented. But Hindustani served no general need as a vehicle for literature, unless perhaps at a popular level. For literature the Muslims of north India had Persian, and from the eighteenth century their highly-developed Urdu style, while the Hindus used the Braj Bhāṣā and Avadhī dialects for the great bulk of their devotional and other poetry. Nor does

[1] A contraction of the expression *zabān-e-urdū-e-mu'allā* 'language of the exalted camp, or court'.

the language of the Hindus' prose-writings have anything closely in common with Hindustani, or literary Urdu, being Sanskritized, rather than Persianized. It is interesting, however, that an increasing use of the Kharī Bolī dialect, rather than Braj Bhāṣā, is found in Sanskritized prose of the late eighteenth century, and this points to the shape of things to come. Paradoxically, modern standard Hindi owes the possibility of its emergence largely to the spread of knowledge of Kharī Bolī in conditions created by the Muslims' presence in India.

A LITERARY CURIOSITY: 'RĀNĪ KETKĪ KĪ KAHĀNĪ'

The Muslims had given the names Hindavī, Hinduī, Hindī to the Kharī Bolī dialect which had become the basis first of the colloquial Hindustani style and later of literary Urdu. They distinguished from it the Braj Bhāṣā of Mathura and Agra, and the other Hindi dialects, both as colloquials and as more formal Sanskritized styles. Several Muslims are well known to have written in Braj Bhāṣā and Avadhī verse. This relative familiarity with Hindu literary traditions is reflected in the preface to *Rānī Ketkī kī kahānī*, a literary curiosity which is generally classed as the first piece of prose fiction in Hindi. Its author, Inśā Allāh Khān, was an Urdu poet who had lived at the courts of Murshidabad and Delhi before coming to Lucknow, where he wrote this tale soon after 1800. In his Preface[1] he says:

'One day as I was sitting about I had the idea of composing a story in which no other language than Hindi would be used; and my heart expanded like a flower-bud. The work should contain no foreign language, or local dialect. A certain literate, conservative, shrewd old fellow of my acquaintance protested at this, and with shaking head, screwed-up face, raised nose and eyebrows, and rolling eyes said, "This can never come off. Your story will neither lose its Hinduī character nor take on

[1] There are minor variations in the text given by different authorities (Grierson, *Linguistic Survey of India*, Vol. IX, i, 103 ff.; Śukla, *Hindī sāhitya kā itihās*, 11th edn., Banaras, 1957, 382 ff.; Vārṣṇey *op. cit.*, 277 ff.). I follow the Hindi edition of S. S. Dās, Nāgarī Pracāriṇī Sabhā, 1925, based on texts in Persian script.

bhāṣā character?[1] You will simply write just as worthy folk generally talk among themselves? Using no admixture of language? It won't succeed!" '

The plot of *Rānī Ketkī kī kahānī* is full of the romantic and supernatural. A prince falls in love with Princess Ketkī, but war breaks out between their houses; a yogi dwelling in the Himalayas is introduced to preside over Ketkī's fortunes, and eventually, after the practice of much magic, the loving couple are united. This subject-matter clearly reflects the same oral narrative tradition hinted at by the *vāta* fragments, and its choice suggests that it enjoyed a certain vogue among Hindus; Inśā's Preface implies, too, that the novelty of his story is in its language, and by no means in the story itself. But he is hardly implying that Hindus habitually tell this type of story in something like the literary form which he gives to it. In the absence of similar tales preserved in the Hindi dialects it seems best to think of this tale as exemplifying a form familiar to Inśā from his own literary background, and told in Hinduī as something of a curiosity.

This conclusion is also suggested by the style of Inśā's Hinduī. His vocabulary is as simple and colloquial as he claims, but in its use there is a verve and flippancy, and also an element of self-display, which is quite unexampled in early prose written by Hindus. Excessive alliteration and a predilection for rhyming syllables, long strings of verbs and exaggerated metaphors are perhaps the most striking aspects of Inśā's prose style. It is probable that he is not taking this Hinduī, with its colloquial vocabulary and Urdu style, very seriously.

It is doubtful if anyone else did so either. The story in its present form perhaps found little favour among the Hindus, if it ever reached them, and seems to have exerted no influence on the development of prose in Khaṛī Bolī. It had apparently been quite forgotten by the time the Hindi prose romances began to appear, and its importance is primarily as an antece-

[1] *Hindavīpan bhī na nikle aur bhākhāpan bhī na ho.* This means most probably 'You will write within neither the Muslim nor the Hindi literary traditions?' i.e. neither Urdu nor Sanskritised Braj Bhāṣā. Persons interested in the interpretation of the Hindi are referred further to *JRAS*, October 1967, 115.

dent of this class of prose fiction, based, like the *vāta* texts noted above, on the same sort of traditional narrative elements.

THE RISE AND CONSOLIDATION OF STANDARD HINDI

By the time *Rānī Ketkī kī kahānī* was being written the East India Company had consolidated its position in Bengal, and had been in contact for some decades with the eastern part of the Hindi language area. Here it had inherited Persian and the Hindustani style as languages of law and commerce. It was therefore natural that Hindustani should have an important place among the subjects taught to the Company's junior civil servants at the new Fort William College, which had been established in 1800 in Calcutta.[1] But from experience it was also realized that some place should be made for the study of a form of language which should not rely on the Perso-Arabic vocabulary of the lingua franca, but come nearer in its vocabulary to the various regional and local dialects of the Hindi language area spoken by the mass of the population. Such a form of language would naturally be written in the Devanāgarī script.[2] Pundits were appointed to the College staff to prepare and give instruction in reading materials answering to these specifications. Since Khaṛī Bolī was now widely understood in northern India, it was perhaps inevitable that Khaṛī Bolī rather than Braj Bhāṣā should become the basis of this new style. The novelty of the style has, however, often been overemphasized. In enlarging the scope of Khaṛī Bolī with words of Sanskritic, rather than Perso-Arabic origin the pundits were working fully within the tradition of both the earlier poetry and the prose texts referred to above.

[1] See the official papers of the College of Fort William in Bengal, London, 1805, 27. The College replaced a seminary for the study of Indian languages founded in 1798.

[2] For an acknowledgement of the value of a study of another form of language than Persianized Hindustani, see a report of a speech by the Acting Visitor of the College in the *Asiatic Journal*, I, 1816, 164–5, 'The study of the Hindi . . . becomes important and even necessary to those who may have to maintain an extensive intercourse and personal communication with all classes of the Indian population; more especially is it requisite for the military officers of the Company's service, because a large proportion of the Sepoys of the army on the establishment of Bengal speak either the Braj Bhāṣā or a dialect of which the Hindi forms a chief component part.'

The word *bhāṣā* or *bhākhā* (meaning language) had been used loosely by the Muslims of northern India to denote the various Hindi dialects, and it was thus natural that at the College, with its emphasis on Hindustani and Persian, the teachers of the Sanskritized style should come to be called bhakha munshis. Their familiarity with the literary Braj Bhāṣā dialect, in which they also composed some texts, must also have been a factor in their acquiring this name. The College did, however, usually make a clear distinction between Braj Bhāṣā and the Sanskritized Khaṛī Bolī which was the bhakha munshis' main responsibility,[1] and this is reflected in the names which it gave to the latter style. At first two names, Khaṛī Bolī and Hindui, were used for this style, the former being somewhat more common, but in the course of time both were generally replaced by the name Hindi.

Lallū Jī Lāl and his colleagues produced numbers of translations and adaptations of Sanskrit and Braj Bhāṣā texts, or parts of them, into Sanskritized Khaṛī Bolī, with a greater or lesser admixture of Braj Bhāṣā forms. But a long period was still to elapse before anything in the nature of prose fiction was attempted, and the importance of these texts is primarily historical. They paved the way for the production right through the nineteenth century of all manner of instructive works in the new prose style, which in the last decades of the nineteenth century began to be used as a vehicle for independent literature.

The missionaries had embraced the new Hindi style, and their activity was of some importance in spreading knowledge of it. The New Testament had been translated into Hindi and printed under William Carey's direction by 1811,[2] and other translations and numerous reprintings followed throughout the

[1] The great majority of the works of Lallū Jī Lāl, the most famous *bhakha munshi*, was in the new style. The title-page to his *Premsāgar*, which was the most widely used of all the texts prepared at Fort William College, states that it was translated into Khaṛī Bolī from a Braj Bhāṣā version of part of the Sanskrit Bhāgavata Purāṇa, at the order of John Gilchrist. Vārṣṇey, *op. cit.*, 384 f., 402 f.

[2] The first edition ran to 1,000 copies; a second edition of 4,000 copies was printed in the following year. Translation of the Old Testament into Hindi had been completed by 1818. Translations into Braj Bhāṣā were a separate enterprise. G. A. Grierson, 'Early Publications of the Serampore Missionaries', *The Indian Antiquary*, 23, 1903, 242.

century. There was a missionary press at Allahabad by 1838, one at Agra by 1840, and one at Ludhiana by 1836.[1] These and other later established presses published much material in Hindi, including instructive cautionary tales which seem to have reached a modest circle of readers.[2]

The School Book Society of Calcutta, founded in 1817, had also published a certain amount of material in Hindi from an early date.[3] In 1823 the foundation was authorized of a college in Agra,[4] which should teach the new Hindi, along with Sanskrit, Persian and Arabic;[5] we learn, however, that its Hindi and Sanskrit studies were early embarrassed by a shortage of text-books.[6] These difficulties were to be increased with the growing interest being shown in the study of English,[7] culminating in the Government's decision of 1835 to promote the spread of Western education through English and no longer to devote public funds to printing in Indian languages. In spite of this, however, such a body as the School Book Society of Agra was able to print books in Hindi from soon after its inception in 1837, and the second half of the nineteenth century saw pamphlets and manuals in Hindi being issued from many of the main centres of the Hindi language area.

Hindi suffered a serious set-back in 1837, with the change from Persian to Urdu as the official language of the departments of law and revenue in the new Agra presidency. This was a natural step in the waning days of Mughal overlordship. But the increased importance of Urdu meant a corresponding diminution in the attention paid to Hindi as a formal style of expression. And the use of English from 1835 onwards for higher government business and in the higher law courts was

[1] B. H. Bradley, *Indian Missionary Directory*, Lucknow, 1876, 75, 131.

[2] One such story was printed in an edition of 5,000 copies by the Church Vernacular Education Society of Allahabad, in 1876.

[3] See reports of its activity in the *Asiatic Journal* for January 1835 and October 1836. Between January 1835 and May 1836 it issued 4,000-odd copies of books in Hindui, compared with 32,000- and 3,000-odd copies of books in English and Hindustani respectively for the same period.

[4] B. K. Boman-Behram, *Educational Controversies in India*, Bombay, 1943, 111.

[5] Its aim was 'the instruction of Mahomedan and Hindu youths in Persian and Hindi, chiefly, with provision for more advanced studies in Arabic and Sanskrit'. See *Asiatic Journal*, February 1825.

[6] See the report of an address by the Acting Visitor of Fort William College, *Asiatic Journal*, March 1828.

[7] B. K. Boman-Behram, *op. cit.*, 269 ff.

an even more important factor discouraging the cultivation of Hindi. In these circumstances it is hardly surprising that the new style took the best part of a century to consolidate itself.

There is, however, evidence from the later 1860s onwards of an increasing desire on the part of Hindus for a greater measure of recognition and public use of Hindi and the Devanāgarī script, and it is to this feeling that the ensuing gradual expansion of the sphere of use of Hindi can be traced. The feeling is first noted in Banaras, but its early effects are more evident outside the North-Western Provinces. They include the use of Hindi from 1873 in subordinate government offices in the Central Provinces, and from 1881 for administrative and legal purposes in Bihar, replacing Urdu. The use of Sanskritized Hindi by the Ārya Samāj reform movement founded in 1875 must also reflect a growing feeling in favour of the style, and contributed in turn to its consolidation and further acceptance, especially in the Punjab. It is interesting, too, that there was support at this time in Bengal both for the use of Hindi by Hindus within northern India, and for its adoption on a wider scale as a means to encouraging a sense of unity between northern Hindus and those of Bengal and western India. Growth of feeling in favour of the use of Hindi clearly played a part in stimulating the production of Hindi prose in the 70s, and of the novels of the 80s and thereafter.[1]

The first newspaper in Hindi appeared in Calcutta in 1826,[2] and was followed belatedly by one or two in the North-Western Provinces round about 1850. But it was not until the 1870s that numbers of newspapers and magazines began to appear all over the Hindi language area. One of the most successful

[1] For the facts referred to in this paragraph see further S. M. Ikram, *Modern Muslim India and the birth of Pakistan* (1858–1951), 2nd edn, Lahore, 1965, 35–6; A. K. Majumdar, *Advent of Independence*, Bombay, 1963, 41–2, 57; A. Seal, *The emergence of Indian nationalism*, Cambridge, 1968, 325–6; P. Gaeffke 'Zur Entstehungsgeschichte der indischen Reichssprache', *Die Sprache* XIV 1, 1968, 28–9; S. K. Chatterji, *Indo-Aryan and Hindi*, 2nd edn. Calcutta, 1960, 154–9.

[2] A weekly called *Udant Mārtaṇḍ*, it ran from May 1826 till December 1827. Baṅkaṭlāl Ojhā, *Hindī samācārpatra sūcī*, Pt. 1, Hyderabad (Deccan), 1950. Five hundred copies of the first number were printed. See *Lists of publications registered in N.-W. Provinces*, 1867– , India Office Library (some omissions). In the present essay details of editions are given from this source.

of the early journals was the *Kavivacansudhā*, edited by the playwright and poet Bhārtendu Hariścandra (1850–85), of Banaras. This ran from 1868 till 1885, first as a monthly and later as a weekly, and carried poetry, dramas and translated novels as well as social and political comment. An associated journal carrying articles in both English and Hindi was *Harishcandra's Magazine*, first published in 1873; this described itself in its opening number as 'a monthly journal published in connexion with the *Kavivacansudhā* containing articles on literary, scientific, political and religious subjects, antiquities, reviews, drama, history, novels, poetic selections, etc.' But the relative success of these two periodicals depended in very great measure on the energy and ability of Bhārtendu Hariścandra himself. Despite the growing interest in Hindi noted above most of the early newspapers and magazines, right through the century, seem to have had very short lives and very small circulations, and one reason for this was the entrenched position of Urdu and English. Another was that most people who might have read them were interested chiefly in the traditional dialect poetry. They were not accustomed to reading prose, to say nothing of news in prose. However, the newspapers were helped on slowly by the spread of education and a growing interest in social, religious and political questions, particularly after the foundation of the Ārya Samāj movement. A number of monthly journals had appeared by 1880, and later many Hindi novels were first published in such journals in serial form.

Translations from Sanskrit had been important for the new style since the time of Lallū Jī Lāl and before, and continued to appear throughout this period. In the second half of the nineteenth century we find numerous translations into Hindi from English, Urdu and Bengali also. The *Arabian Nights* from Urdu in 1876, *Robinson Crusoe* by way of a Bengali version as early as 1860, *Sandford and Merton* in 1877 and *Lamb's Tales from Shakespeare* in 1883 are among the earlier examples. Translation of independent Bengali novels had begun by about 1880,[1] and was an important influence in acclimatizing

[1] The first part of the Bengali novel *Durgeśnandinī* appeared serially in translation in the *Kavivacansudhā*, and thereafter in book form in 1882 in an edition of five hundred copies. Its translation had been encouraged by

the novel in Hindi as a form. There were two translations, at least, from Marathi.[1]

PROSE TALES

Among the miscellaneous writings published at this early stage are a few improving tales composed as reading material for students, and possibly independently written, though it is often unclear whether the Hindi texts are original, or translations from Urdu or English. Illustrative of the type is *Dharmasiṃh kī kahānī* by Śrī Lāl, first published in 1851 and reprinted frequently until at least as late as 1877. This tale comprises three short sketches of village life, united only by their didactic character and by the figure of Dharmasiṃh, who appears in each as an example of prudent or virtuous conduct, or of thoughtless conduct later made good. Apart from an introduction of about a page giving a rambling description of the virtues and repute of Dharmasiṃh, the writer shows no interest in anything but the sequence of events and the morals which can be drawn from them. The language used is simple Hindi, i.e. Sanskrit words are used as necessary and common Persian and Arabic words not excluded. This type of tale must have enjoyed considerable popularity, as collections of similar didactic tales, translated from Urdu, were still appearing at the very end of the nineteenth century.

A more interesting piece of fiction from the same period is *Devrānī jeṭhānī kī kahānī*, Meerut, 1870, by Gaurī Datt. This is a didactic tale illustrating the life of women in a joint family and written from an orthodox viewpoint for an overwhelmingly conservative public. Questions such as the place of women in society, the role of education, and widow remarriage had clearly been raised, but it would seem from their treatment in this work that they did not greatly exercise the Hindi-reading public at this time, and there is little consciousness of the threat posed to orthodox society by Western influences. Technically, the author is groping towards the novel form, achieving

Bhārtendu Hariścandra. It is a fairly close translation of the original; there are one or two alterations which are calculated to meet a more conservative taste. There were many other translations from Bengali until well into the twentieth century.

[1] See Vārṣṇey, *op. cit.*, 177 f.

some touches of realism in delineation of character and background, and a reasonably supple prose style.

EARLY DIDACTIC NOVELS

The first work in Hindi which can fairly be described as a novel is *Parīkṣā guru*, by Śrīnivās Dās, 1882. This was followed by a number of similar works of didactic intention. The didacticism of these works extended now to comment on social attitudes, as well as on individual behaviour. Their general outlook was conservative, and their central aim to fortify orthodox Hindu society against the effects of Western influence; but we also find, in some of the novels in particular (such as *Parīkṣā guru*, and *Tīn patohū*, discussed later in this essay) a degree of welcome to certain aspects of Western influence and criticism of aspects of orthodox society. Both these attitudes are reflected in the contemporary Braj Bhāṣā verse and drama of Bhārtendu Hariścandra and his colleagues.

The novel *Sau anjān aur ek sujān*, first published in 1892,[1] may serve as an example of the main didactic tradition in the early Hindi novel, reflecting an outlook in which consciousness of ill effects of Western influences on Hindu society is relatively strong. This slow-moving tale gives the history of two sons of an orthodox Hindu. We learn of their traditional education and early promise, marred by their revolt against their orthodox background at adolescence. They squander their fortunes, sink to crime, and are arrested, together with the villain of the story who has engineered their downfall. He is severely sentenced by the court, but the two wayward sons are saved by the intervention of a friend (the *sujān* of the title) who pleads their case successfully, having exacted a promise from them that they will mend their ways.

Much can be said about the achievement of this novel, as a representative of the genre, from a consideration of the first chapter alone. It begins:

'It was at the end of the monsoon. Just as the wealth of a dissolute man is fated to dwindle and disappear, so the clouds were now beginning to clear away in the sky. Autumn was

[1] By Bāl Kṛṣṇa Bhaṭṭ, 5th edn., Lucknow, 1928.

beginning, and soon the cold weather would be on the way. It was the month of Kārttik, and a clear night. Eleven o'clock had struck. A stillness had settled over everything, as though the goddess of nature, exhausted by her day's toil, were now longing for rest. The moon was almost full, and seemed to smile on the face of the night, his beloved. . . .'[1]

And so on, through many a figure of speech, until we are introduced to a man on horseback who is described in general terms; and at the close of the chapter we learn of his secret, unspecified, mission.

This is quite unlike anything seen in the Hindi prose predating *Parīkṣā guru*. The author clearly has an idea from reading of some of the potentialities of the novel form as it is understood in the West. Thus he attempts setting his scenes in time and place, and introducing his characters within them, in exactly the tradition of the European historical novel. But these introductions are in very general terms, and the short sentences of the scene-setting passages have a perfunctoriness about them which suggests that he is doing this somewhat as an obligation, and generally has little real interest in creating elaborate, realistic settings. Any elaborateness of presentation is rather in style, and is connected much less with the borrowed Western prose tradition than with the native tradition of Hindi poetry. Hindi poetry had become decidedly uninventive by the end of the Mughal period and had compensated for this by adopting an increasingly florid and rhetorical style. In the absence of a developed prose tradition a writer trying to create a literarary prose style would inevitably be influenced by traditional poetry. Hence the frequent exaggerated figures of speech, the ritual piling-up of adjective phrases, and the frequent description of female characters in something of the old *nakh-sikh* tradition of the rhetorical poetry, although this has by now taken on a prosaic respectability.

Another point of contact with older literary traditions is to be seen in the way the introductory passages are often set in time. Following quite quickly on the first chapter with its tableau of the end of the monsoon, we find other chapters set in the cold season and the hot season, and by the end of the

[1] *Sau anjān aur ek sujān*, ed. cit., 1.

book have reached and passed the beginning of the next monsoon. These different time-settings have no particular motivation in the story, but they link up easily with the descriptive tradition of the *bārahmāsā* in older Hindi poetry, in which the changing seasons form a framework within which the heroine's changing emotions are presented. It is noteworthy that the most florid specimens of Sanskritized diction in this novel are found precisely in conjunction with such chapter introductions.

The novel as a whole is less interesting than some of its component parts, however. In the opening chapters the various main characters are introduced one by one, and are sufficiently well established at that stage, but, as it turns out, often in a way that is irrelevant to their use in the subsequent story. The author seems to glimpse their potentialities without ever trying to realize them in any degree, and the result is that the first chapters seen in the perspective of the whole resemble rather a series of independent sketches than the introductory part of a novel. As one's somewhat favourable impression of them recedes the novel becomes very tedious. There is little dialogue until quite late in the book. The reader is much more a passive spectator of the events described by the author than a vicarious participator in them, and the author's didactive theme becomes increasingly the single unifying feature of the whole.

An interesting aspect of the technique of presentation of the narrative, in this and most of the early Hindi novels, is the borrowing from the earlier-founded drama of its convention of representing dialogue. In this particular novel the indebtedness goes even farther, for we find what amount to complete stage directions inserted in the dialogue.

THE ROMANCES

We turn now to a very different work, much more influential and representative of the taste of its time than the few didactic novels which were in the field before it. This is the romance *Candrakāntā*,[1] which is the inheritor in Hindi of the tradition hinted at ninety years earlier by *Rānī Ketkī kī kahānī* and continued in Urdu literature in the nineteenth century.

[1] By Devkī Nandan Khatrī, Banaras, 1892 (1,000 copies).

Candrakāntā was first published in 1892, had run to a twentieth impression of eight thousand copies by 1936 and was certainly in print until quite recently. No Hindi novel can have been more successful, and thousands of people are said to have learned the Devanāgarī script for the sole purpose of reading it. This is both understandable and revealing of the current state of knowledge of literary Hindi, for Devkī Nandan Khatrī wrote not in formal Sanskritized Hindi but in the simple language known to all in northern India who would have been likely to be readers at that time. To him, Hindi meant simply this style of language written in Devanāgarī script. This style was an easier proposition to almost everyone than Sanskritized Hindi, which though in theory closer to the various dialects in vocabulary, differed sufficiently in practice in the range of its Sanskritized words for the lingua franca to be a better medium of communication. Sanskritized Hindi is to some extent still faced with this difficulty today.

Devkī Nandan Khatrī writes in his preface of the magicians of the royal courts of old who could 'change their form, deal in magic potions, sing, play, discharge commissions, bear arms, spy, and had many arts besides. When war broke out they would bring it to an end with their cunning, and not allow blood to be spilt and the lives of soldiers wasted. They enjoyed great respect. . . . Up till now no Hindi book has given an account of these magicians. If readers of Hindi would take note of their amazing deeds they would be advantaged in several ways. The chief of these is that the reader of such stories will not easily let anyone deceive him. Bearing all this in mind I have written this novel *Candrakāntā*.' The author then summarizes the story, which deals with the love of Prince Bīrendrasingh for Princess Candrakāntā, the embroilment of their houses, their subsequent adventures and eventual marriage, and adds that 'because these kingdoms were in mountainous country there has been ample scope to write of hills, rivers, passes, fearsome jungles and beautiful and entrancing valleys'.

There is little in this fanciful tale, except presumably the most general conventions of the novel, which derives from contact with the West, and its enormous success reminds us forcibly that even by 1890 Western standards of taste had not been assimilated in any significant degree in the Hindi language area. Its author's hopeful suggestion that worldly prudence may be learned from *Candrakāntā* was a sop to the serious 'improving' literature of the type of *Sau anjān aur ek sujān*. *Candrakāntā*, with its traditional story material and its unique mixture of sentiment and sensationalism, enjoyed a very much wider reading public than any didactic novel, and this is its real importance for us. It was the popularity of romances of this kind which created for the first time a public eager to read fiction in Hindi, and thus paved the way for the Hindi work of Premcand.

An extract from *Candrakāntā* will give an idea of Devkī Nandan Khatrī's melodramatic style.

'Only the prince can know what were his feelings at this sight. Like one beside himself he began to weep and complain, "Oh, Candrakāntā! How have you come to this end? Surely it was the wolves I heard howling before I reached this place which robbed you of your life. The wolf which devoured you was all too eager! He would have found me more to his liking, for in my blood there is mingled the sweetness of love. . . . Do my eyes tell me the truth, or is this all a dream? How can this sight be real? But real it is, for there is the canal below this cliff. . . . What is there more for me in this life? Wait, princess! I will follow you. I will not fail to die with you! . . . My life is run, and my time in the cruel world is at an end! I follow you, Candrakāntā!"

'With these words he went to hurl himself to his death in the abyss, while the three hidden sorcerers looked on in silence. Suddenly the adjoining wall split apart with a deafening noise, and an aged holy man stepped forward and seized the prince by the arm.'

The success of *Candrakāntā* led to a sequel called *Candrakāntā santati* (1896), on a much enlarged scale. This was followed in turn by *Bhūtnāth* (1908), purporting to be the life-story of the principal sorcerer in *Candrakāntā santati*. The whole series runs to several thousand pages.

These romances embody many elements which are traditional in the mixed culture of the Hindi language area. But there was also another romantic tradition building up in this area at the time the early Hindi novels were being written.

This new romanticism has its origin in the confrontation of the Indians with Western ways of life. The members of the small, somewhat superficially Westernized middle class which had grown up in the Hindi language area in the course of the nineteenth century owed their new position entirely to their English education, and their success in assimilating Western values. Details of English life, authentic or otherwise, thus held a fascination for many people (and not only members of this class), which was at least equal to that exercised by the motifs of the traditional romances. This must be part of the reason for the success at this time of Hindi translations of such novels as G. W. M. Reynolds' *Mysteries of London.*[1] The sensationalism of this kind of work was of much the same brand as that of Candrakāntā, but for many Indian readers of this period they held the extra allure of depicting the semi-mythical world of England, and the exciting ways of what was taken to be real English life. Contact with the West had not been so long-lasting in the Hindi-speaking area as in some other parts of India, and probably there was never so much general approval or true understanding of Western ways there as in Bengal, for instance. If numbers of people did see the need for and welcomed some social changes, many were impressed simply by the apparent freedoms offered by Western society, and were happy to cultivate them in their imagination. Out of all this comes something of a new character type in the novel: the semi-Westernized hero, whose foreign ways may be largely spurious, but who is raised by them to a status above his humbler contemporaries. Such a character lives life to the full, endures tribulations bravely, and foils the stratagems of lesser men with ease. But this type is unstable, and except in the borrowed genre of the detective novel, usually merges with that of the traditional romance hero, who marries and lives hapiply ever after.

A hero of this kind is found in the initial chapters of the novel *Nūtan caritra.*[2] From either a European or an orthodox

[1] G. W. M. Reynolds (1814–79), a prolific writer of melodramatic novels and serialized sketches of London life between 1835 and 1860.

[2] '*New People*'. By Ratnacandra,1893 (1,000 copies).

Hindu viewpoint the leading character of this work has little to commend him as he is portrayed at the outset of the novel. His brashness clearly engrosses the author, however, who early makes him into something of a young hero when the train in which he is travelling is derailed. Soon he duly appears in another role, rescuing the girl whom he has met in the train, and fallen in love with, from the series of melodramatic dangers which befall her in Delhi. But the author has only a superficial interest in what may be new in this 'new character' and his background, and once well launched into his novel is far more concerned with weaving an intricate plot in the manner of the old romance tradition. His language, too, looks back to pre-Western tradition with its occasional very elaborate figures of speech. For instance, a description of his heroine's astonishment at an unexpected meeting can be translated as follows:

'When he saw that the vessel of Citrakalā's mind had foundered in the vast ocean of her amazement, and that she too was about to be engulfed, he contrived to rescue her with the lifeline of his word; and when he saw that she had somewhat recovered, he continued. . . .'[1]

The traces of modernism in *Nūtan caritra* do reflect changing social attitudes on the part of a section of Hindi speakers, but their superficiality reminds us that their taste remained essentially conservative at this time. *Nūtan caritra* is fundamentally a romance of the same literary lineage as *Candrakāntā*.

A work called *Āścarya Vṛttānt*[2] shows a more interesting range of reactions to late-nineteenth-century life than does *Nūtan caritra*. This well-named compilation is basically a picaresque sequence of the supposed adventures of the narrator, involving such items as descents into unfathomable wells, encounters with holy men of magical powers, a remarkable subterranean cavern, and so on. There are no divisions of any kind in the 94 pages of printed text. What unity of theme the narrative has is given chiefly by the person of the narrator, and this is formal rather than real; no interest is taken in the narrator as a character, although his emotions of amazement,

[1] 3rd edn., 1922, 55.

[2] '*An astonishing tale*'. By Ambikā Datt Vyās, Bhagalpur, 1893.

fear and bewilderment at each of his successive adventures lend some show of colour to his personality.

This tale apparently looks back in its structure and certain of the motifs it uses to the tradition of the Sanskrit tales and romances, reinforced by the nineteenth-century translations. Nevertheless even in this context we come on interesting reflections of the modern age. We meet an American professor pursuing scientific research, a Westernized Bengali, and an English archaeologist, who is discovered poring over a Sanskrit text deep in the mysterious cavern. The last of these encounters gives the narrator the chance to reflect that the English are indeed to be found everywhere nowadays. But he is gratified by the archaeologist's interest in Indian culture, and heartily approves of his broken Hindi, which is a token of his affection for India. This Englishman believes in the sayings of the old Hindus, the first the narrator has ever met who does so. He even berates the Westernized Bengali for his distrust of Hindu beliefs. The narrator is properly amazed at this, as at his other adventures. But whether the author was indulging in sarcasm here or no, he clearly has every disposition to share his pride in Hindu culture with a well-disposed foreigner. We meet a very different attitude in some of the social novels of this early period, in which pride in Hinduism is more militant and allies itself with a separate felling of discontent which had begun to rise against Western institutions in general.

HISTORICAL NOVELS

Novels and novelettes with a general historical background began to appear in Hindi in increasing numbers from the last decade of the nineteenth century, largely under the influence of translations from Bengali. Frequently these works were designated historical novels by their authors. Their actual scope throws further light on the aspirations of Hindi writers of this period.

Illustrative of the class is the novel *Jayā*.[1] The heroine of this work, Jayā, is a betrothed Rajput princess who is coveted by the Muslim suzerain 'Alā-ud-dīn. The narrative of some hundred and fifty pages details her various adventures as the prize of

[1] By Kārttik Prasād Khatrī, Banaras, 1896 (1,000 copies).

the ensuing Rajput-Muslim struggle, and concludes with her happy marriage to her Rajput fiancé.

The events described in the novel are not historical, and the historical background against which they are set is very generalized and of little intrinsic importance for the development of the narrative. The Rajputs of the past are presented as noble and admirable figures, but there is little of the historical romanticism of nineteenth-century Western literature in the author's approach to his material. If the Rajputs of his novel are admirable, it is as much because they serve as models of traditional Hindu virtue as recognized in the author's time as because they symbolize a glorious Hindu past. Jayā's virtue recalls first and foremost that of Sītā in the *Rāmcaritmānas*, not the fame of any historical Rajput princess, and her relations with Dhīrsingh and Bīrsingh those of Sītā with Lakṣmaṇ and Rām. Equally, although a Rajput victory is desired and anticipated throughout, the Muslims, who are frequently described as *yavanas* or barbarians, behave none the less with honour; the author is not at all concerned in this work to preach any political moral for the present in his treatment of the past. (There are, however, references in other novels to Hindu resentment of and resistance to Muslim dominance, and similar references are frequent in the Braj Bhāṣā verse and drama of this period.)

There are many details of treatment in this novel which illustrate its author's ability.[1] There is evidence, too, of a nascent interest in character portrayal. But what strikes the reader of *Jayā* first and foremost is once again the author's overriding interest in the sequence of the incidents which form his narrative. We read comparatively little about either characters or historical background which does not bear directly on advancing the plot, and as a result the whole novel takes on an air of breathless haste. It is chiefly over his generalized descriptive chapter introductions that the author seems willing to delay, and, as it were, write at leisure. If some of his characterizations recall the idealized figures of the *Rāmcaritmānas*, the florid, highly Sanskritized language of

[1] He wrote a number of novels, biographies and other miscellaneous works in Hindi. Bāl Mukund Varmā, *Bābū Kārttik Prasād Khatrī kā saṃkṣipt jīvancaritra*, Banaras, 1904.

these set-pieces reminds us for its part once again of the close connection between the new narrative prose tradition in Hindi and the old poetic tradition. A translated specimen follows.

'The moon's hours of labour were at an end. Preparing to yield up her place, she awaited the coming of the sun. Yesterday, when first she had resumed her toil, what varied preparations nature had made in her honour! How wondrous the splendour which had enveloped her at the instant of her rise, and what ineffable radiance her beams had cast from moment to moment upon the earth! On all sides mankind had sung her praise, and tender nature had done her honour. . . . Now as the sun made ready to come forth, her splendour faded and steadily grew wan. The world awoke, and to those who had lain inert consciousness returned. At dawn's approach the *cakvā* birds' hours of separation ended, and the *cātak* birds, male and female, flew up and blessed the sun.[1]

KIŚORĪ LĀL GOSVĀMĪ (1865–1932).

Apart from Devkī Nandan Khatrī the one prose writer who is remembered from this early period is Kiśorī Lāl Gosvāmī. His many novels, fables and novelettes, from the very end of the nineteenth century and the first years of the twentieth, reflect most of the tendencies discussed so far, but add little that is new to them. Kiśorī Lāl Gosvāmī is fond of calling his works social novels, but in fact the real centre of their interest is melodramatic, and he can be linked more closely with Devkī Nandan Khatrī than he would maybe have wished to acknowledge. In the preface to one of his early novels, *Sukhśarvarī*,[2] he writes that the novel has been recognized as supreme among literary forms because of the scope it gives for analysis of the forms of love. He does imply in a vague way that this in its turn should throw light on character, but it is clear that the main characters in his full-scale novels are of melodramatic interest only.

Kiśorī Lāl Gosvāmī's novels were not nearly as influential as those of Devkī Nandan Khatrī in spreading a knowledge of Devanāgarī Hindi, although (and perhaps because) Gosvāmī

[1] 3rd edn., Banaras, 1913, 90–2.

[2] Banaras, 1894 (1,000 copies).

was a more conscious protagonist of Hindi than Khatrī. He writes in the above-mentioned preface that because of the lack of interested people who can read Hindi almost all of his previous ten or fifteen novels have found no public. If only the rajahs, maharajahs and other worthy folk would lend their support, he would publish numbers of large novels and endeavour to redeem the honour of Hindi. Gosvāmī may have been the first Hindi writer to give voice to this feeling of grievance over the lack of recognition accorded to Hindi, which is still in evidence today.

Sukhśarvarī is described on its title-page as a novel of coincidence adapted from Bengali[1] into pure Hindi.[2] It may usefully be discussed here, since what merits it has serve to emphasize the current weaknesses of original prose fiction in Hindi. The story centres on the adventures of an orphaned girl, from the time of her father's death until her happy marriage, and is full of coincidences and eerie and violent events reminiscent of the romances. These are used blatantly to excite the reader's interest in the opening chapters of the novel. And from time to time the old exaggerated conceits make their way in, generally in descriptions of nature at the beginning or end of chapters. The involutions of the narrative are again the author's primary interest, although he does allow himself some casual observations on contemporary social conditions.

The novel represents some small improvement on others of the time, however, in that its author's attention is not completely monopolized by the requirements of the narrative. For perhaps the first time in Hindi fiction we find some interest in human character for its own sake. This interest may be fleeting, and rarely bear on the main personages of the story, but it is nonetheless worth noting. In particular it brings life

[1] To some extent from B. C. Caṭṭopādhyāy's novel *Kapālkuṇḍalā* (1866), with which it shares the character of a murderous tantric hermit. But the two novels differ widely in the use they make of this character.

[2] *śuddh āryabhāṣā*; literally, pure 'Aryan' language. The expression insinuates that modern Sanskritized Hindi is a form of language traditional in the central Ganges plain, the 'heartland' of ancient Hindu India. Hindi had evolved in answer to a modern need, but was valued by some people (and not only Arya Samajists) less as a means of general communication than as a vehicle suited to the expression of traditional cultural values.

to a court scene in which suspense is made truly dependent on motivation and character, and the potentialities of the novel form begin to be realized.

Some of the credit for this would appear to be due to influence of the Bengali source, or sources. One realizes this on considering Gosvāmī's other novels, one of which, *Līlāvatī*,[1] may serve as a fair specimen. This novel traces the fortunes of the virtuous Līlāvatī through an involved course of events culminating in her marriage. Līlāvatī's fortunes are contrasted with those of her sister Kalāvatī, who breaks with all the traditions of orthodox society and eventually drowns, a leper, in the river Jumna.

This work is primarily a story of love and intrigue, another melodramatic romance set in the modern world. But its middle-class heroes and heroines share the values of traditional society. The type of youth who longs to shake off the restraints imposed on his conduct by Hindu society is abhorrent to Kiśorī Lāl Gosvāmī here. To this extent only, however, can *Līlāvatī* claim to be a social novel; in fact it deals hardly at all with the workings of society. Its author's aim in his description of society is didactic only. The characters are approached from a moralistic standpoint, and opportunities to develop them realistically and allow them to assume the burden of the novel are neglected. The reader is left only with the melodrama, the moralizing, and a truly fantastic plot to make what he can of. The plot is virtually complete two-thirds of the way through the book, the remaining third being mainly taken up with recapitulations of parts of the story from the points of view of different characters. A marvellous episode deals with an enchanted underground vault in the best tradition of Devkī Nandan Khatrī, and the whole is rounded off by a description of the marriage of Līlāvatī.

The manner in which the author handles this last episode further indicates the conservative taste of his readers. He disclaims any ability to emulate the Sanskrit poets in a description of the heroine's charms, and then proceeds to give just such a description, in the manner of the *śṛṅgāra* poetry of the eighteenth century.[2] Although he protests that to do this is

[1] Banaras, 1901. (A second edition of 750 copies in same year.)
[2] *Līlāvatī*, ed. cit., 447 f.

only the way of *anargal baknevale kavi*, foolishly chattering poets, he cannot bring himself to do differently.

Among Kiśorī Lāl Gosvāmī's minor works are what he terms a historical novel, *Indumatī*,[1] and two detective stories.

The latter, *Candrikā* and *Candrāvalī*[2], are of a very contracted form, running to twelve and eleven two-page episodes respectively. They deal with the exploits of a Bengali, a B.A. of Calcutta University, in solving murders in up-country Delhi and Banaras. The stories themselves are trivial and poorly told, again because of their author's characteristic weaknesses as a writer, but the attitude underlying their telling is worth noticing. We find here again the same excited interest in things Western, particularly trivialities of Western life, which is hinted at in *Nūtan caritra*. Such details as the reading of an English magazine, the sending of a telegram, the reservation of a train compartment, and at a different level the type of the educated, urbane, successful Bengali detective must have been calculated to appeal particularly to the growing Indian middle class who had put their stake into Western education. The point is emphasized when detective Mukurji receives his English superior's commendation, as a sort of accolade, before returning to metropolitan Calcutta. It is an interesting commentary on the general climate of social and political opinion in the Hindi language area at this period that such a scene could have the tacit approval of the author of *Līlāvatī*.

LATER PERIODICALS: DETECTIVE FICTION

Shortly after the beginning of the twentieth century several new periodicals devoted wholly or in part to Hindi prose fiction were appearing regularly. A considerable number of novels were first printed serially in these. A first part of *Candrakāntā santati* had appeared in this way by 1896 (it was also printed separately in that year), and in the same year the Allahabad periodical *Ratnākar* carried a sequel to the first volume of *Nūtan caritra*. Prominent among the later journals was the *Upanyās māsik patrikā* of Banaras, edited by Kiśorī

[1] 3rd edn, Vṛndāvan, 1914.

[2] *Candrikā, vā jaṛāūcampākalī upanyās; Candrāvalī, vā kulṭākutūhal;* Banaras, 1904. (3rd edn of 1,000 copies, 1914.)

Lāl Gosvāmī from 1901. Many of Gosvāmī's writings, including *Līlāvatī*, were first published in this periodical, which ran to 40 pages per number and aimed at a circulation of five hundred. Other more ephemeral periodicals are recorded as printing three or two hundred copies per number. More successful, and of much greater prestige, was the *Sarasvatī* of Allahabad, a general literary monthly whose editor, Mahāvīr Prasād Dvivedī, played a dominant part in standardizing modern Sanskritized Hindi.

Of a different class was the popular periodical *Jāsūs māsik pustak*.[1] More or less sensational crime and detective stories were already enjoying a vogue in Hindi by this time, no doubt because of their essential similarity to the romances. The majority were much more substantial than Kiśorī Lāl Gosvāmī's two essays in the genre. Gopāl Rām Gahmarī, editor of the *Jāsūs māsik pustak*, was a prolific producer of such works as well as a writer of prose fiction of other kinds. One of them may be noted briefly for its author's attitudes to his subject material.

This novel, *Cakkardār corī*,[2] is set in Mewar Udaipur at the end of the Mughal period. In setting his scene in time and place the author goes out of his way to comment on the past and present condition of India. Of the Mewars he says: 'One should not be surprised that before the English came they could run their affairs without supervision. Marwaris and Mewaris have always been famous for this.'[3] And he describes the late Mughal period as a time 'when Hindustan was in anarchy, and the English, French, Maratthas and Sikhs were trying to seize it. And the Afghans would come like mountain rats from the north-west, gather up whatever they could find in Bharat[4] and take it back across the Punjab.'[5]

This is implicit criticism of present conditions in India, and shows a political consciousness which has hardly come to expression in the writing considered up to this point. And more

[1] It first appeared in 1901 and printed a thousand copies of fifty pages per number.

[2] First published serially in the *Jāsūs māsik pustak* in 1903–04. (1,000 copies.)

[3] *Cakkardār corī*, intro.

[4] The word *Bhārat*, now used in Hindi to denote the modern state of India, is here used as a synonym of *Hindustān*, which means properly northern India.

[5] *Cakkardār corī*, intro.

explicit criticism of the *status quo* is not wanting. Elsewhere in his introduction the author has the following comment to make, in describing an artefact in the palace at Udaipur:

'Now, with no customers, the Indian craftsmen, potters, smiths, goldsmiths, weavers and the like have given up their trade and accepted slavery. Foreign workmen give us boxes, chests, locks, keys and cloth to relieve our want and shame.'

The attitudes here hinted at may be connected with those underlying a small class of didactic works in Hindi which began to appear from about the mid-1890s. These works are discussed below. They express violent opposition to the inroads made by Western influences in India.

LATER DIDACTIC WRITING UP TO 1905: ANTI-WESTERN, AND CONSERVATIVE

One finds adverse or quizzical comments on Western influences in India in several of the novels already discussed, and as pointed out above the general purpose of the didactic novels was to bolster traditional Hindu society against the ill effects of these influences (either with or without recognition of ways in which they might also be beneficial).

It seems to have been only a few novels that vaunted the values of traditional society aggressively, and fiercely denied that Western influences could benefit India in any way.

An early work of this kind is *Naye bābū*[1] by Gopāl Rām Gahmarī. This short novel is in effect a farce directed against the abandonment of traditional Hindu practices in general, and the allowing of widow remarriage in particular. The narrative describes the fate of a Westernized young Indian who supports widow remarriage, and, perhaps inevitably, has a disreputable friend. In defiance of Hindu custom he arranges the marriage of his friend to his widowed sister. The friend acquiesces willingly in this, as he has designs on the hero's own wife. These he eventually fulfils, and the unfortunate reformer leaps in despair into the river Narmada. The tale is told in a vein of strong satire, which is very effective, and seems strangely

[1] Jubblepore, 1894. (1,000 copies.)

well practised for the period. Its success comes not from any skill the author shows in character portrayal, but from the pungency of his indictments and scathing comments on Western ways, together with the ridiculous nature of a scrape the hero gets himself into half-way through the plot. Presentation is blatantly one-sided, and understandably so; the author shows in a later work that he has a real ability to develop character interest, but to do so here would have impeded his case. The virtuous female characters do occasionally bewail their plight in a traditional way, but in these circumstances the traditional has a new significance. This is not merely the traditional embraced unthinkingly, but the traditional exalted, perhaps for the first time, in the face of the alien culture. The style of language used is also not without significance in this connexion. With its doctrinaire Sanskritization, this is Hindi as the standard-bearer of 'Indianness', a role in which it has frequently been cast since.

A later novel expressing the same attitude to Western influence is *Hindū gṛhastha*[1] by Lajjārām Śarmā. This describes the early life of a promising son of orthodox merchant parents, who has been corrupted by his English-style education. He falls into bad company; his marriage proves a failure; he goes to England, where he is instantly successful and has various amatory adventures. Returning to India, he is as quickly discredited, but is regenerated by a journey to Japan where he is impressed by the respect and admiration which the Japanese show for Indian culture.

This moralistic work admits no possibility that its author's views may not meet with acceptance, which suggests that it speaks for a considerable body of orthodox opinion. The lack of real knowledge of English life we have met with before; what is perhaps new here is the wilful underrating of the values of English life themselves, as opposed to the effect of English influences on India. The writer clearly shows the extent of his prejudices when he takes his story outside India. The Japanese theme is understandably even more unrealistic than the English, and the manner of its use is revealing. It serves ostensibly to project the ideas that the countries of Asia have

[1] Bombay, 1902–3: first published in a Bombay journal, *Śrī Veṅkaṭeśvar samācār*, in 1901 or 1902.

an essential community of interest and culture, and can readily achieve mutual understanding, but in fact the understanding shown in this novel is all on the part of the Japanese. What we are really dealing with here is once again the assertion of Hindu, rather than Asian, values in their superiority to the imagined values of the West.

However, the main trend of the didactic writing of this period is better described as conservative than as aggressively anti-Western. The novel *Tīn patohū*[1] is representative of this later, generally conservative work, and is worth discussion both because of its intrinsic merit and as being from the pen of the same Gopāl Rām who had earlier written the satirical *Naye bābū*. Gopāl Rām is here concerned to uphold the prestige of the traditional joint family, but now in his attitude to Western influences he shows a tolerance which was quite lacking in his earlier work. The most villainous characters in this novel are the ones who scorn Western education most, it is a Calcutta student who is one of the foremost in practising the virtues of restraint, filial affection and self-sacrifice, and a Calcutta-trained lawyer who restores the family fortunes after the ignorance and jealousies of its members have allowed it to break up. The attitudes expressed in this novel are thus a corrective to any judgement of Gopāl Rām's general outlook which might be formed on the basis of his other works. His writing taken as a whole is ambivalent in its attitude towards the West.

The introduction to this novel stresses what its author hopes may be its instructive value. There is no shortage of novels in Hindi nowadays, he writes,[2] but few are suitable for reading to one's relatives or using for their instruction. For this reason, and also since interest in reading is increasing with the change in the times, he offers his novel to lovers of literature as a fair account of the regrettable changes which have been taking place in the social system. The narration follows much the expected pattern in its general outline. The disasters which may attend the dissolution of a joint family are pointed out, and the traditional social virtues commended. The junior branch of the family, which practises them, ultimately achieves an implausible prosperity.

[1] Bombay, 1904.
[2] Ed. cit., intro.

But while the novel as a whole suffers from Gopāl Rām's didactic approach, much of the first section detailing the break-up of the family is memorable in the context of this early fiction. The deterioration of relationships within the family to the point where its disintegration becomes inevitable is treated with a sensitivity, and an eye for detail, which perhaps no other writer of this period can rival. The chief characters are invested with something of an individual personality, and as a result the best part of this novel has a vitality which raises it into a different class from anything in the 'social' novels of Kiśorī Lāl Gosvāmī.

The following extract, from early in the novel, begins with a bantering conversation between Suśīlā, the heroine, and the wife of her husband's friend, Sarasvatī. With them is the two-year-old son of Mahāmāyā, Suśīlā's sister-in-law, whose jealousy is the root cause of the family's difficulties.

'Jokingly Sarasvatī put her hand under Suśīlā's chin and began to push her head from side to side.

'All right,' she said, 'are you going to show me the letter, or not?'

Suśīlā: All right then, you can see it. But first you'll have to do something for me.

Sarasvatī: I'll do anything you like, if you promise to show me that letter.

Suśīlā: Well, your first task is to try some of these sweets.

With these words Suśīlā pushed the brass tray of sweets over in front of Sarasvatī.

'Really, I can't manage any more just now, my dear,' Sarasvatī said.

Suśīlā: What do you mean, you can't manage any? Is eating in your poor friend's home going to lose you your caste, or something?

Sarasvatī saw the fleeting smile on her friend's face.

'If you say that I'll eat the lot.'

'I'd be honoured!'

'Don't joke, my dear. It would be no laughing matter.'

'Well, we'll both have some, and so will Śrīgopāl. There aren't too many here.'

'Try this one!' Sarasvatī took a sweet from the tray, broke off a piece, and put it in Suśīlā's mouth. The rest she began to eat herself, giving a small corner to Śrīgopāl.

Suśīlā got up to get some water, passing Śrīgopāl over to Sarasvatī, but the little boy, seeing himself abandoned by his aunt, began to wail miserably. In a moment she was back, kissed him, and calmed his crying.

'Evidently Mahāmāyā had heard Śrīgopāl crying. Suddenly she burst into Suśīlā's room, and without a word snatched her child in fury from his aunt's lap. Again Śrīgopāl protested loudly. This time he was cuffed twice and cursed for his pains.

'Don't you get enough to eat without filling up on that stuff, you brat? Are you never satisfied?' Again his mother struck him.

The wretched Śrīgopāl called imploringly to Suśīlā, 'Auntie, Auntie!'

'Say that once more and I'll wring your neck!' Mahāmāyā was beside herself with rage and started beating him again, while all Suśīlā could do was look on in anguish.'[1]

If contrasts are posed rather artificially and some scenes are overdrawn, pathos and suspense are well invoked in others and there is much graphic and convincing description. The following is one of the accounts which the novel contains of the actual moment of the joint family's dissolution.

'At this final insult your father turned furiously on your two elder brothers, berating them and cursing them too in his rage, and finally ordered them from the house. The two brothers saw that this was their chance to make the break for good. Finding lanterns, they disappeared into the darkness. No one in the house ate food that night, and all night your sisters-in-law were up bundling and packaging their things. When Rādhā, Śrīgopāl and the other children asked for food, a beating was their only answer. The rice remained untouched. Your parents and Suśīlā went hungry too. How could they eat and leave the children unfed? Early next day your sisters-in-law took all the children and went off with your brothers to their

[1] Ed. cit., 14 f.

parents' homes. The boys didn't want to go, but what could they do? They were beaten for their pains. Śrīgopāl went off looking back all the time at Suśīlā, and shouting "Auntie, Auntie!" '[1]

Although *Tīn patohū* is an unequal work, the living interest of much of it marks it out very clearly from most contemporary productions in Hindi prose. For perhaps the first time we gain from a work of prose fiction some vital understanding of a section of Indian society. From this point of view we may fairly see in this novel a forerunner of the work of Premcand.

The essential conservatism of *Tīn patohū* is shared by Ayodhyā Singh Upādhyāy's novel *Adhkhilā phūl*.[2] The plot of this novel details the fortunes of Devhutī, a virtuous married lady who is coveted by one Kāminīmohan, and is attracted towards him. Kāminīmohan's designs are frustrated by an unknown stranger, Devsvarūp, who is eventually revealed to be Devhutī's lost husband. Kāminīmohan dies repentant, bequeathing his wealth to Devsvarūp, who uses it to found schools, hospitals and charitable institutions.

The didactic approach of this work resembles that of its contemporary *Tīn patohū*, and the earlier *Parīkṣā guru*, in that the conflict between virtue and villainy is not between persons representing unwesternized and westernized aspects of Indian life. The villain Kāminīmohan belongs to the unwesternized village milieu as much as Devsvarūp. What is distinctive in so late a work is that in content it is relatively so unaffected by Western influences. There are admittedly various touches which imply a consciousness, largely inspired by contact with the West, of the abuses which have crept into traditional society, and the conclusion in particular shows clear influence of reformist ideas and of the ideal of service to society which was gaining strength in the early years of the twentieth century. This ideal was to receive greater recognition in Ayodhyā Singh Upādhyāy's *Priyapravās*, a long poem based on aspects of the traditional Krishna story, which appeared in 1914. But in this novel, published nine years earlier, it is less prominent; and the conclusion of the novel is far from being an integral part of its structure. As for more direct Western

[1] Ed. cit., 56 f.

[2] Patna, 1905.

influence, the work shows little curiosity or concern about Western life and its values. There are one or two passing references to commonplaces of Western science, but these are in a tone, and are used in a way which suggests that science and scientific attitudes are of little real importance to the author or his public. With its plot almost solely an account of the preservation of a virtuous woman's *dharma*,[1] *Adhkhilā phūl* is remarkable above all for its confidence in traditional values.

The language of the novel is something of a curiosity in the field of Hindi prose, in that it shows little or no borrowed Sanskrit vocabulary. Both this and a previous novel, *Ṭheṭh hindī kā ṭhāṭh*, were written in the first instance to demonstrate their author's conviction that Hindi prose need not be highly Sanskritized to be effective. The expressive use which he makes of colloquial and dialect words is what one would expect from a practising poet versed in the traditional literature, and goes far to proving his case, if only for a work of the type which he was trying to write.[2] The effectiveness of his writing here stands in sharp contrast to the artificiality of most of the Sanskritized prose of this period.

With its conventionalized, rhetorical style and its characterization both stereotyped and scanty, *Adhkhilā phūl* is deficient as a novel. But the homogeneity of its chief component elements makes it seem perhaps better realized in its own terms than any other novel which had appeared up till its time. This again suggests how essentially conservative literary endeavour in Hindi prose had remained up till 1905.

THE EARLY WORK OF PREMCAND[3] (1880–1936)

The work of Premcand far surpasses that of his predecessors, and finally establishes the novel as an independent genre in Hindi. The greater part of his early writing, however, was in

[1] The complex of religious and social obligations which a devout Hindu is required to fulfil; also the spiritual merit deriving from their fulfilment.

[2] The author expounds his theory of non-Sanskritized Hindi in a preface abounding with Sanskrit expressions. He justifies this by saying that the ideas he is advancing are complicated (adding defensively that he has had to write the preface quickly). A better proof of the potential stylistic value of Sanskritized Hindi could hardly be found.

[3] The pseudonym of Dhanpat Rāy Śrīvāstav for most of his career.

Urdu. It was not until after the publication in Hindi of *Sevāsadan*,[1] his first mature novel, that he wrote regularly in Hindi. Most of his general literary background he also acquired through the medium of Urdu rather than within the young Hindi prose tradition, although he knew Devkī Nandan Khatrī's prose romances in Hindi. An early work of Premcand's, *Vardān*,[2] illustrated both his promise as a novelist and some of the lines of development the Hindi novel was to take in his hands.

This novel relates the history of one Pratāp, starting with his childhood in a middle-class home and his friendship and later love for Virjan, the daughter of a neighbouring household. Virjan returns his love, and on her marriage being arranged with another youth, Pratāp is in despair. He becomes a student at the University of Allahabad. Here he is a great success, but always he retains his devotion and respect for his family and the traditional way of life. Virjan's husband soon dies in dishonourable circumstances. Virjan, who had striven to be an ideal wife and give her love to her husband as a duty, now becomes a poetess devoted to the service of India, while Pratāp is moved to renounce the ties of worldly life and devote himself to contemplation and the service of the people. After visiting his family amidst great acclaim he withdraws to minister to a neighbouring flood-stricken area, and his mother, who had asked the goddess Kālī that her son might serve his country, finds her boon granted.

Many of the motifs of this plot are familiar from earlier Hindi novels, although the plot taken as a whole reflects a wider social consciousness than we have seen before, and a new ideal of social service within the framework of traditional society. This new ideal and enlarged social consciousness reflect a movement of opinion away from the simple conservatism expressed in the earlier didactic novels. However, it is not the

[1] This work was written in Urdu (as *Bāzār-e-ḥusn*), but published first in Hindi, probably in late 1918 or early 1919; see Amṛt Rāy, *Kalam kā sipāhī*, Allahabad, 1962, 654; also Premcand's letter of April 24, 1919, referring to the success of the Hindi version, *Premcand ciṭṭhī-patrī*, ed. A. Rāy and M. Gopāl, Allahabad, 1962, I, 82.

[2] Translated from the Urdu *Jalva-e-īṣār* (1912), but perhaps based on a draft of an earlier novel, see M. Gopal, *Munshi Premcand; a literary biography*, New York, 1964, 86. The Hindi version appeared in 1921, A. Rāy, *op. cit.*, p. 654.

scope of the novel or the new direction of its didacticism which first attracts attention so much as the potentialities of Premcand's writing as compared with that of, say, Kiśorī Lāl Gosvāmī. These are evident in the evocative first chapter of the novel, which describes Pratāp's mother's seeking her boon from Kālī in a dark temple, and also in the following chapters dealing with Pratāp's childhood and his friendship with Virjan. The treatment here may perhaps sometimes seem cursory, and sometimes over-emotional, but in general it shows a sensitivity and an understanding of the way incident may be used to throw light on character which is rare in the earlier novels.

'Suvāmā was about to add something more when suddenly dizziness overcame her once again. Pratāp, seeing how his mother was, felt helpless and afraid. He ran to the doorway of Virjan's house, and stood there in tears.

'He would usually come to see Virjan at about that time of day, or earlier, and today she was wondering why he had not yet appeared. Suddenly, looking up, she saw him standing in the doorway with his face buried in his hands. Why is he laughing, this must be some trick, she thought. Then, when she pulled his hands away, she saw the tears.

'"Lallū! Why are you crying? What's the matter?" Pratāp went on sobbing.

'"Aren't you going to tell me? Did your mother scold you? . . . Well, if you're not going to tell me I don't care."

'"No Virjan, she's very ill!"

'Virjan dashed out at this, and in a moment had reached Suvāmā's side.'

The attention given to the presentation of minor characters is also new, and welcome. Such treatment would hardly have seemed worth its space to Kiśori Lāl Gosvāmī. It would have taken him too far from the description of a sequence of events which was his chief concern. Premcand, however, succeeds in eliciting our sympathy for his characters, and we share emotionally in the trials and the happiness of their lives.

However, the novel in its entirety belies the promise of the opening chapters. The theme is confusing. In describing the separation and sufferings of Pratāp and Virjan the author seems first to stress the shortcomings of the traditional arranged marriage system and to advocate reform. But as he follows through the mental processes of the protagonists the point of his treatment of the subject is not quite clear. From seeming to deplore the bad features of the system he swings to a consideration of the traditional virtue of accepting the marriage arranged for one by one's parents. Then in describing Virjan's transfiguration and Pratāp's sacrifice of his personal life in the disinterested service of the people Premcand shifts the narrative to an ideal plane, proclaiming his vision of a transformed Hindu society, and implying incidentally a growing consciousness on his readers' part of Hindu society as the chief determinant factor in Indian life. The narrative is developed with increasing unreality, and the author soon quite loses sight of the living characters which he had so realistically begun to create. The construction of the novel leaves no doubt, however, that Premcand was serious in his view of the development of Pratāp's character. This conflict between the idealism of his approach and the realism of his observation was to persist throughout the greater part of his work.

Before Premcand the subject of village life had received only incidental attention from prose writers. Premcand was to make it an important motif in modern Hindi literature. The present novel breaks new ground with its vivid descriptions of aspects of village life in the form of a series of letters from Virjan to her husband. These show in abundance the realism lacking in the conclusion of the novel, as well as a consciousness of the need to improve village conditions, which reflects the influence of the Ārya Samāj movement. But the villagers' ignorance and grinding poverty is not yet construed as the outcome of oppression or exploitation, and there is nothing of the idealization of the long-suffering peasant which was to appear later in Hindi literature after the advent of Gandhi.

'What a difference there is between hearsay and reality! Seeing what I do here, I simply want to get away—tumble-down straw huts, earthen walls, rubbish piled high in front of every house, oxen fresh from the wallowing-hole, cows feeble for want of food. As for the people, they are in a frightful state, starving, destitute, poverty-stricken. Not a man of them wears clothes that are not in tatters, and though they sweat all day and half the night too they never earn enough to fill their stomachs.'

(On superstitions)—'How benighted these superstitions are! But they hold a terrible power. If a boy falls ill, the villagers try to placate the spirits. In agriculture, in the arranging of marriages, in fact in every sphere of life, these spirits hold sway. The people here know nothing of gods, or goddesses, for the spirits reign supreme. If the very god of death were to set foot in this village the spirits would make an end of him, or so they would think. What can be done to stamp out these superstitions?'[1]

CONCLUSION

In the course of the nineteenth century there developed a style of language, written in the Devanāgarī script, which was able to subsume the potentialities of all the dialects of the Hindi language area as vehicles for literary expression. Throughout the century this standard Hindi style was both in competition with, and dependent on, Urdu and English in developing itself as a medium for prose literature within the area. The ensconced position of Urdu and the growing importance of English in the area meant that for most people practical incentives to learn the style remained small, while on the other hand the absence of a developed prose tradition in any of the Hindi dialects encouraged the early practitioners of the style to have recourse to English for a form of expression, and to Urdu for some narrative themes. Other themes and motifs they endeavoured to draw from contemporary life, or occasionally from traditional, historical or translated sources.

Although almost all the early works of prose fiction in Hindi are organized on the pattern of the Western novel, their authors generally have a very superficial idea of the possibilities of the novel form. They succeed in differing degrees in assimilating aspects of the novelist's technique, but rarely grasp the fact that the novel form demands a fundamental concern on the part of its author with aspects of human personality and

[1] *Vardān*, 3rd edn., 1953, 90–2.

character. Very often the central theme of their novels is merely narrative, or melodramatic, or didactic, while the eager use of pseudo-poetic language and conceits taken over from traditional verse points to the essential literary conservatism of most writers.

The Hindi reading public for its part showed a generally undeveloped literary taste throughout this period. The only class of prose fiction to enjoy much popularity before the appearance of Premcand was the romance. This was based on traditional material, but could also easily accommodate motifs and themes drawn from India's contacts with the West; whatever its range of theme, it was dependent for its success essentially on its qualities of melodrama. The popularity of the chief romances was an important factor in the development of standard Hindi, as it first brought into being a sizeable public literate in the new style.

Thus until the twentieth century Hindi writers had made comparatively little of the novel as a borrowed form, while Hindi readers had remained generally unaware of its possibilities. Hindi lagged far behind Bengali, and also behind Urdu, in the domain of prose fiction. It is revealing of the cohesion of much of northern India as a mixed culture area that Premcand, who was almost the first writer to produce more promising work in Hindi, owed far more to Urdu for his development than to literary importations from Bengal. The development of Hindi, when it came, was in a certain sense an internal process.

Premcand's thirty-odd years of literary production were to consolidate the position of the Hindi novel, as well as to establish the short story in Hindi literature. He brought to his work the fundamental interest in human character which had been lacking in the writing of almost all his predecessors, and in portraying his characters in action within the whole framework of society gave more fitting themes to the Hindi novel than it had hitherto known. If his treatment of both themes and characters was often marred by an uncritical idealism, this did not mean that the Hindi novel was not now established on the right lines.

THE TAMIL RENAISSANCE AND THE BEGINNINGS OF THE TAMIL NOVEL

by R. E. ASHER

Tamil literature, particularly the earliest writing, is notoriously difficult to date. The body of factors influencing a decision in the matter is complex, and the degree of parochialism of the writer is not always the least important. Age is often assumed to be a synonym of quality, and it therefore appears desirable to push the beginnings as far back in time as possible if quality is to be proved. Without such efforts, however, an objective observer can safely say that Tamil contains literary works of a high standard dating from a period much further back in time than any other Indian language apart from Sanskrit. How far back is another question.

There are traditions in South India to the effect that under the ancient Tamil kings there existed three 'Sangams' or academies in which Tamil literary compositions were 'heard' and assessed—the first lasting for 4,440 years, the second for 3,700 and the third for 1,850. This gives a total for the three academies of 9,990 years, and if the view is accepted that the last phase of the third Sangam was round about the beginning of the Christian era, then poems were being written in Tamil as early as 10,000 BC. It is unnecessary to labour the point that serious literary historians no longer give expression to such opinions. The tradition is first recorded in a medieval commentary on a work on poetics, and many peoples have myths about the beginnings of their civilization.[1] Such early Tamil poems as are extant are traditionally ascribed to the third Sangam, and this is more reasonably dated. One distinguished scholar puts the beginnings at 500 BC.[2] Others

[1] Compare the notion, based on the forgeries of Annius of Viterbo and current in sixteenth-century France, of the advanced civilization, with its great poets, musicians and architects, flourishing under the ancient kings of Gaul as early as 3000 BC. See H. Gillot, *La Querelle des Anciens et des Modernes en France*, Paris, 1914, pp. 125–55.

[2] M. Varadarajan, 'Tamil', in *Indian Literature* [*Short Cultural Surveys of 12 Major Indian Languages and Literatures*], ed. Dr Nagendra, Agra, 1959, p. 13.

are quite happy to start in the course of the second century AD.[1]

The earliest works of the so-called Sangam period have come down to us in collections of poems by various writers. These poems, generally quite short, fall into two fairly distinct groups, one dealing mainly with the theme of love, the other with heroism in war, just government, praises of gods and kings, and so on. Strict conventions are observed in the writing of these verses, and the rules for them were systematically stated in the earliest Tamil grammar, the *Tolkāppiyam*. In common with the poems of the anthologies it contains only a very limited number of Sanskrit loan-words.

In contrast the fair number of ethical works of the Sangam age, among them the famous *Kuṟaḷ*,[2] contain a greater admixture of Sanskrit and for this reason are commonly considered later compositions. So, too, are the two great 'twin epics' of classical Tamil literature, *Cilappatikāram* and *Maṇimēkalai*, held by some to belong to the sixth century, though they may well have been composed as much as four centuries earlier. Much of the second of these is taken up with discussions on the principles of Buddhism.

This must be regarded as exceptional, since early Tamil poetry is almost completely secular in content, whilst the writings of the thousand years from the beginning of the seventh century are nearly all of a religious nature. There is a large corpus of Vaishnavite and Saivite hymns (devotional poems in praise of the god Viṣṇu on the one hand and of the god Śiva on the other), and with the flowering of Hinduism come the first Tamil translations of the great Sanskrit epics. The *Rāmāyaṇam* of Kampan, however, is not to be considered so much a mere translation or adaptation of Vālmīki's work, as an original poem on the same theme by a master poet.

One important development in the late medieval period was the formulation and systematization, in verse form, of the

[1] E.g. S. Vaiyapuri Pillai, *History of Tamil Language and Literature* (*Beginning to 1000 A.D.*), Madras, 1956, p. 22. *A History of Tamil Literature* by C. and Hephzibah Jesudasan (Calcutta, 1961) and *A History of Tamil Literature* by T. P. Meenakshisundaram (Annamalainagar, 1965), both date the first stratum of extant verses somewhat earlier.

[2] There are numerous English translations. The best-known is G. U. Pope's: *The 'Sacred' Kurraḷ of Tiruvaḷḷuva-nâyanâr*, London, 1886.

Śaiva Siddhānta, the major Tamil contribution to Hindu philosophy. It was at this time, too, that were written the greatest of the commentaries on the older secular works.

In the period preceding the arrival of substantial numbers of Europeans in South India purely literary activity seems almost to have faded out, and in fact one literary historian finds no writers or writings to mention at all between 1600 and 1700.[1] European contacts began in earnest with the considerable expansion of missionary activity towards the end of the seventeenth century. The influence of western culture, however, was not seriously felt until almost two hundred years later—the start of the Tamil Renaissance.

One major justification for the use of the term 'renaissance' in the realms of art or literature must necessarily be the consciousness of the artists or writers of a certain time that they are taking part in such a process. The decision to talk of a rebirth is not left simply to the historian. Tamil writers for the whole of the present century at least have been very conscious of their role in restarting massive literary activity in their language. The use of the term is also justified for other reasons. For it is plain that there had been not merely a falling off in the quality of writings, but a complete gap—a substantial period during which little or nothing of permanent value was written. Awareness of being involved in a renaissance also implies looking back on a flourishing state in the past, and at the turn of the century much attention was given to the earliest known Tamil literature. Collections were edited and printed, and a number of works that had been forgotten, but not entirely lost, were unearthed and published.

In the renewal of literary activity European influence was important in two ways: firstly in reminding the Tamils of the contrast between their heritage and their present failure to produce new writings; and secondly in putting before them the possibility of using Tamil for new literary forms.

Among the earlier European missionaries was the best-known, the Italian Jesuit Beschi, who died in the Tinnevelly district in 1747 after almost forty years in South India.[2] He

[1] M. S. Purnalingam Pillai, *Tamil Literature* (rvsd. edn.), Munnirpallam, 1930.

[2] See L. Besse, S.J., *Father Beschi of the Society of Jesus. His Times and Writings*, Trichinopoly, 1918.

called himself by a Tamil name and dressed like a Tamil. After studying Tamil for some ten or twelve years he wrote grammars of the language in both Latin and Tamil. More significant was his ability to write original works in Tamil, among them a lengthy epic poem about the life of St Joseph.[1] He even instituted important reforms in the Tamil script.

Later missionaries, though less original, showed great interest in Tamil literature, producing translations of the main ethical works and the best of the Saivite hymns. One nineteenth-century missionary, Bishop Caldwell, rather more than a hundred years ago published a comparative grammar of the Dravidian languages,[2] clearly showing that the languages of Southern India were in origin completely independent of Sanskrit. This and all such objective comments from outsiders helped to increase the desire to repeat past glories.

Because of the gap already mentioned, however, and because of the contacts with the west, bringing awareness of hitherto unknown literary genres, it was not possible to continue solely in the path that had been all but lost. Hence the obvious fact that the bulk of twentieth-century writing is in the fields of the novel, short story, and drama—none of which is to be found in the writings of earlier periods. That prose fiction should be attempted by those who had read and admired European models is not surprising. Other evident factors contributing to its introduction and development should not be forgotten. Novels do not lend themselves to being memorized and passed on by word of mouth. Nor are they suitable for public reading in the way in which the great epics are still read and expounded. The possibility of producing large numbers is essential. The setting up of a Tamil printing press in Tranquebar in 1710 is therefore important, even though it was not for half a century used outside the mission field.[3] The spread of education

[1] *Tēmpāvaṇi*. An abridged edition was published quite recently: C. G. E. Beschi, *Tēmpāvaṇi curukkam*, edited with commentary by V. Mariya Anthony, Tuticorin, 1960; and this has been followed by an edition of the complete work by R. L. Ārōkkiyam Piḷḷai, 3 vols., Tuticorin, 1961–64.

[2] Robert Caldwell, *A Comparative Grammar of the Dravidian or South Indian Family of Languages*, 3rd edn, University of Madras, 1956 (revised centenary edition).

[3] See J. S. M. Hooper, *The Bible in India*, Oxford University Press, 1938, pp. 46–55. A modest amount of printing in Tamil was done before this date, even as early as 1578. See M. Siddiq Khan, 'The Early Bengali Printed Books',

during the nineteenth century is also relevant here, in that if people are to be taught extensively to read and write, reading matter in prose must be readily available.[1]

The use of prose in original literary composition in Tamil is recent. All literary works in the classical and medieval periods, with the exception of the commentaries on the classics, were in verse.[2] Some of the earliest prose works in Tamil were, in fact, written by the Italian Beschi, the best known being the set of comic stories about an absent-minded *guru* and his five half-witted disciples.[3] Other early printed Tamil books in prose are translations of Sanskrit epics and tales, and versions of traditional Tamil stories.[4] Rather less expected is the translation of parts of a French children's periodical, Berquin's *L'Ami des Enfans*, of which the first of many editions appeared in 1838.[5]

In the early days of Tamil printing, most books came from the mission presses, and so were mainly translations of the whole or parts of the Bible, or religious tracts, with the

Gutenberg-Jahrbuch 1966, pp. 200–8, and Xavier S. Thani Nayagam, 'The First Books printed in Tamil', *Tamil Culture*, Madras, vol. VII, No. 3 (July 1958), pp. 288–308.

[1] It is worthy of note that more than one publisher expressed the hope at the beginning of a novel that the work would be found suitable as a set text for an examination (as a number indeed were). See, for example, the introduction to T. M. Ponnucāmi Piḷḷai, *Vijayacuntaram*, Madras, 1910, p. 10.

[2] *Cilappatikāram*, mentioned above, p. 180, is a rare exception in that with the verse are mingled frequent passages of rhetorical prose.

[3] *Paramārtta kuruvin̲ katai* (The Story of the Guru Paramartta). English (by B. G. Babington), French and German versions were published during the nineteenth century. The Tamil text, based on a manuscript in Beschi's own hand in the Library of the British Museum, was recently republished by Dr Rama Subbiah, with a brief introduction on Beschi's orthography. See *Tamil Oli*, Journal of the Tamil Language Society, Univ. of Malaya, No. 5 (1965–66), pp. 105–27.

[4] There is a valuable list in John Murdoch, *Classified Catalogue of Tamil Printed Books*, Madras, 1865. For brief accounts of the development of Tamil prose from the earliest times, see V. S. Chengalvaraya Pillai, *History of the Tamil prose Literature*, Madras, 1966 (first published 1904), and R. E. Asher, *Some Landmarks in the History of Tamil Prose*, University of Madras, forthcoming (The Dr. R. P. Sethu Pillai Silver Jubilee Endowment Lectures, 1967–68).

[5] T. Vytheanatha Moodelair (Vaityanāta Mutaliyār), *The Looking-glass for the mind; . . . stories . . . from . . . L'Aim* [*sic*] *des Enfans. With analysis & close translation in Tamil*, Madras, 1838. It appears to have been popular in other parts of India. See I. M. P. Raeside, *Early Prose Fiction in Marathi*, this volume, p. 79.

inevitable Tamil version of *Pilgrim's Progress* appearing in 1793. Gradually, however, the balance changed, and with the coming of the Tamil novel the overwhelming majority of books published was soon to be made up of original Tamil works, mainly in the field of prose fiction.

The first quarter of a century in the history of prose fiction produced a large number of novelists. In the present paper only the more significant works of the five most important and well-known novelists writing in this period will be discussed.

Samuel Vedanayakam Pillai (1826–89) is firmly established as the author of the first Tamil novel, *The Life and Adventures of Prathapa Mudaliar*, first published in 1879.[1] A book calling itself 'an original Tamil novel' had appeared four years before this, but it was in verse.[2] Vedanayakam Pillai wrote his novel after retiring from his position of District Munsiff.[3] He had published other books earlier, but these were non-narrative verse. Quite a clear idea of the nature of this pioneer work is given in the author's Preface:

'My object in writing this work of fiction is to supply the want of prose works in Tamil, . . . and also to give a practical illustration of the maxims of morality contained in my former works. . . .

'The scene is laid in Southern India. The hero is a well-educated native gentleman of brilliant parts, wit and humour. He gives an account of his birth, parentage, education, marriage and other important events of his life and the narrative is intermixed with various scenes of humour and pleasantry, and observations of a moral tendency.

[1] *Piratāpa Mutaliyār carittiram*. The English title is that given by the author. A difficulty arises with the transcription of Tamil into roman, in that an exact transliteration is often a poor guide to the pronunciation. When books have an English title (as most of the early novels do), this title will be used in the body of the paper, and a transliteration of the Tamil title will be given in a footnote. A similar compromise will be adopted with the names of authors. Thus a transliteration of the name of this government official turned novelist would be Vētanāyakam Piḷḷai.

[2] D. V. Seshaiyangar (Cēṣaiyaṅkār), *Athiyuravadhani, or the Self-made man. An original Tamil novel, delineating pictures of modern Hindu life*. Madras, 1875. (*Ātiyūr avatāni caritam*.)

[3] For a rather more detailed account of his life and his other writings see Francis Morais, 'Vedanayagam Pillai', *Tamil Culture*, Madras, Vol. X, No. 2 (April–June 1963), pp. 30–41.

'The principal personages who play important parts in this novel are the hero's mother, *Sundara Anny,* and his wife *Gnanambal,* both being ladies of high birth and fortune, with every accomplishment both personal and mental, and endowed with every estimable quality that could adorn the female sex. . . .

'The father and the father-in-law of the hero are types of uneducated native gentlemen in high life, with all their eccentricities and singularities of character. They are, however, made by the gentle artifices of *Sundara Anny* and *Gnanambal,* to exhibit traits of latent good feelings, and to perform praiseworthy acts. There are many subordinate characters . . . affording examples of *filial affection, fraternal affection, conjugal affection, chastity, universal benevolence, integrity, gratitude, &c.*

'In writing this story, I have not followed the example of those novelists who depict human nature as it is, not as it ought to be, and who thus exhibit bad specimens of humanity which are often mistaken by the young and inexperienced for objects of imitation. I have represented the principal personages as perfectly virtuous, in accordance with the opinion of the great English moralist Dr Johnson. . . .

'. . . I have endeavoured to exhibit the inherent beauty of virtue, and to expose the deformity of vice, in such a manner as to create a love of one and a detestation of the other. . . .'

His story is basically a very simple one, though the book is long and rambling. Like so many of the novels that were to follow it, it is the life story, told in the first person, of the main character. Vedanayakam Pillai goes further back than most of his successors in beginning his novel with an incident in the life of the hero's grandfather. Soon after the British came to South India, we read, a stranger riding near Prathapa Mudaliar's grandfather's village was knocked from his runaway horse. Most of the villagers were afraid to go to his aid, fearing that he was a fakir, to help whom might have harmful results. Ekampara Mudaliar, conscious of his duty to his fellow men, went to his aid. Now it so happened that the stranger was the local Nabob in disguise, and because of this happy circumstance, Ekampara Mudaliar was soon after the incident offered the post of minister of state.

The social standing of the family being thus established, we pass rapidly to the hero's birth, childhood and education. Among his boyhood companions is his mother's twin brother's daughter, the brilliant and virtuous Gnanambal. They are always together, as long as they are young enough for this to be socially permissible. Later the respective parents discuss the possibility of their marriage, and it appears that the necessary arrangements will be completed. A dispute arises between the two fathers, however, as to where the couple shall live, a quarrel develops, and everything is called off. As the children are of marriageable age, other matches are planned, and by coincidence the two marriages are fixed to take place in the same village on the same day. Fate takes a further hand, when both the wedding parties, Prathapa's and Gnanambal's, are prevented from reaching the appointed place. There the difficulty is resolved by the waiting young man and girl being married to each other. After further vicissitudes, including the abduction of Gnanambal and her rescue by Prathapa Mudaliar, the marriage of these two is happily celebrated, the earlier point of dispute being settled by an agreement that they shall spend alternative periods of six months with their respective families. This takes us no more than a third of the way through the book. There are further family disputes, among them a lengthy one as to which grandfather shall have the expected child.

The last section of the book is taken up with Gnanambal becoming queen, or rather 'king', of a nearby state.[1] Her husband failed to come back from a hunting expedition. His elephant, however, returned and took her to where he was. For safety's sake Gnanambal dressed as a man. In a large town she joined the crowd, and before she realized what was taking place an elephant put a garland round her neck. She was then hailed as king, for this was how the people had decided to choose a new one. She accepted the position, thinking this would make it easier for her to find her husband. He was

[1] The purpose of this section is explained in the Preface: 'By a fortuitous combination of circumstances over which she has no control, *Gnanambal* rises to sovereign power in the disguise of a man, and administers the Government with great wisdom and ability. She is raised to the highest pinnacle of human greatness, with a view to meet the taste of the Hindu readers, who are very fond of kings and queens.' (Vētanāyakam Piḷḷai was a Christian.)

in fact imprisoned, and she of course had him released. With his help she ruled the state in an enlightened fashion and introduced many necessary reforms. Good government being well established, they returned home together (though not before further complications have been introduced into the plot). After fears that Gnanambal, who became very ill, would die, there is a 'happy ending'—the title of the last chapter.

It has seemed worth while to summarize the story at some length, since it appears relevant to an understanding of the nature of the work. Whatever else the book may be, it is plainly not an example of realism in the novel. There are, nevertheless, brief lifelike scenes in the midst of improbabilities. An example is the description of an incident that took place when Prathapa Mudaliar and his wife were staying in a distant town after a quarrel with their fathers. The description forms quite a good study in growing exasperation:

'One afternoon I was sitting having a pleasant chat with Devaraja Pillai and Kanakasapai, when one of the drivers who had come with us from Sattiyapuri rushed in puffing and blowing and said to us, "Good news! Good news!" jumping around all over the place as he spoke. When we asked him what the news was, he continued to jump about saying, "Sirs, through running a couple of miles to get here I am quite out of breath. As soon as I get my wind back I'll tell you." In a threatening tone I asked him, "What are you talking about? Can't you even give a hint as to what the good news is?" Without saying anything about what he had come to tell us, he went on talking without rhyme or reason. Losing control of my temper, I lifted my hand as if to strike him. Moving away he said, "Is this the reward I get for bringing you good news? Am I to be treated like this? How long have I been in your service? Even your father and your mother never spoke harshly to me. And certainly they never once struck me. Is it right that a young man like you should strike me and abuse me?" All this, and a lot more meaningless talk besides—but not a word about the news he brought. I became really angry and started to thrash him.'[1]

[1] *Piratāpa Mutaliyār*, pp. 160–1. Reference will be made to the 1952 edition published in Madras by the South India Saiva Siddhanta Works Publishing Society.

The various family quarrels in the book show quite acute observation, though a realistic picture is often followed by a rather romantic note, as on the occasion when the fathers quarrel at the time of the first attempt to marry the hero and heroine. A slight lack of good feeling leads gradually to a fierce exchange of abuse:

'From that day on there was no contact between Sampanti Mudaliar and us. We never went to their house, they never came to ours. Their friends became our enemies, their enemies became our friends. There was enmity between their servants and ours. There was enmity between their cattle and sheep and ours.'[1]

This novel has been described above as rambling, with the implication that it is badly constructed. There are a number of subsidiary themes concerning other characters who move closely with the principal ones, and we are told quite a lot about them. No serious attempt is made, however, to bind plot and sub-plots together at any point in the story.

The 'observations of a moral tendency' mentioned in the preface are frequent and more often than not are illustrated by an appropriate story. There are a great number of these, most of them drawn from the collections of traditional stories published earlier in the century, and there is at least one from the *Arabian Nights*. Schoolchildren in all countries have their own lore—jokes, trick questions, stories[2]—and the sections on Prathapa Mudaliar's childhood include many of these. One might even suspect that the author gave every one he could remember from his own boyhood. The following is a typical example:

'When some children and I were playing in the street, one boy asked me whether I could do with both eyes open a trick that he would perform with both eyes closed. I replied, "Shall I not be able to do with my eyes open a trick that you do with both eyes closed?" and agreed to stake so much against

[1] *Piratāpa Mutaliyār*, pp. 77–8.

[2] An interesting study of those current in various parts of Great Britain is contained in Iona and Peter Opie, *The Lore and Language of Schoolchildren*, Oxford, 1959.

my not doing it. Immediately the boy sat down in the middle of the street, closed both his eyes and, scooping up handfuls of dust, put them on his eyes. Then, asking me if I could do this trick with both eyes open, he gave me a handful of dust. Thinking it better to lose money rather than my eyesight, I paid him the bet.'[1]

Digressions consisting of the expression of opinions are frequent, particularly in the long final section, where good government is discussed. A section on the need to use Tamil only in education and government in the Tamil country could well have been quoted word for word by a post-Independence politician.

This first Tamil novel, in fact, might seem to fail by trying to do everything. Nevertheless, it was and is widely read for its easy style, its occasional effective character sketches, its touches of humour and, let it be admitted, its quaintness. Because of the favourable reception it was given, Vedanayakam Pillai published another novel, *Sugana Sunthari*,[2] eight years later, but the success was not repeated, perhaps because he had packed so much into the first one that he had very little left to say. *Sugana Sunthari* is, however, of some importance because of its attempt to expose the evils of certain social customs, among them the practice of early marriages. There are hints, too, of a belief in female emancipation. Similar views are implicit in the idealized portraits of the women in his first novel, and in particular in the heroine's success in government.

The case of Rajam Aiyar was very different from that of his predecessor. Trained in law, he devoted a great part of his short life (1872–98) to writing of various kinds. He was the editor, for the last two years of his life, of *Prabuddha Bharata*,[3] a monthly journal devoted to religion and philosophy, and he contributed a wide variety of articles to other periodicals, both English and Tamil. Among his English writings is an unfinished novel.[4]

[1] *Piratāpa Mutaliyār*, p. 10.

[2] *Cukuṇacuntari carittiram*, Madras, 1887.

[3] He was also the main contributor, using a large number of pseudonyms. The bulk of these writings were reproduced in book form as *Rambles in Vedanta*, Madras, 1905. This contains a brief sketch of his life (pp. xxxii–xxxix). The only biography appears to be A. S. Kastūriraṅka Ayyar, *Rājam Ayyar caritai*, Madras, 1909.

[4] *True Greatness, or Vasudeva Sastri*. In *Rambles in Vedanta*, pp. 617–734.

His only Tamil novel, *Kamalambal, or the Fatal Rumour*,[1] was first published in serial form in the *Viveka Chintamani*, a monthly magazine in Tamil 'devoted to the diffusion of general knowledge'. It is somewhat surprising to find that *Kamalambal* is exceptional among early Tamil novels in having been first published in serial form. This development, as a common practice, plainly came later in Tamil than in certain other Indian languages. Though *Kamalambal* appeared in twenty sections during the years 1893–95, publication in this form seems to have had little effect on the shape of the novel. Chapters are to some extent self-contained, but this is in any case one of the implications of chapter division. There is no tendency at all for them to be of equal length, and it would appear that the editor normally allowed Rajam Aiyar the amount of space that he required. There is no building up of suspense at the end of an instalment, and in fact one chapter—presumably when space was limited—appeared in two successive months. By thus being untypical as a serial, *Kamalambal* was probably a better book.

Kamalambal has very little in common with *Prathapa Mudaliar*. The plot is complex, concerning as it does a large number of characters whose lives are closely interrelated. It is not possible, as it was with *Prathapa Mudaliar*, to pick out the main plot and say that the sub-plots are barely relevant to it. All that *is* there seems to be essential to all the rest. There are humorous episodes, but the humour is often of a whimsical kind not found in Vedanayakam Pillai. Moreover, the episodes are bound up with the telling of the story and with the depicting of character, and are not introduced with a 'That reminds me of the story of so-and-so', so frequent in *Prathapa Mudaliar*. The portrait of the teacher of Tamil is quite typical of Rajam Aiyar's style:

This and other selections from Rajam Aiyar's writings in English were recently reprinted in a cheap popular edition: *True Greatness, Stories that inspire, Parables of Wisdom, God Seekers*—all four published in Madras (Pastime Pleasure Books), 1967.

[1] B. R. Irājam Ayyar, *Āpattukkiṭamāna apavātam, allatu Kamalāmpāḷ carittiram*, 3rd edn, ed. C. V. Swaminatha Iyer, Madras, 1910. The first reprint in book form came out in 1896. Though not changing the substance of the book, modern editors have made a good number of minor textual changes (e.g. 7th edn, Madras, 1947).

'We shall now leave Sirukulam and go to Madura, where we have a little business to attend to. . . . In Madura is a government college generally known as the District School. In the middle of some benches in a corner of the school verandah were placed a chair and a table. On the table were some inkstands. As soon as the "ding-dong" of ten o'clock was heard, about twenty boys assembled there. Within five minutes of their arrival there came a man, tall and dark, with pockmarked face. He was the school's Tamil pandit, his name Ammayappa Pillai. He would be about fifty years old. He came from Adusapatti, a large town of five or six houses and a tamarind tree. He was a real character. If he began impromptu singing,[1] he would reel off a rapid succession of verses, like monkeys shaking figs from a fig-tree. If anyone who knew Tamil fell into his hands, he would straightway, before they could breathe, pierce their ears with songs to the number of three or four hundred, like arrows from Rama's bow.'[2]

Because he is something of a character, he is much liked by his pupils, who are allowed to tease him up to a point, but always with the risk of making him lose his temper. He has a way of getting the worst of any situation. Thus, while in Madras, he falls an easy victim to a confidence trickster and pickpocket, who relieves him of all his money, while the pandit holds forth about his skill as a versifier.

Ammayappa Pillai is introduced mainly because in one of his classes is the boy who, it has been agreed, shall marry Kalyani. She is ten years old, and the book opens with a discussion between Kamalambal and her husband, Muttuswamy Aiyar, about the girl's marriage. Rajam Aiyar does not follow Vedanayakam Pillai in giving his eponym's life story from birth, but gives a picture of south India Brahmin home-life based on an account of Kamalambal's middle years.

It has been noted above that such realism as there was in

[1] A free translation. The Tamil has, 'If he began to sing *yamakam* and *tiripu*'. *Yamakam* is 'Repetition, in a stanza, with changes of meaning sometimes effected by changes in the division of words'. *Tiripu* is a 'Stanza whose initial letters excepting the first are identical in each line' (*Tamil Lexicon*, University of Madras, 1924–39).

[2] *Kamalāmpāḷ*, 1910, pp. 48–9.

Prathapa Mudaliar was mainly in snatches of dialogue. Rajam Aiyar's seems no less true to life. He does, in fact, go considerably further in the pursuit of realism in introducing dialect colloquial forms. This to some extent, however, defeats its ends, in that it quite often necessitates the placing of the standard form in brackets, so that readers who are not from Tanjore shall understand.[1] Rajam pursues realism in incident, too, and avoids the improbable coincidences and fantastic happenings that are found so frequently in *Prathapa Mudaliar*. That is not to say that the book merely describes routine incidents of everyday middle-class family life. There is robbery, arson, manslaughter, and no shortage of extremely malicious gossip. Towards the end of the story all the male members of Kamalambal's family are missing. Her small son, Natarajan, has been kidnapped and is presumed dead. Her son-in-law, Srinivasan, has been wrongfully arrested. Her husband, who has allowed himself to be convinced of a rumour that his wife had been unfaithful, has, after an abortive suicide attempt, disappeared on a pilgrimage to Benares. Nevertheless, in spite of such incidents, there is no departure from the possible—except, perhaps, in the extraordinary strength and vigour displayed by the bandit, Peyandi Thevan, before the police succeed in taking him.

The looking back at past glories is an essential feature of any renaissance, and *Kamalambal* has an important link with earlier Tamil literature. Kampan's version of the *Rāmāyaṇa* overflows with rich descriptions, and his wide vocabulary causes Tamil scholars to speak of him, with justice, in the same breath as Shakespeare and Goethe. A great admirer of the epic, Rajam Aiyar attempts to popularize it by giving a new birth to words and expressions used in it but not commonly found in later literature. Where reasonably appropriate certain characters quote from Kampan, and the author states that many of the figures of speech and descriptions in his own narrative are drawn

[1] There is a wide difference, as regards the phonetic and grammatical structure, between 'spoken' Tamil (as used in conversation) and 'written' Tamil (which is also the standard style for public speaking and broadcasting), and it is difficult to give an accurate representation of the colloquial in terms of the Tamil script. A number of writers have attempted it (e.g. P. Sambanda Mudaliyar in his farce *Sabapathy* and other plays), but most still give up the task as hopeless—just as Shaw did the representation of Cockney in *Pygmalion*.

from the Tamil *Rāmāyaṇam*. At appropriate times, too, various persons are found reading the *Kamparāmāyaṇam*.[1]

Since Rajam Aiyar's death editors have attempted to show the profound philosophical truths lying behind the action of the novel. Moreover, the author stated in an Epilogue, 'In writing this novel, my main purpose was not the story',[2] and in *Kamalambal*, as in almost everything he wrote, aimed at popularizing the Vedanta. For all that, the novel rarely reads like a deliberately moralizing and didactic work.

It is true that the content of one chapter, relating to the conversion of Muttuswamy Aiyar, is such that the reader is warned that those who are interested only in the story and have no faith in the spiritual heritage of man need not read it.[3] Then, at the end of the story, most of the characters, among them Muttuswamy Aiyar, Kamalambal, Ammayappa Pillai and even the robber, Peyandi Thevan, have become sincere seekers after spiritual truth. Nevertheless, the book lives on as a work of fiction, not as a philosophical treatise.

Rajam Aiyar, though not simply interested in telling a story, showed no signs of wanting to be a social reformer. On the few occasions when he discusses social customs directly he seems, on the contrary, to be very satisfied with things as they are. Thus:

'Nowadays there are some people among us who think that only if they marry after passing the age of twenty can women live happily with their husband. Knowing so well the mutual love of Srinivasan and Lakshmi, I do not subscribe to this opinion.'[4]

Mandaviah,[5] the next important figure in the history of the Tamil novel, did display a reformist tendency to a marked degree, and so might be said to be taking up where Vedanayakam Pillai left off. His literary career, certainly, had something in common with Vedanayakam's. He held a government post (in the 'Salt, Abkari and Customs Department, Madras'), and

[1] E.g. *Kamalāmpāḷ*, 1910, Chap. 1, pp. 4–5 (Kalyāṇi) and Chap. 27 pp. 242–4 (Śrinivācaṉ and Leṭcumi). Kalyāṇi is also known as Lakshmi (=Leṭcumi). [2] *Kamalāmpāḷ*, 1910, p. 307.

[3] *Ibid.*, p. 258: Chap. 30, 'God is the nectar that feeds my loving heart. What should I fear?' (Rajam Aiyar gives his own English translation of his chapter headings.) [4] *Ibid.*, p. 182. [5] A. Mātavaiyā (1874–1926).

writing was a spare time occupation. He wrote one novel by way of experiment 'in hours of fitful leisure',[1] as he put it, with no very serious intention of ever writing another, for he did not expect it to have the success of *Prathapa Mudaliar*. In the event it was well received, and he therefore wrote others. Having started earlier in life than Vedanayakam Pillai and being perhaps more gifted, he produced quite a few more novels in both English and Tamil, as well as volumes of verse and translations of Shakespeare. One of his English novels,[2] like *Prathapa Mudaliar*, opens before the hero's birth and gives an account of his life from the beginning. It includes, too, a lengthy statement of political views, though the story is not as often interrupted by such digressions as Vedanayakam Pillai's work. His first completed Tamil novel, *Padmavati*, tells the story of two cousins, who as children wanted, like Prathapa Mudaliar and Gnanambal, to marry, but who found there were many obstacles, not least of them the prison sentence that the boy's father received for quarrelling with and striking a man. The main digressions here are on the elements of a good education and on the need for women to be educated. In *Vijayamarthandam*[3] such passages are made up of attacks on the extravagant living of ignorant and improvident zemindars.

Muthumeenakshi,[4] by no means lacking in social criticism, shows the beginnings of a new technique. Instead of merely interrupting the narrative to make his point, Madhaviah here does his preaching mainly by weighting the action so that it becomes clear from what takes place, what institutions and social customs he is criticizing. The book is a powerful attack on the marriage customs of Madhaviah's community, on child marriage, the commercialism involved in arranging marriages, the treatment of widows (even those who have never lived with their husbands) and on the joint family system.

Muthumeenakshi is a Brahmin girl, whose husband, Rama,

[1] Preface to *Patmāvati carittiram, oru tamil̲ nāṭṭuk katai* (*Padmavati charitram. A story of the Tamil country*), 2 vols, Palghat, 1898–1900. (7th edn, Madras, 1958.)

[2] *Thillai Govindan: a posthumous autobiography*, London, 1903. Using the pen-name 'Kusika', Madhaviah also wrote a number of short stories in English with a reformist bias. Collections appeared in book form in Madras in 1916 and 1924.

[3] *Vijayamārttāṇṭam*, 2nd edn, Madras, 1922. (1st edn, 1902?)

[4] *Muttumīnākṣi, oru pirāmaṇappeṇ cuvacaritai*, Madras, 1903.

son of her maternal uncle, was picked for her soon after her birth. As a child she often played with her elder brother and his friend Somasundaram, both of whom taught her Tamil and English. In fun Somasundaram used to speak of her as his wife, but she was in fact married off to someone else. The original plan to marry her to Rama was spoilt by his death by drowning just before the proposed date of the marriage, but at the age of nine she was married to a widower of thirty. In a sense she was quite glad to leave home, for her stepmother, some five years older, treated her very badly. Her mother-in-law, however, treated her much worse, especially when, after she had reached the appropriate age, she failed to produce a child. She was given many types of treatment to remove her barrenness—all dictated by tradition and superstitition, and including the swallowing of a certain kind of insect. Neither this nor *pūjās* and *mantras* had any effect, and the treatment was ended by her husband's death from cholera. This only made her condition worse, for as a widow she was more harshly treated than ever, and regarded as a useless mouth to be fed. After a suicide attempt she was driven out and went to live with her now married brother. One day her childhood friend came to see her brother, and after a time he wrote asking her to marry him, which after due consideration she did. There the story ends, except for a concluding description of the social ostracism they suffer because she is a remarried widow.

If the action of the story is weighted, it is not in the improbability of any given incident, but merely in the heaping of misfortune on one person's head. The picture can be taken to be a realistic one, and this effect of realism is heightened by Madhaviah's simple and fast-moving prose. This comes over quite effectively in the translation of the work made by one of his daughters:

'My father was fifty years old when my mother died. When he was a young man of twenty, he had married a child of four years who died of small-pox six years later. Then he married my mother and I have heard my relatives say that they were a very loving couple. The year after my mother's death, my father married again. I shall relate how it all happened from what I know and have heard about it. In those days, the bride (not the bridegroom) had to be bought, and a girl of the Tanjore district was settled as my brother's bride for a dowry of a thousand rupees. The wedding day had been fixed when my father changed his mind and inquired what the price would be if he was to marry the girl himself. The girl's parents considered that they should not let slip such an opportunity of getting a fair reward for their care of their daughter for eleven long years, and somehow comforting the girl's grief at the change, demanded a dowry of Rs 2,000 in cash and a settlement of lands to the same value on the girl. My father agreed and the wedding took place on the date originally fixed and the daughter-in-law elect became his own wife. I cannot bear my bitter shame and grief in recording this.'[1]

The action moves at its rapid pace without digressions until the final happy marriage is agreed upon. Then comes a violent and breathless attack on the illogicality and hypocrisy implicit in certain social attitudes and customs. The heroine has received a letter from Somasundaram:

'. . . Must not the world approve? Is that all your objection? What matters it if this wretched, mad world approves or does not approve? When an old man of sixty marries a child of six; when an infant girl of three is married to an infant boy of four before the sacred fire and they both are ushered into family life; when men who have their first wives living marry at will another wife and even two or three wives more . . . ; when parents sell their daughters to the highest bidder, without any shame; . . . when men go into temples, into the holy abode of the Deity Himself, to enjoy the dance and song of public women and there learn to love them; when these and other like evils prevail, is not this the world that approves and applauds them as ancient institutions? Is not this the world that considers a wretched Brahmin stained with every sin as superior to a virtuous, worthy and honourable Sudra? . . . Is not this the world that detests and casts off a widow who

[1] *Muthumeenakshi. The Autobiography of a Brahmin Girl*, Madras, 1915, pp. 3–4. First published in the *Social Reform Advocate*. A Telugu version appeared soon afterwards, first in the *Hindu Sundari* in the course of 1915 and then in book form (Kākināḍa, 1916).

re-marries and lives honourably, but countenances and respects a widow who secretly lives a life of shame?'[1]

One recurrent feature of Madhaviah's novels is his attempt to portray the world of children. His interest in this was foreshadowed in his first shot at prose fiction, the first six chapters of a novel (which was never completed) published in serial form in 1892.[2] There are details such as the rather naïve comic device of a semi-illiterate letter written by a young girl (with a footnote giving a literate version) to be repeated in *Padmavati*.[3] More interesting is the link with *Muthumeenakshi* in Savitri's sufferings after her mother's death:

'When I was six, my aunt from Tanjore came to our house. She was thirteen. . . . Once when I came home I asked, "Where's mummy?" My aunt replied "You have no mother, no grandmother. She's gone." I burst out crying, whereupon she said, "Don't get under my feet", and taking hold of me she struck me on my back and pushed me outside. I stood sobbing in the street. Then my father came. He said nothing. He did not even look round. My sorrow increased. Then indeed I knew the meaning of the words, "Mother is dead". I thought of jumping into the pond to die. But the frogs would bite me. If I were to jump into the well, the tortoises would bite me. What was I to do?'[4]

There are signs in this early unfinished novel, too, of Madhaviah's interest in the 'social novel', in that it contains a dissussion on whether women should be educated or whether their place is entirely in the home.[5]

Like Madhaviah, Pandit S. M. Natesa Sastri[5] wrote novels

[1] *Muthumeenakshi*, pp. 104–6.

[2] *Savitri. An Autobiographical Sketch* (*Cāvittiri carittiram*) in *Viveka Chintamani*, Madras, Vol. I, Nos. 2–7 (June–November 1892).

[3] *Patmāvati*, Madras, 1958, p. 42.

[4] *Cāvittiri*, in *Viveka Chintamani*, Vol. I, No. 2, p. 54.

[5] The plots of many South Indian novels are still woven round this question of woman's place in society. In the neighbouring Malabar (now Kerala) it was the theme of one of the first novels to be written in Malayalam, O. Chandu Menon's *Indulēkhā* (1889. English translation by W. Dumergue, Madras, 1890). See this volume, pp. 208–16.

[5] C. M. Naṭēca Cāstiri (1859–1906). For a more detailed account of Natesa Sastri's novels, see R. E. Asher, 'Pandit S. M. Natesa Sastri (1859–1906), pioneer Tamil novelist', *Proceedings of II International Conference-Seminar of Tamil Studies*, Madras, 1970 (forthcoming).

depicting certain aspects of South Indian Brahmin family life. His purpose, however, was not so much to reform and instruct as to entertain. There are therefore no lengthy sermons or digressions, but merely pictures of the reactions of certain types of person in certain types of situation. Of the writers discussed in this paper Natesa Sastri was easily the most prolific. In the large number of his books—over a score each in English and Tamil—the novels are among the latest. Combined with his earlier works they make him a link between the commonest type of Tamil prose fiction published earlier in the century and that published at the end. He produced versions of the traditional Tamil collections of stories: of Tenaliraman, the Court Jester, of the King and his Four Ministers, of the so-called Dravidian Nights Entertainments, all of which were very popular throughout the nineteenth century. He collected South Indian folk-tales and published versions in Tamil and English. There were also Tamil prose versions of Sanskrit poems and plays, of Persian story cycles, of tales from Shakespeare.

Then, in his early forties, he had the idea that Tamil prose literature would be more quickly advanced by the production of novels. In his introduction to *Dinadayalu* we read:

'Each month thousands of stories called "novels" are written in English. Our countrymen say to those who know English, "Novel. Novel. What is all this craze for 'novel'? It's only the same thing as a story." So that those who are ignorant of English shall know what a novel is, I am publishing a novel I have written. The meaning of the word "novel" is "new".'[1]

This is hardly a useful definition. To Natesa Sastri a novel was simply a book of the same sort as *Dinadayalu*, which work, says the author, is the first novel in Tamil. Had he not read the earlier ones, or did he merely have a poor idea of their merits?

So that it should be judged without prejudice (for the author was already a well-known figure in Tamil letters),

[1] *Tīṉatayāḷu*, 2nd edn, Madras, 1902. Introduction. The pun inherent in the word appealed to Vētanāyakam Piḷḷai too: 'I crave the indulgence of the public for any shortcomings I might have been guilty of in a novel attempt of this kind.' (Preface to 1st edn of *Piratāpa Mutaliyār*.)

Dinadayalu was first published, in 1900, under a pseudonym, with the promise that other novels of a similar sort would follow if this was well received. That Natesa Sastri's optimism was justified was shown by the appearance of the second edition two years later.

It is the story of the first son of a Brahmin family whose mother died when he was very young. As his father married again, he was brought up by an aunt, given a good education up to degree standard and eventually appointed as a clerk in public service at a salary of Rs 25 a month. Only a short time after his appointment his father died, leaving him with rather more debts than his assets would cover and, because he was the eldest son, the responsibility for the whole of the joint family, including his own wife and four children. His step-mother made life more difficult by her constant demands for more money and by her criticisms, and his half-brother, an idle and somewhat spiteful person, was a constant nuisance. Added to this, his progress in his work was hindered by the actions of a jealous superior. By the end of the book, however, he has achieved a salary of Rs 1,000 a month and solved all his family problems.

In outline, therefore, the book would appear to be just another complete life. Natesa Sastri, however, does not start at birth and work his way through a complete biography. The book opens with Dinadayalu's receipt of a telegram whilst at his post in the hills, saying that his father is ill; and the whole of the first half is taken up with his attempts to arrange effective treatment. He works up through the indigenous doctor, the 'dresser' from the neighbouring village, a fully qualified doctor, and a specialist—but his father is not saved. So we pass to the second half of the book, which shows how over a short period of years he solved the family's financial problems.

Where Madhaviah kept the reader's interest by means of a swiftly moving narrative, Natesa Sastri holds his interest by successfully building up suspense. The reader's reward for the calamity of the first section is the ultimate success of the hero's efforts in the second. One characteristic feature of Natesa Sastri's novels is his refusal to divide his characters into simply good and bad, with the ultimate benefits going to the perfectly good. Dinadayalu is a worthy hero in his persistent efforts and general kindness, but he occasionally shows sympathy amounting to weakness, makes a number of stupid mistakes, and is sometimes needlessly quick-tempered. His difficult step-mother is not a totally unsympathetic character, nor his step-brother the complete villain. Perhaps such features led to the book having a sufficient success for the author to carry out his promise to produce others. In view of their close succession,[1] one might expect them to be cast in precisely the same mould. In fact, they are unexpectedly varied. The *Mother-in-law in Council* is 'an eighteenth-century Hindu life novel', *The Rejuvenation of Komalam* is described as 'a farcical romance', whilst *The Two Orphans* is a sad, sentimental story which is at the same time not without an element of melodrama.

Just as he had claimed to be writing the first 'novel' in Tamil, so Natesa Sastri claimed to have written the first 'romance'. Certainly *Komalam* was a new type of story in Tamil. It concerns two sisters, former dancing-girls, Komalam (aged sixty) and Tanam (aged fifty-five), who, feeling envious of their younger fellows, spent large sums on a drug to make them young again. Komalam took an overdose, and Tanam returned home to find only a very young baby there. Complications ensued, including the suspicion that Tanam murdered her sister. The situation got more and more confused and would never have been straightened out but for the fact that the effects of the drug eventually wore off.

The last work of prose fiction to be published by Natesa Sastri was an adaptation of an English model, a trend that was soon to become a predominant feature of the Tamil novel. Thus his *Talaiyaṇai mantirōpatēcam*[2] was based on Douglas Jerrold's *Mrs Caudle's Curtain Lectures*. Some years earlier he had published a derivative work as his first attempt at prose fiction. This was a set of five stories telling of cases solved by a South Indian detective.[3] Here, too, he was breaking new

[1] The second edition of *Tīṉatayāḷu* and the first editions of five others came out in the space of two years. *Kōmaḷam kumariyāṉatu*, Madras, 1902; *Tikkaṟṟa iru kuḻantaikaḷ* (The Two Orphans), 1902; *Matikeṭṭa maṉaivi* (A Wife Condoned), 1903; *Śri māmi koluvirukkai* (The Mother-in-law in Council), 1903; *Talaiyaṇai mantirōpateēam*, 1903.

[2] First published 1903. 3rd edn, 1907. English title: *Curtain Lectures*.

[3] *Tāṉavaṉ eṉṟa pōlīsnipuṇaṉ kaṇṭupiṭitta atputa kuṟṟaṅkaḷ*, Madras, 1894. 2nd edn, 1914.

ground, for his Tāṉavaṉ (after the English Donovan) was the first fictional Tamil detective.

Other new tendencies in the early-twentieth-century Tamil novel were foreshadowed in the works of T. M. Ponnusami Pillai, an approximate contemporary of Natesa Sastri. Like Vedanayakam Pillai and Madhaviah he was not a full-time writer, for he did not retire from his post of Treasurer in the Paper Currency Office, Rangoon, until after the publication of his second novel.

All Ponnusami Pillai's novels are of a similar pattern.[1] Their most original feature is their form: the chapters are a succession of dialogues, with relatively brief narrative introductions to set the scene, and the dialogues are set out as in a play.[2] This is perhaps rather surprising in that there are no dramatic works—extant at least—in earlier Tamil literature. Such preliminary descriptions as occur in Ponnusami's novels tend to be somewhat stereotyped. The heroine of the first one, *Kamalatchi*, is described as

'. . . a worthy girl of seventeen or eighteen, with a lemon-like complexion, a flat face, large eyes, thick, black, wavy hair, broad forehead, long nose, small mouth, small, red lips, slightly full cheeks, a not too prominent jaw, a row of white pearl-like teeth, full breasts, small waist, and a slender body.'[3]

The hero, Vijayarangam, is

'. . . an admirable young man of twenty or twenty-one, about five feet six inches tall, with a complexion the colour of sandal wood, flat face, broad forehead, thick eyebrows, long nose, an even row of pearl-like teeth, a mouth with a ready smile, the beginnings of a moustache, broad shoulders, thick chest, and long hands.'[4]

[1] There are at least six: *Kamalākṣi*, Madras, 1903; *Vijayacuntaram*, Madras, 1910; *Ñāṉacampantam*, 1913; *Ñānāmpikai*, 1913; *Ñānappirakācam*, 1920; *Civañāṉam*, 1920.

[2] Rajam Aiyar, Madhaviah and Natesa Sastri had all made occasional use of this way of presenting dialogue, in order to surmount the difficulty caused by the fact that the normal position of a verb of saying in Tamil is *after* what is said; but they use it sparingly.

[3] *Kamalākṣi*, 2nd edn, Madras, 1910, p. 7.

[4] *Ibid.*, p. 11.

Ponnusami Pillai's plots are complicated in the extreme:[1] there are disguises, mistaken identities, melodramatic incidents in quick succession. Characters are either virtuous or vile.

Kamalatchi opens with a scene on the edge of a forest 'ten o'clock at night on the tenth day of the Tamil month of Tai in the English year 1830'. A young man and woman are talking together. Meanwhile two men have come into the forest to kill and bury a baby. It goes without saying that their plans are foiled by the young man. So, after a jump of twenty years to the next chapter, the story goes on.

Plainly we are here well outside the South Indian family life portrayed in a number of the other Tamil novels mentioned above. Thieves, crooks, prostitutes all play their part in the tangled web of the story. At the same time the book is not without its serious purpose. In the course of his work Ponnusami Pillai had close dealings with the Nāṭṭu Kōṭṭai Cheṭṭis, a trading and money-lending class in the Ramnad district, and each of his novels gives a detailed picture of their customs with some criticism of their practices. He also developed a deep interest in Śaiva Siddhānta philosophy, and the nineteenth chapter of every novel is devoted to some aspect of this.

The introduction to *Vijayasundaram* gives a definition of the purpose of the novel which Ponnusami Pillai plainly tried to follow:

'The modern novel converts abstract ideas into living models; it gives ideas, it strengthens faith, it preaches a higher morality than is seen in the actual world; it commands the emotions of pity, admiration and terror; it creates and keeps alive the sense of sympathy; it is the universal teacher; it is the only book which the great mass of reading mankind ever do read; it is the only way in which people can learn what other men and women are like; it redeems their lives from dullness, puts thoughts, desires, knowledge and even ambitions into their hearts; it teaches them to talk and enriches their speech with epigrams, anecdotes and illustrations. It is an unfailing delight to millions, happily not too critical.'

Parts of this are reminiscent of the Preface to Vedanayakam

[1] By way of exception the plot of *Ñānāmpikai* is relatively simple.

Pillai's *Prathapa Mudaliar*. He too, it will be remembered, presented an ideal of virtue not normally found among men; and he too considered it appropriate to intersperse his narrative 'with many amusing anecdotes and interesting stories'. In spite of this the differences between the first Tamil novel and the works of Ponnusami Pillai are greater than the similarities. With Ponnusami we are much closer to the world of G. W. M. Reynolds, a Victorian novelist who was widely esteemed in India even after being forgotten in England.[1] His name is coupled by Tamil writers with the greatest of his contempories, though in fairness to A. Madhaviah at least, it should be noted that his Thillai Govindan says, 'When Reynolds was discarded, Scott, Thackeray, Dickens and George Eliot took his place'.[2] It is with the increasing influence of Reynolds that a deterioration in the quality of the Tamil novel sets in. Many early-twentieth-century novels are acknowledged adaptations of Reynolds' works, and even those that are not tend to be characterized by the same preponderance of melodrama and sensationalism. It is not for almost a generation that another really competent novelist arrives on the scene in 'Kalki',[3] famous for his sense of comedy and his historical novels recreating the Tamil past. Novels on historical themes were written as early as 1901, but none of these are remembered.

The reasons for the falling off in the quality of the Tamil novel after its early flowering are not easy to assess. Perhaps it was largely because, by the time Ponnusami Pillai came on to the scene, the majority of readers were in fact 'none too critical'.[4] A further contributory factor may well have been the failure of novelists to take their task particularly seriously.

[1] Most of the novels of Reynolds (1814–79), a prolific writer, were first published in the 1840s and 1850s. A number of translations into Tamil have appeared over the last seventy years, including one adaptation by N. Nācciyappan in 1959. A translation of *Leila* into Malayalam by C. Mādhavan Piḷḷa was published in 1960. It is not easy for the modern English reader to understand why anyone should still want to read his works in any language. Reynolds was no less popular in Northern India. See, for instance, the papers by Ian Raeside and R. S. McGregor in this volume, pp. 91 and 158.

[2] *Thillai Govindan*, p. 16.

[3] R. Kriṣṇamūrtti (1899–1954).

[4] For a discussion of the reasons for a similar 'fallow period' in the history of the English novel, see Walter Allen, *The English Novel*, Penguin Books, 1958, pp. 80–1. Cf. also Ian Watt, *The Rise of the Novel*, Penguin Books, 1963, p. 302.

Natesa Sastri published his novels under the general title *Pandit Natesa Sastri's Popular Novels*; Madhaviah's were *Light Literature for Tamil Homes*. As these titles imply, the authors were not aiming at the aesthetic sense of the reader, but wished above all to entertain him. It is only in very recent years that there has been an attempt to treat the novel seriously as an art form, a tendency exemplified by the novelist and critic K. N. Subramanyam.[1] For many others the novel only barely qualifies to be considered as literature, if at all. The failure to aim so high did not prevent the production of competent and interesting novels up to the turn of the century, for until then all Tamil novelists were in some sense pioneers, and hence likely to show originality and vitality. Once they had prepared the way and created a market for works of prose fiction, the gates were open for imitators. The Tamil Renaissance may have started quite well with the early novels, but there was to be a considerable period of stagnation before others showed signs of consolidating their work.[2]

[1] See his article 'The Tamil Novel: Symptoms of a Stalemate', *Quest*, Bombay, Vol. III, No. 1 (August–September 1957), pp. 33–7. Since the first draft of the present paper was written, K. N. Subramanyam has also published a short study of 'The First Three Novels in the Tamil Language' (*Prathapa Mudaliar*, *Kamalambal* and *Padmavati charitram*). See *Quest*, 30 (Summer 1961), pp. 29–32.

[2] Some of the tendencies in the writing of those successfully continuing this work of consolidation since Indian independence are discussed in an account of the novels of Professor M. Varadarajan, justifiably admired both as a scholar and a writer. See Xavier S. Thani Nayagam, 'The Novelist of the City of Madras', *Tamil Culture*, Madras, Vol. X, No. 2 (April–June 1963), pp. 1–18.

THREE NOVELISTS OF KERALA

by R. E. ASHER

If a literature is little known to outsiders, the reason is commonly that none of the works on which its claim to fame would be based is readily available in translation.[1] It can also be the case that it does not deserve to be known, because it contains nothing that is worthy of translation. This is emphatically not true of the literature of Kerala, and the motivation for the production of this paper is the conviction that the contemporary literature of Malayalam can stand comparison with that of any other living language. These remarks do not imply a wish to enter into the controversy as to which is the outstanding literature of modern India. It is a commonplace that speakers of almost any important language of India will often claim that their language has the greatest literature in India outside of Sanskrit—a claim that is commonly made without direct knowledge of what is being published in any of the other languages. It is not the purpose of this paper to dispute the claims of Bengalis, Tamilians, or the speakers of Urdu, Hindi or Marathi, but merely to claim that no account of what is most interesting in modern Indian literature can ignore Kerala.

Observers from outside frequently speak of Kerala as 'the problem state of India'. If this is at all justified, it is largely because Kerala is so conspicuously alive. One soon gets the impression when staying in this beautiful region of southern India, that controversy is as important to a Malayali as food, whether it be controversy about religion, about politics, or

[1] This study owes much to the friendliness and encouragement of most of the writers mentioned when I have been privileged to meet them in Kerala. My interest in their writings was first kindled by Dr J. Minattur in London and Mr C. K. Nalina Babu in Ernakulam. I am indebted to all of these. The present paper is a revised version of a talk I gave at the Michigan State University on June 24, 1968. I am grateful to Miss Achamma Coilparampil for valuable comments at all stages of its preparation, to Mrs Bonnie R. Crown for help towards having it included in this volume, and to Mr Vaikom Muhammad Basheer, Mr Thakazhi Sivasankara Pillai (the two contemporary novelists among the three referred to in the title) and Dr K. M. George, who were kind enough to read through and comment on the paper before it went to press.

about literature. No book, however great, can possibly be universally acclaimed there unless the author is well and truly dead. Vigorous criticism may on some occasions be based on prejudice, envy or even spite, but most often will be the result of an attempt to judge the work in the light of well-thought-out notions as to what makes good literature and what a writer should aim to do.

There can be no simple explanation of the causes of this liveliness in the literary scene. The very varied nature of the population of Kerala—the fact that it is an amalgam of so many different groups—may have something to do with it. The level of literacy is clearly an important element also. For the percentage of literacy has within living memory, and probably much longer, been substantially higher in Kerala than in any other part of the sub-continent. In this context it should be remembered, however, that though the proportion of potential readers among the population of Kerala is high, the possible readership for a book in Malayalam remains relatively low by world standards. When, some three or four years ago, three novels in Malayalam each sold more than a thousand copies within a period of six months, they were making history for serious works of literature.[1] It is an unusually successful writer who makes a good living out of writing alone.

The literature of Malayalam has, like that of all the languages recognized by the Indian Constitution, a very honourable past. The traditions are there on which to build and from which inspiration can be drawn. At the same time it does not have to carry the burden of a classical literature of such supreme excellence as that of Tamil. If it is to stake a claim to be one of the great literatures of the world, a claim that could with justice be made by Tamil even if nothing had been written in it for the last thousand years, it is bound to be forward-looking. However impressive the achievements of Malayalam poets of three or four centuries ago, what really matters is what is being done in modern times. This is reflected in the fact that a well-balanced survey of the history of Malayalam literature must

[1] See *NBS Bulletin*, National Book Stall, Kottayam, Vol. XIII, No. 2 (August 1965), p. 5. The largest sale (1,115 copies) was for Thakazhi's *Ēṇippa-ṭikaḷ*, discussed below, pp. 224–6.

devote about two-thirds of its length to what has happened during the last century or so.

If the literature of Malayalam is known at all in the west, it is as the language in which Thakazhi Sivasankara Pillai's *Chemmeen* was written.[1] But it is far from being a language having only one writer of note (just as Thakazhi is far from being a man of one book). No attempt will be made here to demonstrate this point by providing impressive lists of names, for two recent books in English give excellent accounts of the history of Malayalam literature.[2] Attention will instead be concentrated almost entirely on the work of three particularly significant novelists, with a few hints about trends and scattered references to other writers.

Though the frequent use of prose as a medium for creative writing goes back less than a century, Malayalam literature does have some prose works of considerably greater antiquity. Thus as far back as the tenth century there was produced a prose version in a somewhat Tamilized Malayalam of Kauṭilya's *Arthaśāstra*. In later centuries, notably in the fifteenth, a number of *purāṇas* were retold in prose. But it was the Jesuit missionaries, following in the wake of Portuguese traders from the early part of the sixteenth century onwards, who encouraged the extensive use of prose for writing in Malayalam. Though the Jesuits were naturally concerned with the propagation of the Christian faith, their work encouraged the production of prose writings in other fields. Equally important from a long term point of view was their setting up of a printing press at a seminary near Cochin in 1563. Two further presses were established in 1580. It is true that only one or two books were

[1] Takaẓi Śivaśaṅkara Piḷḷa (b. 1914). In the text of this article names will be given in the form used by the author when writing in English. A transliteration of the Malayalam spelling will be given in a footnote when a name is first mentioned. *Cemmīn* (*Shrimps*), first published in Kōṭṭayam (National Book Stall) in 1956, appeared in an English translation under the title *Chemmeen* in 1962 (London: Gollancz; New York: Harper).

[2] P. K. Parameswaran Nair, *History of Malayalam Literature*, translated from the Malayalam by E. M. J. Venniyoor, New Delhi (Sahitya Akademi), 1967; K. M. George, *A Survey of Malayalam Literature*, Bombay (Asia Publishing House), 1969. The last third of Dr George's book (pp. 229–336) is made up of translations of contemporary poems and short stories. The work of a number of important novelists is studied in greater detail in Verghese Ittiavira, *Social Novels in Malayalam*, Bangalore (The Christian Institute for the Study of Religion and Society), 1968.

printed in Malayalam (and Tamil) before the end of the sixteenth century and that it was very many years before these presses were used extensively for printing in Indian languages. The fact remains that their existence 'signalled a new epoch in the literary history of Kerala'.[1]

One feature that persists throughout the whole history of Malayalam language and literature is its willingness to borrow and assimilate the best of cultures with which it comes into contact. Earlier phases came under the strong influence of Tamil and Sanskrit. The effects of the coming of English to this part of India were even more extensive. Perhaps with still greater certainty than for other regions of India, it is possible to say that in contemporary Malayalam literature 'all the present forms and movements owe their origin to English literature' (or, to a lesser extent, to other literatures of Europe that became known through English translations). 'The whole range of it—novel, short story, drama, essay, literary criticism, biography, history, travelogue—is conceived after English patterns.' And certain indigenous poetic forms, for it must not be supposed that older traditions have been entirely forgotten, 'have taken their tone from the same source'.[2]

It is merely to state the obvious to say that the most cultivated field in contemporary letters in Malayalam is that of prose fiction. The beginnings of this were well under a century ago, for the first Malayalam novel appeared some considerable time after the earliest ones in Bengali and almost a decade after the first one in Tamil.[3] Most of the earliest ones, which were published in the late eighties, are now largely forgotten. But one that came out in 1889 is still widely read and referred to, and is held by all critics to be the first significant novel in the language. It is Chandu Menon's *Indulekha*.[4]

[1] Parameswaran Nair, *op. cit.*, p. 83, in a chapter on 'Early prose literature' (pp. 79–85). [2] *Ibid.*, p. 122.

[3] See the papers by Clark and Asher in the present volume. The first Malayalam novel to be published would seem to be T. M. Appuneṭuṅṅāṭi's *Kundalata*, which appeared in 1887. See Parameswaran Nair, *op. cit.*, p. 122. This novel is discussed in some detail in M. P. Pōḷ (1904–52), *Nōvalsāhityam*, Kōṭṭayam (National Book Stall), 1963, pp. 164–71 and 269–75. M. P. Paul's study of the novel with special reference to significant works in Malayalam first came out in 1930.

[4] Oyyārattu Cantu Mēnōn (1847–99), *Indulēkhā. Imglīṣ nōval mātiriyil eẓutappeṭṭiṭṭuḷḷa oru katha*, Kōẓikkōṭu (Spectator Press), 1889. An English translation by W. Dumergue, Chandu Menon's superior in the Madras Civil

Indulekha has been said to be based on Benjamin Disraeli's *Henrietta Temple* (1836). But the two have in common not much more than the fact that they are both love stories—and the story of overpowering emotions. In both cases, too, misunderstandings delay but do not prevent a happy ending. Chandu Menon, however, could not be accused of lifting his plot from Disraeli. *Henrietta Temple* is a love story pure and relatively simple: *Indulekha* has a substantial part of social criticism. All the chief characters in Disraeli's book are idealized and highly virtuous, showing a barely human unselfishness that is suspended only when mistakes and misunderstandings provide a justification: Chandu Menon's characters show a wide range of human weaknesses and failings.

Chandu Menon himself has explained clearly the place of *Henrietta Temple* in his own work as a novelist. In the preface to the first edition of *Indulekha* he tells how he only 'began to read English novels extensively after . . . the end of 1886'. He continues:

'I then devoted all the leisure which my official duties left me, to novel reading. Thereupon I found that my circle of intimates with whom I had been accustomed to pass the time in social conversation and amusement considered itself somewhat neglected, and I accordingly endeavoured to find means by which I could conciliate its members without in any degree foregoing my novels. With this object in view, I attempted at first to convey to them in Malayalam the gist of the story contained in some of the novels I had read, but my hearers did not seem particularly interested in the versions which I gave them of two or three of these books. At last it happened that one of these individuals was greatly taken with Lord Beaconsfield's *Henrietta Temple*, and the taste then acquired for listening to novels translated orally, gradually developed into a passion. . . .'

Service, was published by Addison & Co., Madras, in the following year (reprint by Mathrubhumi, Calicut, 1965). All quotations will be given from the 1890 edition of this translation. The translation is preceded by the translator's preface and the author's letter to the translator (pp. ix–xix) in addition to a translation of the author's preface to the Malayalam edition (pp. i–vii). There seems to be no study of Chandu Menon's work in English; but in Malayalam see P. K. Bālakṛiṣṇan, *Cantumēnōn, oru paṭhanam*, Kōṭṭayam (National Book Stall), 1957 and M. P. Paul, *op. cit.*, pp. 180–200.

'Finally, I was urged to produce a written translation of the novel by Beaconsfield . . . , and I consented.'[1]

But he eventually decided against it; for a straightforward translation from English to Malayalam seemed inadequate, yet the necessary commentary would spoil the work as a translation. He therefore decided 'to write a Malayalam novel more or less after the English fashion'.[2] After some delay he got down to the work and completed the whole book in a period of two months.

One important feature of the book stems from his decision to use the language he 'would ordinarily speak at home'.[3] If he brought in Sanskrit words, he attempted to use them in the manner and to the extent in which they were used colloquially by Malayalis. The result is that his language is far less stilted than that of the book that inspired him. His decision had further implications for the future, for all the more outstanding of the novelists who followed him have benefited from the avoidance of pedantry.

In a letter addressed to his friend and translator, W. Dumergue, Chandu Menon made clear that he was motivated not simply by a desire to please the Malayali friend whose interest he had aroused in the art of the novel—nor even by a wish to please his wife, whose 'oft-expressed desire to read in her own language a novel written after the English fashion' he also mentions. There was in addition

'a desire . . . to try whether I should be able to create a taste amongst my Malayalee readers, not conversant with English, for that class of literature represented in the English language by novels, of which at present they (accustomed as they are to read and admire works of fiction in Malayalam abounding in events and incidents foreign to nature and often absurd and impossible) have no idea, and to see whether they could appreciate a story that contains only such facts and incidents as may happen in their own households under a given state of circumstances.'

He also wanted

[1] *Indulekha*, trans. Dumergue, pp. i–ii.
[2] *Ibid.*, pp. ii–iii.
[3] *Ibid.*, p. vi.

'to illustrate to my Malayalee brethren the position, power and influence that our Nair women, who are noted for their natural intelligence and beauty, would attain in society, if they are given a good English education';

and finally

'to contribute my mite towards the improvement of Malayalam literature, which I regret to observe is fast dying out by disuse as well as by abuse.'[1]

The story is set in the southern part of Malabar at the time of its telling. It is concerned with a part of the history of a Nāyar joint family. The chief characters are Panju Menon, a narrow-minded old man of seventy and head of the household, his granddaughter, Indulekha, and his sister's grandson, Madhavan. The book opens with a quarrel between Panju Menon and Madhavan over the education of a nine- or ten-year-old boy, the great-grandson of Panju Menon's grandmother's sister. Madhavan, who has had the benefits of a good education, thinks that this boy too should have them. But the old man does not wish to waste money in this way, particularly as the boy is a somewhat distant relation. The two quarrel and Madhavan speaks in a much more outspoken way than he, in normal circumstances, would be considered to have any right to speak. This so angers Panju Menon that he decides not to let his granddaughter, Indulekha, marry Madhavan, to whom she some time earlier got engaged—an engagement entered into without anyone else being consulted. Panju Menon swears an oath that he will never permit this marriage to take place. Instead, he tries to get Indulekha to make a match with a rich Nambudripad who, says the author, 'represents the rich, licentious, profligate, unsteady Nambudripad so often found in Malabar'.[2] Panju Menon's hope is that this middle-aged man will be able to win Indulekha's heart and, therefore, make her willing to marry him and not have her forced to marry him. But he fails entirely in this attempt and

[1] *Indulekha*, trans. Dumergue, pp. ix–x.
[2] *Ibid.*, p. xvii.

in the end, in order to please the Nambudripad, Panju Menon lets him marry one of his nieces, 'an ignorant, helpless girl'.

After his marriage the Nambudripad, in order to take revenge on Indulekha for not giving in to his advances, spreads a rumour that she has become his concubine. Through a sequence of unhappy coincidences Madhavan is led to believe this, and he is so disturbed that he decides to take a long journey away from Malabar, a journey which takes him up to Bombay and afterwards to Calcutta.

Eventually Madhavan finds out the truth. He returns home to marry Indulekha. The old man, who is not quite as hard and unfeeling as he appeared in the early parts of the book, agrees to it. He yields to circumstances and retracts his oath by a penance prescribed by a number of 'avaricious Brahmin priests for their own good'; that is to say that, in order to be relieved of the need to adhere to his oath, he has to have each letter of the oath made in gold or silver, these letters to be given to the priests.

The story moves at a fairly rapid pace, but there are several digressions from the narrative of events. Some are simply to allow the painting of a portrait of important characters. Thus:

'Madhavan was a young man gifted with great abilities and a remarkably handsome exterior. The fame which he had acquired by an uninterrupted series of triumphs in the schools from the time he began to learn English until he graduated in the arts, clearly and fully proclaimed the rare talents with which he was endowed. He had never failed in an examination, be it what it might. . . . All his tutors firmly declared that none of their pupils ever surpassed Madhaven in mental power and aptitude. With regard to his external appearance, all who knew Madhavan were of the opinion that nature had indeed provided in his form and features a fitting habitation for an intelligence so exceptional. . . . His complexion was like refined gold, and as he had daily attended to his physical development by the use of gymnastic exercises, his appearance, in all the glory of youth, was most attractive and elegant. . . .

'It follows from what has already been recorded that Madhavan had a sound knowledge of English. He was at the same time an adept at lawn tennis, cricket and other athletic games, and had moreover, since the days when he was a boy, been inured to the toils of field sports.'[1]

Indulekha is described after an enumeration of the qualities that make a truly beautiful woman:

'Such a woman as this is indeed beautiful, and among such women, Indulekha was supreme.

'A few words descriptive of Indulekha's complexion will not be thought out of place here. Her skin resembled so closely in colour the golden border of the embroidered robe, which . . . draped her limbs . . . , that it was impossible to distinguish the one from the other by sight. Her hair, black as the raven's wing, was soft, long and luxuriant and, except possibly among the fair ladies of Europe, rich red lips like hers were never seen. Her eyes were long and the colours therein were clearly defined, while only those who had felt the lightning of her glances could know how deeply they burned into the hearts of men.'[2]

So the description of her external appearance, based explicitly on the author's reading of Sanskrit and English poetry, continues. Her 'mental attainments and amiability of character' are equally deserving of admiration.

'Indulekha was . . . . thoroughly grounded in English; her Sanskrit studies included the works of the dramatic authors; and in Music she not only learned the theory of harmony, but also became an efficient performer on the piano, violin and Indian lute. At the same time her uncle did not neglect to have his charming niece instructed in needlework, drawing and other arts in which European girls are trained.[3]

Other digressions are formed by the discussion of the merit of certain social customs and, for example, the desirability of education—for women as much as men.[4] In this context Europe and America are held up as shining examples.

Because of the base designs of the Nambudripad who plays

[1] *Indulekha,* trans. Dumergue, pp. 2–3.
[2] *Ibid.*, pp. 7–8.
[3] *Ibid.*, pp. 8–9.
[4] *Ibid.*, pp. 33–5.

an important part in the narrative, it might be assumed that the book represents a general attack on the Nambudiri brahmins as a class. Aware of this, Chandu Menon digresses to explain, perhaps not entirely convincingly, that this is not so:

'There is . . . no class of men in Malabar for whom I entertain greater respect than I do for the Nambudiris. I am acquainted with several who are distinguished for their intellect and ability, and I am proud to reckon some of them among my intimate friends. But in every caste we see shrewdness and stupidity, wisdom and folly, side by side, and the caste of Nambudiris is no exception to the rule. . . . I am confident that the intelligent and impartial reader will fully and freely absolve me from any intention of maliciously exposing to contempt and derision a section of the community which is so generally regarded with veneration and honour as are the Nambudripads and Nambudiris in Malabar.'[1]

The longest interruption to the action is a chapter written, as the author explains, 'at the request of some of my Malayalee friends'.[2] This chapter of over eighty pages in the first edition is commonly omitted from modern editions as being not strictly relevant to the theme of the book.[3] It is nevertheless of some interest to the social historian. One half of it is devoted to a consideration of atheism as it prevailed among educated Malayalis of the time, and the other half to a discussion of the merits and demerits of the National Congress. The chapter is called 'A conversation'[4]—the participants in which are Madhavan's cousin (anti-Congress and atheist), his father (a devout Hindu) and Madhavan himself (not an atheist, but less bigoted in religious matters than his father). Madhavan, though a moderate supporter of Congress, found various faults in the present constitution and action of the Congress which he would advise the organization to remove. The three argue the relative importance of sovereignty and social reform. If

[1] *Indulekha*, trans. Dumergue, p. 76. [2] *Ibid.*, p. xviii.

[3] First edn, 1889, pp. 385–470. In a 1960 reprint (Kottayam: National Book Stall) it covers pp. 304–66. In the reprint by the same publisher of 1963 it is summarized in five lines (p. 276).

[4] *Indulekha*, trans. Dumergue, pp. 238–85.

sovereignty is desirable, should it be sought by constitutional means or by force of arms? And so on.

Such questions are argued in considerable detail. All this, however, is not an essential part of the book *as a novel*. And it is as the creator of the first real novel in Malayalam that Chandu Menon's worth as a writer should be judged. Though many better novels have been written since, Chandu Menon's first effort was a most auspicious beginning. He invented an interesting plot and created a varied set of characters, none of whom is painted in too extreme colours. He wrote realistic dialogue and showed convincing motivation for the actions of his personages. He succeeded for the most part in his plan to depict events that might happen. Improbabilities are rare, though one is a little surprised to read that Indulekha 'bent over Madhavan with a sob of joy, and as she laid her lovely face on his, their lips met in a kiss of fervent rapture'.[1] On a later occasion, we read, 'Madhavan impetuously caught her in his arms and pressed her to his breast in a close embrace'.[2] The setting, after all, is middle-class Malabar of the late nineteenth century. An incident in Calcutta, when 'Madhavan drew his revolver from his pocket' and shot an escaped panther dead, is not entirely convincing.[3] Such cases are, nevertheless, uncommon. Similarly, coincidence is not normally strained too far. One exception is an evening in Bombay when Babu Kesab Chandra Sen, a Bengali whom Madhavan got to know in Calcutta, saw Madhavan's cousin, Govinda Kutti Menon, near the esplanade, 'and recognizing in his face a likeness to Madhavan, went up and spoke to him'.[4]

Chandu Menon himself had some doubts as to whether the reader would accept the whole of his novel as realistic. In particular he noted that, 'Some of my readers may object that it would be impossible to find a young Nair lady of Indulekha's intellectual attainments in Malabar'. But the objection would not be justified:

'I myself know two or three respectable Nair ladies . . ., who in intellectual culture . . ., strength of character and general knowledge, can well hold comparison with Indulekha. As for

[1] *Indulekha*, trans. Dumergue, p. 38.
[2] *Ibid.*, p. 46.
[3] *Ibid.*, p. 214.
[4] *Ibid.*, p. 233.

beauty, personal charms, refined manners, simplicity of taste, conversational powers, wit and humour, I can show hundreds of young ladies in respectable Nair Tarwads who would undoubtedly come up to the standard of my Indulekha.'

Only her knowledge of English is remarkable, and this was introduced because one of the author's purposes in writing the book was

'. . . to illustrate how a young Malayalee woman, possessing, in addition to her natural personal charms and intellectual culture, a knowledge of the English language would conduct herself in matters of supreme interest to her, such as the choosing of a partner in life.'[1]

Chandu Menon gave similar justification for his account of the love and courtship of the book's hero and heroine, claiming that 'there is . . . nothing in the conversation or manners of the lovers which can be construed as strange in a pair of the educated class of Nairs'. As for their making their own decision about whom to marry, he states:

'Twenty years hence there may be found hundreds of Indulekhas in Malabar who would be able to choose their own husbands for pure and sweet love. My narrative of the love and courtship of Madhavan is intended to show to the young ladies of Malabar how happy they can be if they have the freedom to choose their partners.'[2]

Once again the point is underlined that Chandu Menon wished his novel to 'instruct' as well as to 'amuse'.

Like so many of the earlier novelists in south India, Chandu Menon was not a young man when he first tried his hand at writing prose fiction. Moreover, his career as a writer was further cut short by his relatively early death. He did, however, attempt one more novel, *Śārada*,[3] which was never completed. The fragment of this ambitious project that was published is enough to show that the author's early effort had given him a real mastery of the novelist's craft.

[1] *Indulekha*, trans. Dumergue p. xiii. [2] *Ibid.*, pp. xiv–xv.
[3] First published 1892 and dedicated to W. F. Dumergue.

Where *Indulekha* gave a picture of the section of Malabar society to which Chandu Menon belonged, *Śārada* reflected his life as a member of government services. He had begun his career as a clerk in a collector's office. Later he became a district munsiff and eventually a sub-judge. The action of the part of the book that was printed leads up to the start of a big law-suit and the author's intimate knowledge of the background is very apparent in his realistic portraits of the people involved in a piece of litigation.

Though he lived some years after the publication of this fragment, Chandu Menon seems not to have found the time to continue the story. The tantalizing nature of the unfinished portion, however, has led more than one of his admirers to attempt, *Edwin Drood*-like, to complete it.[1]

At the time of the publication of *Indulekha* C. V. Raman Pillai was working on the first of his historical novels.[2] Worthy of mention though they are, I shall pass them rapidly by, as also the historical novels of Sardar K. M. Panikkar.[3] The latter is known outside India solely as a historian and an international statesman. He did, however, make substantial contributions to Malayalam literature in the fields of fiction, poetry, drama, criticism and autobiography.

The next really important stage in the history of prose fiction was made by a large group of writers all born during the second decade of this century. One or two of them, such as Vettoor Raman Nair and Ponkunnam Varkey,[4] have made their names mainly as distinguished short story writers. There are representatives from all communities—perhaps one of the reasons why modern Malayalam literature is so varied. Thus Ponkunnam and the prolific Muttathu Varkey are Christians; Basheer, clearly, is a Moslem; and so on.[5]

[1] E.g. Payyampeḷḷil P. Gōpāla Piḷḷa, *Śārada. Putiya raṇṭām bhāgam*, Kollam [i.e. Quilon] (S. T. Reḍyār & Sons), 5th impression, 1957.

[2] C. V. Rāman Piḷḷa (1858–1922). His first novel, *Mārttāṇḍavarmma*, probably completed by 1888, came out in 1891.

[3] K. M. Paṇikkar (1895–1963).

[4] Veṭṭūr Rāman Nāyar (b. 1919); Ponkunnam Varkki (b. 1910). On the latter, see K. M. George, 'Ponkunnam Varkey', *Indian Literature*, Vol. IX, No. 3 (July–September 1966), pp. 73–6. This is followed by Dr George's translation of one of Ponkunnam Varkey's stories, 'Veeran' (pp. 77–85).

[5] Muṭṭattu Varkki (b. 1915); Vaikkam Muhammad Baṣīr (b. 1910). On Basheer, see below, pp. 226–34.

Most of the outstanding members of this fraternity of writers were founder members of the Progressive Writers' Association. This means that social criticism forms an essential part of perhaps the greater bulk of modern novels. It means, too, that most of them also have a humbler setting than the middle class background of *Indulekha* and *Śārada*. A typical example is Kesava Dev's *From the gutter*, the hero of which is a rickshaw-puller.[1]

It goes without saying that the political sympathies tend towards the extreme left. Thus S. K. Pottekkatt was for some years a Communist M.P.[2] He now seems to have decided, however, that his true vocation is as a writer.

Closely associated with Kesava Dev in their early days—and arguably the most distinguished of the 'Progressive' group—was Thakazhi Sivasankara Pillai. Thakazhi was born, and still lives, in the small village of Thakazhi, a few miles south of Alleppey. While still at school he started writing verse. But he was persuaded by the scholar and critic, Kainikkara Kumara Pillai,[3] that his real talent lay in prose; and the six hundred or more stories and score of novels he has written since then have amply borne this out.[4]

Not only does Thakazhi not write verse now; like his friend, the critic Joseph Mundassery,[5] he sees little place for the poet in the contemporary literary scene. One cannot be in their company long before the conversation turns to the subject of literature, and soon after that Professor Mundassery may well be heard lashing out at the many 'scribblers' who disfigure the literary scene. In these contexts 'scribbler' seems almost to be a synonym of 'poet'. What, one might ask, is the objection to poetry? The argument is very straightforward. Literature must be concerned with life and its problems. These problems can only be effectively discussed in prose. Hence versified literature is destined to die out. It goes without saying that in his critical writings Mundassery discusses questions of literary theory with much greater subtlety than is implied by such a bald summary

[1] P. Kēśava Dēv (b. 1905), *Ōṭayilninnu*, Kōṭṭayam (National Book Stall), 1942.

[2] S. K. Poṟṟekkāṭṭ (b. 1913).

[3] Kaiñikkara M. Kumāra Piḷḷa (b. 1900).

[4] There is a translation of one of Thakazhi's stories, 'Father and Son', in *Tales from Modern India*, ed. K. Natwar-Singh, New York (The Macmillan Company), 1966, pp. 199–220.

[5] Jōsaph Muṇṭaśśēri (b. 1904).

of a conversational exchange. He is, moreover, not only a critic, but also a creative writer and has published a number of novels. He was a college professor before becoming Minister for Education in the state government and his first novel, *Professor*, was concerned with the problems faced by teachers in the private colleges of Kerala.[1]

Generations of literature students have been asked to pass judgement on such pairs of quotations as Chateaubriand's 'On ne vit que par le style' and Zola's 'La forme est ce qui passe le plus vite'. There is no doubt where Thakazhi stands in any such discussion: what matters is what a writer has to say. But, as he explained in 1964 when I first met him, this view is not accepted by all writers in Kerala. One contemporary group has gone back to stressing form as against content. So such writers as Thakazhi are once again being forced to fight the old battles. For him, Zola remains an excellent model of what a novelist should aim to do.

This does not mean that social propaganda is a prominent feature of all Thakazhi's work, which is extremely varied in its choice of theme. He has drawn his characters from among fishermen, agricultural labourers, untouchable municipal workers, administrators. His *Children of Joseph*,[2] as the title suggests, deals with the Christian community of Kerala.

One of his earliest novels (and one of his favourites, though to my mind a good way short of his best) is *Realities*,[3] which contains no social comment at all, but is an attempt at a profound psychological study. It tells of Patmanābha Pillai, who offered to marry a pregnant girl, convinced he was making a very clever move. For he would not need to question whether he was marrying a virgin. Jānaki Amma's condition saved him from that sort of doubt. He did, however, charge a high price for his willingness to marry her. The child was not to form any part of his life. So this boy, Prabha, grew up fatherless and prohibited from calling Gōpan, the child of the marriage, 'brother'. Prabha, when a man (and after a love affair as a result of which he has made a girl, Vijayamma, pregnant), learns

[1] *Prophasar*, Trichur (Mangalodayam), 1948. This novel is briefly discussed by Thakazhi Sivasankara Pillai in 'The Professor', *Indian Literature*, Vol. X, No. 2 (April–June 1967), pp. 66–8.

[2] *Ausēppinṟe makkaḷ*, Trichur (Current Books), 1959.

[3] *Paramārtthaṅṅaḷ*, Trichur (Mangalodayam), 1945.

that his birth was the result of the raping of his mother by a gypsy. Clearly this is a story unrelieved by cheerfulness, and with no chance of a happy ending. Indeed, on her death-bed, Jānaki Amma punished her husband by leaving him in doubt as to whether he was Gōpan's father. The plot is one that allows an easy descent into the novelettish—a trap that Thakazhi only just avoids.

Scavenger's Son of two years later is much more assured.[1] Here the attack on the structure of society is explicit. It is the story of three generations of night-soil carriers in Alleppey town and their dismal, intolerable existence. The story opens with old Ishukkumuttu on his death-bed. On his death his son Chudalamuttu took over his job. No one knew Ishukkumuttu's real age, but he had clearly lived longer than was usual for a scavenger. For hard work and disease normally carried off much earlier those whose birth destined them to earn their living in this way.

Chudalamuttu, a proud young man, decided that he would not die a scavenger and that any son he had would have a better life than had been his own unhappy lot. So he and his wife, Valli, keep themselves and their house neat and clean. He saves money, partly by resisting the scavenger's temptation to forget life's troubles by spending all he had at the toddy shop, but more by lending money to his workmates at somewhat high rates of interest. For it is his ambition to have a plot of land and a house of his own. Such a goal involves his being a traitor to his class; not only because it by its nature sets him apart from the rest of the scavengers, but also because it can be achieved only with the help of his superiors—such as the overseer of the town's scavengers and sweepers and the chairman of the town council. It is to the latter that he entrusts, unwisely, his savings, until the accumulated amount shall be enough for his house.

Earlier he had agreed to help his friends to form a union. But when he realized this would upset his plans as an individual, he drew back from the venture. Later he was to be used by the authorities to break up another union in the process of being formed.

When Valli bears him a son, nothing is too good for the child. As a symbol of their hopes and aspirations they give him

[1] *Tōṭṭiyuṭe makan*, Trichur (Mangalodayam), 1947.

a name that no scavenger had ever had (Mohanan)—and more than that, a pet name (Baby). They are determined he shall learn to read and write, but social prejudice makes it difficult to get him admitted to school. Eventually admitted through the payment of a bribe, he is the brightest and cleanest boy in the class. This does not prevent him from being ostracized; in fact envy means that he is treated even worse than he might otherwise have been. His parents despair of making a good life for him, though a faint note of optimism is introduced when Chudalamuttu gets a job other than that of scavenger, as watchman at a burial ground.

A few years earlier a smallpox epidemic had killed off many of the town's scavengers. Now there is an outbreak of cholera, in which Chudalamuttu and Valli die. The orphaned Mohanan thus inevitably becomes a scavenger. He is not, however, a submissive and long-suffering one like his grandfather. The end of the book shows him leading a demonstration at the time of a general strike. While carrying a banner at the head of a procession, he is one of those killed by the bullets of an army detachment brought into town to maintain order.

The message of the book is clear. Two methods are used to get it across, the direct and the indirect. The direct approach consists of the author addressing the reader in various ways. Thus, after a description of Chudalamuttu as an untypical scavenger, we read:

'If we look at him closely once again, we shall observe that in the depths of his eyes the cowardly and humble expression of a scavenger is not to be seen. He is a determined sort of person. He will not unnecessarily bow his head.

'You will not care for a scavenger like that. You definitely will not like a scavenger who takes a bath every day, a scavenger who shaves, a scavenger who wears dhoti or shorts that he has either washed or had laundered. . . . Your scavenger must be a drunkard; there must be no sort of system or order in his life. He must always be in some sort of trouble.'[1]

Similarly, in the account of the mass popular demonstrations come such passages as the following:

[1] *Tōṭṭiyuṭe makan*, 6th impression, 1963, pp. 38–9.

'The poor worker who lives starving and deprived in the low huts that are to be seen around us—him we do not fear. What is there he can do to us? Are we afraid of the beggar who comes, supported on a crude stick, and stands at our door calling for alms? Till today has the low-caste worker who toils in the fields beneath the rain and the hot sun ever stood up against anybody? . . . But today we are afraid, not of those individuals, but of the sum total of their emotions.'[1]

And in the early part of the book, when the proposed municipal labourers' union has been taken over by municipal officials and so its effect neutralized, Thakazhi intervenes directly in the narrative to address the reader in these terms:

'See how nowadays religion, with its consoling message of life after death, makes its approach with so much more enthusiasm and sincerity than in former days; are not even the powers-that-be willing to make concessions? Do not big millionaires donate huge sums to charitable institutions? Thinkers are trying to revise their philosophies! Some people go so far as to say there is communism in the Bible. What lies behind all this? It is because the reverberating of the dissatisfaction lying in the depths of the hearts of millions of people in the world can be heard! It is greater than the roar of the mighty ocean!'[2]

The passages from which these extracts are taken, however, make pretty well the sum total of the real direct intervention within the narrative, and there is not quite as much preaching as a simple reading of these two or three excerpts might suggest.

The basic theme of the book is the hopeless lot of these low-class workers until they really got together and took firm and vigorous steps to look after their own interests. The social ostracism they must endure is shown throughout the book. No one will walk by a scavenger without holding his nose; no one will live near one; no one wishes his child to attend school along with a scavenger's son, if this can possibly be avoided. Then they are cheated by their superiors, and do not even know how much they are really supposed to get as wages.

[1] *Tōṭṭiyuṭe makan*, 6th impression, 1963, p. 223.   [2] *Ibid.*, p. 64.

Even clearer is the constantly recurring theme that these people, too, are *men*—the reminders that members of this community, too, in spite of the numbing effect of their job, are human beings capable of experiencing human emotions. One effect of this is that the book is punctuated with scenes meant to show the love of father for son, husband for wife, children for parents.

Because of all these features, there is never a moment's doubt where the author's sympathies lie. Yet there is a complete avoidance of what might seem an almost inevitable tendency—to contrast an entirely noble labourer with an entirely evil superior. Scavengers are shown as being on occasion not only loyal and loving, but feckless, ignorant, superstitious, cringing, treacherous and quarrelsome. This is, of course, not merely an attempt to imitate nineteenth-century French realism, but also a way of stressing that not people but the system is essentially at fault. *Scavenger's Son* insists on both the existence of and the need for class warfare (though not failing to note that some participants are motivated as much by a desire for personal revenge as by any principle of class solidarity).

Two Measures of Rice, published a year later, is in a sense another battle in the same war.[1] It, too, is concerned with the struggles and humiliations of a community of outcastes. This time they are the workers in the rice fields of Kuttanād. Like *Scavenger's Son,* this book gives an essentially accurate picture of the harsh conditions under which the members of the lower strata of Kerala society worked. But the characterization is perhaps somewhat more biased. In the barest of outlines the story tells of Kōran, a good and submissive worker, who killed his master, Pushpavēli Chacko, when he tried to rape Kōran's wife Ciruta. Jailed, Kōran asks a friend, Cāttan, to look after his wife. Cāttan does this, and hands back Ciruta—unspoiled, as the saying is—when her husband is free again. The book ends with the shouting of the slogans, 'Long live the revolution. Long live the union. Agricultural land for the agricultural labourers!'

Two Measures might be described as left-wingery and realism tempered by a sort of romanticism. Thakazhi's best-

[1] *Raṇṭiṭaṅṅaḻi,* Trichur (Mangalodayam), 1948.

known and most successful novel, *Chemmeen*, published in English translation some eight years ago, entirely lacks social criticism and leftist propaganda.[1] The *cemmīn* are the shrimps that form part of the catch of the fishermen who scrape a hazardous living off the coast of Kerala south of Alleppey; that is to say, very near to Thakazhi's home. As in all of his writing, Thakazhi here shows his supreme powers of observation—in his portrayal of character, events, conditions of work, and also in representing on paper the dialect of the fisherfolk. *Chemmeen* is further typical of Thakazhi in being concerned with the economically ill-favoured members of Kerala society. But it is entirely untypical in the absence of any attack, either overt or covert, on society.

Like so many of Thakazhi's stories, it is clearly destined from the start to have a tragic conclusion. A love affair between a Hindu fisherman's daughter and a young Moslem fish-merchant is not a promising start to a comedy, particularly when one is reminded of the powerfully held belief of the fishing community that the improper behaviour of a woman will anger the goddess of the sea, Kadalamma, and so endanger the lives of all the men who fish from the shore on which she lives. There is similarly no room on the sea-shore for any sort of non-conformist: traditions must be respected. And the failure of Chemban Kunju, the father of the heroine, Karuthamma, to respect them is another pointer to the book's inevitable conclusion. One's hopes are raised by Karuthamma's determination to be a good wife to the man her father chose for her. But the tragedy can only be delayed; and, in spite of the economical use of words, and the short, bare sentences that are Thakazhi's normal style, it is tragedy on a grand scale.

It is, nevertheless, by no means a long novel. Thakazhi's latest novel, by way of contrast, was conceived on a large scale. *Steps of the Ladder* is in the nature of a social history of Kerala during Thakazhi's life-time.[2] It gives us a cross-section rather than one particular segment of society. It shows the transition from imperial rule to independent government and traces the history of this up to the late fifties.

[1] *Cemmīn*. See above, p. 207, n. 1.

[2] *Ēṇippaṭikaḷ*, Kōṭṭayam (National Book Stall), 1966. First published serially in the *Mātṛbhūmi* weekly, Calicut, 1964–65.

The central figure is Kesava Pillai, a government officer, and we see how he manipulates events, not only to make his way up the ladder but also to stay in his job regardless of what government is in power in Kerala. After graduation he obtained the post of clerk in the office of the Chief Secretary of the government of the State of Travancore. From that time on he steadily climbed up the ladder to become a member of the Chief Secretary's personal staff. In this position he greatly impressed his superiors by the efficient way in which he handled the political situation in the period preceding the attainment of independence by India and by the manner in which he ruthlessly suppressed the National Congress Party, while supporting the move for an independent Travancore. Once India became independent, however, and the National Congress assumed power, Kesava Pillai changed his tactics and even started wearing the homespun *khadi* cloth that had become the symbol of the struggle for an independent and united India. When the Communist party took over the government of Kerala, he was ready to remain in office; but after the party had been in power for a short while he was persuaded to resign.

Steps of the Ladder paints a picture of the realities of politics that is both frank and pessimistic. Nothing is hidden, be it corruption or lack of scruple. We see the brushing aside after independence of those who really suffered in the fight for freedom. We are shown the disillusionment of those who come to think that whether the government is in the hands of the British, the Congress or the Communists, it is still not *their* government. They have no impression of real participation, no feeling that their grievances will be heard or their problems attended to.

This 'historical' part is but one aspect of a well-integrated story that is concerned equally with the private life of Kesava Pillai. As a young man he formed an emotional attachment to Thankamma, a woman clerk in the Chief Secretary's office, who, indeed, was instrumental in his obtaining his first appointment. He nevertheless allowed his family to marry him off to Karthyayani Amma, an illiterate girl from his village. The fact that Karthyayani Amma proves a good wife is insufficient to enable Kesava Pillai to resist the fascination of Thankamma, who becomes his mistress and bears him a child. The complications of this three-cornered relationship are subtly portrayed. It gives, moreover, room for an implicit discussion of the most appropriate basis for marriage, a question that comes up in another form when the daughter of Kesava Pillai and Karthyayani Amma reaches a marriageable age.

Thakazhi used to be thought of by some critics as essentially a short story writer. *Steps of the Ladder* displays his mastery of the technique of a complex novel. Thakazhi's way of writing, regardless of the size of the project, is often to develop a story in his mind, possibly even for years, before committing anything to paper. Such was the case with *Steps of the Ladder*. Sometimes the writing itself may be done in an almost incredibly short time, and we are told that *Chemmeen*, for instance, was written in a mere three weeks.[1] While a book is taking shape in the author's mind, it is seen by him as destined to be his greatest work. This was the case with *Steps of the Ladder* and is now the case with another projected novel. Faced with a mind so inventive as Thakazhi's, one looks forward to the succession of novels yet to come from his pen.

Vaikom Muhammad Basheer, the third and last novelist to be discussed in this essay, is a very different kind of writer. When, on the occasion of a recent visit I paid to his home, he introduced me to M. T. Vasudevan Nair,[2] one of the best among the younger generation of novelists, he warned me that he (Vasudevan Nair) had already written a good number of books, most of them very long. Mr Basheer then pointed out that one could buy almost everything he himself had ever written for little more than twenty rupees. It is impossible to imagine a more rewarding return for the expenditure of such an insignificant amount.

Many writers have claimed that their works are in some way a confession, even where the fictitious nature of events and persons in their writing prevents this from being apparent. When other novelists and critics mention that Basheer writes mainly about himself, it is sometimes not without a hint of disapproval. But they will hasten to add that he has their

[1] See Narayana Menon, 'Thakazhi Sivasankara Pillai', *Indian Literature*, Vol. V, No. 2 (1962), pp. 14–20. Narayana Menon makes the same point in his postscript to his translation of *Chemmeen* (London, 1962, p. 227).

[2] M. T. Vāsudēvan Nāyar (b. 1934).

unqualified admiration as an artist. Thakazhi, for example, does not hesitate to admit that Basheer is his superior in this respect, though he has a very different idea of the correct use of the novelist's art.

Basheer, who is almost as brilliant an oral story-teller as he is a writer, has the enviable gift of being able to see a story in the most ordinary everyday event. Thus he once spent a birthday in a poor sort of lodging with no money even to buy a cup of tea; and this gave birth to one of his best-known stories,[1] which consists of a narrative of the whole day's events, including his realization that if he wrote the day's diary from beginning to end, there were 'possibilities in it for a fairly good short story'.[2] His latest story, which has only quite recently finished being serialized in a Quilon weekly magazine, is about a 'magic cat'.[3] After getting this cat for his small daughter, he noticed that a number of remarkable things happened: such things as a shrub that had never blossomed bursting into flower. It is a very ordinary-looking cat until one hears about its strange powers. Then it takes on a rather special appearance, and many people in the area near its home stop by to see this wonderful animal. In the words of the author, *The Magic Cat* is concerned with 'the "divinity" of Indian life. The only surplus thing that India can boast of is our Gods and their divinity! New prophets and new incarnations appear all of a sudden in every nook and corner. And they vanish in the same way.'[4] Some admirers even wanted to make a 'god' out of Basheer. But any idea that he could work miracles was quashed by the failure of his attempt to turn the sand in his courtyard to gold! Nevertheless, some neighbours saw a sign of his 'divinity' when the kitten, which had been given a female name when it was brought to his house, turned out to be a male cat. . . . There is clearly material here for a little gentle satire.

Sometimes the events of some years ago are worked into a story, as in the case of the one with the rather startling title,

[1] *Janmadinam* in the book of the same name, Trichur (Mangalodayam), 1944, pp. 1–25.

[2] *Ibid.*, p. 3.

[3] *Māntrikappūcca*. Serialized in *Kunkumam*, Quilon, 1967–68. Published 1968 in book form by Mangalodayam, Trichur.

[4] Personal communication.

A Bhagavadgita and some Breasts.[1] The connection between the two parts of the title is not immediately obvious. The second part is related to the tradition that, when Nayar girls went to Nambudiri houses, they did not cover the upper part of their bodies. The relationship between this and the Bhagavadgita is, curiously enough, an elephant that ran amok. This took place at the house of a Nambudripad who was manager of a Trichur book publishing company and who had most writers of the day under contract. Basheer, one of these, used to get a copy of every book the company published. Yet, on the grounds that he was not a Hindu, he did not receive a copy of their edition of the *Gītā*. As it was priced at seven and a half rupees he coveted it, and on a visit to the Nambudripad's house he proposed to ask for one. This was the occasion when the elephant happened to go mad. It was decided to build a wall of fire to control it, and the Nayar girls carried the necessary firewood. It was quite a shock to Basheer, as a Moslem, to see this; but then he took to wondering why only females of the human species found it necessary to cover their breasts.

It might seem from what has been said so far, that Basheer is not a very serious writer. But this is far from the case even in his most light-hearted short stories, of which these are examples. He is never afraid of a little fun; but in his longer works there is at the same time a depth and true seriousness that few of his contemporaries can match.

If one mentions his short stories when in theory aiming to discuss him as a novelist, it is because in his case there is no clear dividing line between what is a short story and what is a novel. In the introduction to *Childhood Friend*[2] M. P. Paul, during his lifetime the most respected of Kerala's literary critics, made the point that this book in particular lies on the borderline between the two.[3] Is it, he asked, a long short story, or a short novel? In its tracing of almost the whole life history of one of the chief actors and in its careful characterization, it has the qualities one might wish to associate with the novel. On the other hand, in its relative shortness and in its avoidance

[1] *Oru bhagavadgītayum kuṟe mulakaḷum*, Kōṭṭayam (National Book Stall), 1967.

[2] *Bālyakālasakhi*, Kōṭṭayam (National Book Stall), 1944.

[3] See M. P. Paul, *Nōvalsāhityam*, pp. 275–9. This assessment of the book is also prefaced to *Bālyakālasakhi*, 13th impression, 1961, pp. 5–8.

of any digression or remotely unnecessary verbiage it shares features with the nature of a good short story.

Though told in the third person and though making no mention of Basheer (it is the love story of Majīd and Suhrā), the book is not pure fiction. Indeed he has put the autobiographical element at '90 per cent', adding, 'Majid's experiences are mine. Like him I left my village when I was a student. For seven years I wandered. I travelled all over India and parts of Africa and Arabia. I have undergone the same trials as Majīd.' Perhaps this is one reason why, among all his books, it seems to be the author's clear favourite and the one he would like above all to be known outside Kerala.

In their childhood the boy Majid and the girl Suhra were good friends. That is to say, they met and fought regularly. Slowly, as they go through school, a tender affection develops and each becomes indispensable to the other's well-being. But one day Majid forgets to do an errand for his father and is soundly beaten on returning home late. He is thrown violently from the house and decides to leave home.

When he returned home after seven years it was to find that Suhra had against her will been given as second wife to a man who regularly ill-treated her. At the time of Majid's return she is no longer living in her husband's house. Majid's mother agrees that he should marry Suhra. But first they must have money as dowry for his two unmarried sisters. So again he leaves home. He accumulates money only slowly, and extremely so after an accident costs him his right leg. Wearily he tries to earn money, and manages to save five rupees a month from his work as dish-washer in a hotel. Then comes a letter from his mother to say that Suhra, whom they all loved so much, has died of consumption.

It is a sentimental story, but by no means a solemn one. The childhood scenes in particular are full of lighthearted touches. We learn that at school the teacher addressed Majid not by his name, but as 'Number One Blockhead', for he is slow to learn. The point is illustrated by an anecdote:

'Once the schoolmaster asked Majid, "What do one and one make?" It is well-known all over the world that one and one make two. But when he heard Majid's remarkable reply, the teacher burst out laughing. The whole class laughed. The reply he gave became his nickname. Before answering, Majid reflected: just as two rivers join together and flow as a broader river, so two ones joined together become a broader "one"! Having calculated thus, he announced proudly:

' "A rather big one!"

'For finding a new theory in arithmetic Majid was made to stand on the bench.

' "A rather big one!" They all looked at him and laughed. Majid still didn't agree that one and one makes two. So the teacher gave him six strokes of the cane on the palm of his hand and asked him to add all of them together and consider them as just one big one.'[1]

The development of the love story, even though it is concerned with feelings that run very deep, avoids flowery and emotional language. The growth of the mutual feelings of Majid and Suhra is shown through a succession of significant incidents and brief, though telling, descriptions of their emotional state. Yet taken in isolation these descriptions may seem very ordinary. Suhra, for example, is quite fond of Majid's family:

'But there is something that she does not feel for them that she feels for Majid. When he is before her, all is well. It is when he is not there! From the time Majid goes to school in the morning until he returns in the evening she feels a kind of uneasiness. If Majid is not well, she cannot sleep. She always wants to be near Majid. She wants to take care of him day and night'.[2]

And later: 'Suhra loves Majid; and Majid Suhra. Both of them are aware of this.'[3] In the same way the sad letter that ends the story is written in very unelaborate terms. Dictated by his mother, it brings Majid the news not only that the family property has been seized and the family evicted, but also that he will never again see Suhra:

'Our Suhra died the day before yesterday, early in the morning.

[1] *Bālyakālasakhi*, 1961, pp. 26–7. [2] *Ibid.*, p. 50.
[3] *Ibid.*, p. 53.

It was at her house. She was lying with her head on my lap. So our only friend and helper has gone.'[1]

Childhood Friend has faint suggestions of disapproval of certain Moslem customs—among them circumcision, the piercing of girls' ears (twenty-one holes per person)—and more especially customs relating to marriage. It is not at all a social tract, however, but a tragic story that is all the more moving for being told so quietly.

Quite otherwise is *Pattumma's Goat*, in which the noise of the action is deafening.[2] It is a spell in the life of Basheer following his return home after being away almost continuously for some ten or fifteen years; there are also several flashbacks to earlier periods, including episodes in his boyhood. His *umma*, that is to say his mother, is there and his many brothers and sisters with their spouses and children (all mentioned by name). Then there are the animals that add to the difficulty of his finding the quiet and peace so necessary to his health—cats, mice, crows, hens, hawks. And, as if that is not enough, his younger sister Pattumma, who lived near the big family home, acquired a goat. Chaos results. The goat tries to eat a copy of *Childhood Friend*, and there is a succession of troubles both before and after it produces a kid.

Pattumma's Goat is a rollicking story of life in a joint family, full of atmosphere and convincing in its detail. Yet, gay as the story is, it has a serious side. The opening sentence tells us that its alternative title is *The Wisdom of Women*; and no matter how much the book makes fun of the female members of the family, it displays beneath the gaiety a sincere respect for their qualities and the sacrifices they make on behalf of the family.

It should be noted, too, that Basheer's sense of humour extends to making fun of himself—especially as regards his dreams of being recognized as a great man of letters. Thus, when a group of high-school girls look through his gate at him on their way home, he imagines the conversation they must be having about him—about the great literary figure Basheer;

[1] *Bālyakālasakhi*, 1961, p. 89.

[2] *Pāttummāyuṭe āṭu*, Kōṭṭayam (National Book Stall), 1959. Completed April 7, 1954. See author's introduction, p. 11.

they will be discussing whether to come and ask him for his autograph. But it turns out that they are not at all interested in him; indeed they show no signs of knowing who he is: they are merely hesitating before coming to ask for a few jambu-fruits off his tree.

In the same way he expects members of his family to appreciate that he has created 'the world's greatest literary masterpieces'. One revealing incident shows that this is not so. It is the occasion when his younger brother Abdulkhadar, a former schoolmaster, looks over one of his stories and then, after underlining several parts 'with his fat pen', returns it with the suggestion that he needs to study grammar and find out about subject and predicate and so on. Basheer, however, like Thakazhi, persists in avoiding the stilted and the pedantic —to an even greater extent than Chandu Menon before them. As far as he is concerned, the sentence in which his brother deplored the lack of a 'predicate' is a 'first-rate sentence'.[1]

One of the reasons for the relatively small volume of Basheer's literary output is his manner of composition. Usually he will not publish anything until he has revised and rewritten it a number of times. The technical perfection of his finest writings is not achieved without thought and hard work. *Pattumma's Goat* is an exception, as his introduction to the book explains. For five years after completing it he did nothing with it. Then he took it out again and read it 'and did not feel that it should be corrected'. So, apart from the addition of the introduction, he published it just as he wrote it. Even more surprising is the fact that this, perhaps the gayest of all his stories, was written at a time of extreme mental depression.

The book that is felt by many to be Basheer's greatest work, *Me Grandad 'ad an Elephant!*,[2] is, more typically, a highly polished gem. This short novel is not autobiographical in the same sense and to the same extent as some of his other stories, though it is not entirely fictitious. The connection with reality is less in the development of the story than in the

[1] *Pāttummāyuṭe āṭu*, pp. 104–5.

[2] '*Nṟuppuppākkorānēṇṭārnnu!*', Kōṭṭayam (National Book Stall), 1951. A translation of these three stories (*Bālyakālasakhi*, *Pāttummāyuṭe āṭu* and '*Nṟuppuppākkorānēṇṭārnnu!*') by R. E. Asher and Achamma Coilparampil will appear as a volume in the Indian Series of the Unesco Collection of Representative works.

portrayal of certain characters. Thus 'Vattanadima [the heroine's father] is a true portrait of my maternal uncle', while into the character of Nizar Ahmad, the man the heroine marries, he put much of himself.

Me Grandad 'ad an Elephant! is, like *Childhood Friend,* a love story—of an ill-educated girl, the daughter of a family once rich and important, but which is impoverished before she is married. Eventually she marries an educated Moslem from an unorthodox family that comes to live in the house next door—a marriage that stems from their feelings for each other. But the marriage is arranged only after Kunjupattumma has become seriously ill at the thought of marrying a man she has neither seen nor chosen.

Neither grandfather nor the elephant appear in the book. Grandfather's elephant is the symbol of the past greatness of Kunjupattumma's mother's family. But times have changed since the great days of grandfather and the family's social position is far from what it was. Hence it happens that at the end of the book Kunjupattumma's mother has to suffer the indignity of being teased by local children with the suggestion that the famous elephant was not a real elephant (i.e. *āna*), but a mere *kuẓiyāna* (an 'ant-lion', an insect whose diet is ants).

This again seems very light-hearted, and the impression is reinforced by the title, which is an extreme and compressed dialectal form of the sentence that translates 'My grandfather [or *uppuppa*] had an elephant'. But the story contains several different elements, that together make it a far from superficial work. There is plenty of typical Basheer fun and humour; there is a restrainedly sentimental and touching love story; there is an ordinary Malayali Moslem's ideas on life, God, destiny and so on; there is criticism of Moslem superstitions and social customs. The modern members of the community are clearly the ones that are admired, even though Kunjupattumma's bigoted mother holds that their very way of dressing by itself makes it impossible to believe that they are really Moslems.

All these different aspects are so carefully woven together to make one piece, that elements that on the surface might seem incompatible are made to seem a necessary part of each other. One would probably seek in vain for a more skilfully and intricately constructed novel in any language. A writer who can create such a work does not need to produce long volumes to find a place in the history of his nation's literature.

In spite of its great merit and its considerable commercial success, *Me Grandad 'ad an Elephant!* has had an uneasy sort of existence. The author gives an account of some of its troubles in the introduction to *Pattumma's Goat*.[1] 'As soon as it came out in book form, two remarkable things happened. One was that the Congress Government [of Madras] gave me five hundred rupees or so, saying that it was the best novel of those years. . . . The second remarkable thing was that the Communist party criticized the book unmercifully, saying that it was against Communist ideals.' Later, however, the Communist Government of Kerala arranged for the book to be prescribed (as a 'non-detailed text') for use in schools. This was an unheard-of thing; no such incident as the selection of a book by a Moslem to be included among the list of prescribed texts had occurred, says Basheer, since the legendary creation of Kerala by Parasurāman. So 'the book was opposed. . . . Everybody opposed it—the Catholic Congress, the P.S.P., Congress, the Moslem League.' The members of the Congress opposition in the Kerala state legislature accused the author of being a Communist. . . . Happily Mr Basheer's sense of humour extends even to these events.

It will be noticed that almost all of the living writers referred to above have passed the half-century mark. It must not be assumed from this that the younger generation of writers have nothing to offer. There are many good ones, and the best of them have more than enough talent to ensure that contemporary literature in Malayalam will continue to hold its high place in the literature of India.

[1] See *Pāttummāyuṭe āṭu*, pp. 7–10.

INDEX